D1414899

THE PIRATE OF TOBRUK

The PIRATE of TOBRUK

A Sailor's Life on the Seven Seas, 1916–1948

Alfred B. Palmer

DSC, MBE, Commander, Royal Navy Reserve

with Mary E. Curtis

Distributed by:
Airlife Publishing Ltd.
101 Longden Road, Shrewsbury SY3 9EB, England

Originally published in a different form as *Pedlar Palmer,* Roebuck Society Publication no. 29, Canberra, Australia, in 1981.

Library of Congress Cataloging-in-Publication Data

Palmer, A. B. (Alfred Brian), 1898–1993
   [Pedlar Palmer of Tobruk]
   The pirate of Tobruk : a sailor's life on the Seven Seas,
1916–1948 ; Alfred B. Palmer, with Mary E. Curtis.
      p.   cm.
   Originally published: Pedlar Palmer of Tobruk. Canberra : Roebuck
Society, 1981. (Roebuck Society publication ; no. 29)
   Includes index.
   ISBN 1-55750-667-1
   1. Palmer, A. B. (Alfred Brian), 1898–1993.   2. World War,
1939–1945—Personal narratives, British.   3. World War, 1914–1918—
Personal narratives, British.   4. Great Britain. Royal Navy—
Biography.   5. Seamen—Great Britain—Biography.   I. Curtis, Mary E.,
1915–   .   II. Title.
D811.P295   1994
940.54′5941′092—dc20   94-10450
                                                        CIP

Printed in the United States of America on acid-free paper ∞

9 8 7 6 5 4 3 2

First printing

Frontispiece courtesy of Australian War Memorial

CONTENTS

NAUTICAL GLOSSARY

aback in an unmanageable condition because of a sudden shift of wind striking the sails from the side opposite that to which they are trimmed

backstay a rope or shroud slanting sharply aft from the top of the mast of a ship to help support the mast

barque (bark) a sailing vessel with its two forward masts square-rigged and its rear mast rigged fore and aft

belaying pin a removable wooden or metal pin in the rail, around which ropes can be fastened

boat falls hoisting apparatus

bowsprit a large tapered pole or plank extending forward from the bow of a sailing vessel, with the foremost stays fastened to it

bulwarks the part of a ship's side above the deck

buntline one of the ropes attached to the foot rope of a square sail to prevent the sail from bellying when drawn up to be furled

capstan an apparatus, used mainly on ships, for hauling in cables and hawsers; consists of a large spool-shaped cylinder with the cable or hawser wound around it, revolving on an inner shafting

chock the woodwork on a ship's deck where the lifeboat rests

close-hauled having the sails adjusted for heading as nearly as possible in the direction from which the wind is blowing

dead reckoning (ded [abbreviation for deduced] reckoning) the finding of a ship's location by using compass readings and data recorded in the log (speed, course, and distance traveled), rather than astronomical observations; used in fog, storms, and other weather conditions

dogwatch either of two duty periods (from 1600 to 1800 and from 1800 to 2000), half the length of the normal period

doldrums equatorial ocean regions noted for dead calms and light fluctuating winds

donkey boiler a small boiler used for generating power to assist in raising a ship's anchor (rarely needed)

fid a wooden instrument used chiefly when splicing rope

fife rail a rail around a ship's mast to hold belaying pins for the rigging

forecastle the upper deck of a ship in front of the foremast

foremast the mast nearest the bow of a ship

foresail the main, square sail on the foremast of a square-rigged ship

gantline a working rope for raising or lowering sails, blocks, or anything pertaining to the rigging

gudgeon a metal pin or shaft at the end of an axle, on which a wheel turns

half deck a separate house in front of the poop, reserved for cadets or trainees

halyard a rope or tackle for raising or lowering a sail

hatch a rectangular opening in a ship's deck through which cargo can be loaded

hawse that part of the bow of a ship containing the hawseholes, through which the cables run for mooring

hawser a large rope or small cable, often made of steel, by which a ship is towed or moored

headsail any sail forward of the mast or foremast

helm the wheel or tiller by which a ship is steered

horse latitudes either of two belts of calms, light winds, and high barometric pressure, situated at about 30° N and 30° S latitude

jigger mast the mast nearest the stern in a ship with four masts

ketch a fore-and-aft–rigged sailing vessel, with a mainmast toward the bow and a relatively tall mizzenmast forward of the rudder post toward the stern; distinguished from yawl

leeward in the direction toward which the wind blows (opposed to windward)

mainmast the principal mast of a vessel: in a schooner, brig, bark, and similar vessels, the mast second from the bow; in a ketch or yawl, the mast nearer the bow

marlinspike a pointed wooden or iron instrument for separating the strands of a rope in splicing

mizzenmast the mast closest to the stern in a ship with two or three masts

parrel a rope or chain loop or a metal collar used to fasten a yard to a mast

pay off to cause or allow the bow of a vessel to veer to leeward

Plimsoll mark a line on the outside of British merchant ships that indicates the lawful submergence level (named after Samuel Plimsoll,

1824–1898, a British statesman who was instrumental in having legislation passed against overloading vessels)

poop the area containing separate quarters for the captain and the steward, large storage space for spare sails, and a separate galley for the captain

poop deck on sailing ships, a raised deck at the stern, sometimes forming the roof of a cabin

port the left-hand side of a ship as one faces forward, toward the bow; larboard, opposed to starboard

royal mast the small mast next above the topgallant mast

scupper an opening in a ship's side to allow water to run off the deck

sheet a rope or chain attached to a lower corner of a sail; it can be shortened or slackened to control the set of the sail

shroud one of a set of ropes stretched from a ship's side to a masthead to offset lateral strain on the mast

stanchion an upright bar, beam, or post used as a support

starboard the right-hand side of a ship as one faces forward, toward the bow; opposed to port, larboard

stay a heavy rope or cable, usually of wire, used as a brace or support, as for the masts of a ship

stem (1) the forward part of a ship, (2) the upright piece to which the side timbers or plates are attached to form the prow of a ship

swell a large wave that moves steadily without breaking

tack to change the course of a ship by turning her with her head to the wind

topgallant adjective used to describe any mast, sail, or spar that is above the topmast and below the royal mast on a sailing ship

topmast the second mast above the deck of a sailing ship, supported by the lower mast and often supporting a topgallant mast in turn

topsail in a square-rigged vessel, the square sail next above the lowest sail on a mast

trade wind a wind that blows toward the equator from the north side of the equator, and from the southeast on the south side

truck a small wooden block or disc with holes for halyards, especially one at the top of a mast

wearing to turn or bring a ship about by swinging the bow away from the wind; opposed to tacking

windward in the direction from which the wind blows

yard (yardarm) a pole or spar fastened at right angles across a mast for supporting a square sail

yawl a small sailboat rigged fore and aft, with a short mizzenmast astern of the rudder post; distinguished from ketch

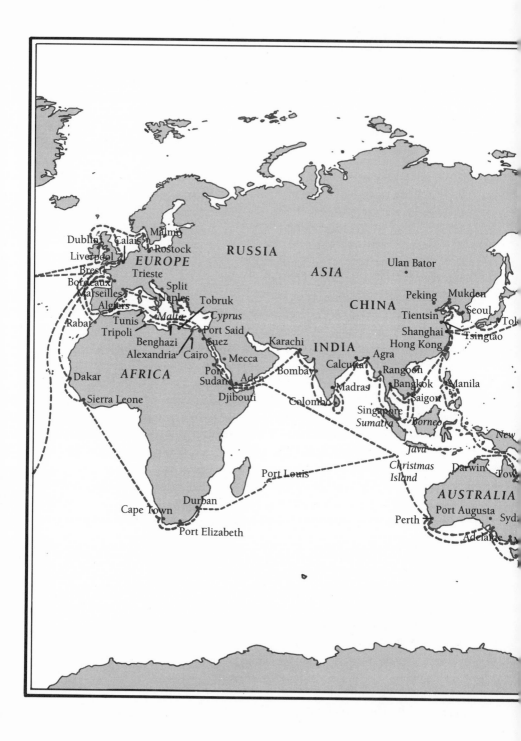

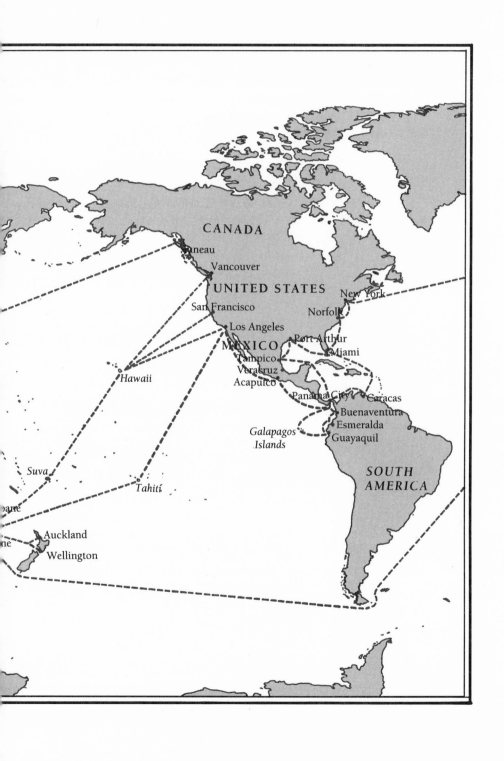

THE PIRATE OF TOBRUK

1

SAILING SHIPS

Sailing ships have virtually disappeared from the ocean. The greatest explorations of this earth were made by these colorful ships from various countries. All contributed their share to world knowledge, and we have all benefited.

Prior to World War I, an extensive and lucrative trade was carried on by sailing ships flying the flags of many nations: British, German, Norwegian, Swedish, Finnish, and a few French. They were competing against steamers and had been driven from the normal trade runs because of their slowness and inability to maintain a set schedule. However, these vessels were able to compete successfully on around-the-world trips, which followed a pattern similar to this: They loaded in Europe with manufactured goods—machinery, steel, copper, building materials, cloth, musical instruments, toys, glassware, china, leather goods, and much more. They sailed to South Africa around the Cape of Good Hope, stopping at Cape Town and Durban, then crossed the Indian Ocean to Australia with stops at Fremantle, Adelaide, Melbourne, and Sydney. The entire cargo would have been unloaded by the time they finished at Sydney. Then, usually under tow, they were taken to Newcastle, New South Wales, for a full load of coal. Newcastle was rated as

1

the greatest sailing ship harbor in the world, and a common sight was ships three abreast, tied to the long piers awaiting their turn to load coal.

With their holds crammed full, the ships sailed across the Pacific to South America, where the cargo was discharged by the crew at Chilean ports Iquique and Pisagua, and Callao in Peru. When all the coal was out, they loaded phosphate and sailed around the Horn into the Atlantic Ocean for record runs to Liverpool, Rotterdam, Hamburg, or Bremen or to whatever port their cargo was assigned. These ships were all large, well-fitted, and made many records for fast passages. In fact, if the skipper did not make a fast passage he was relieved of command.

The story of this voyage is true in every detail. The ship was under German flag during World War I and, without the benefit of radio, sailed into Newcastle Harbor, New South Wales. A naval boarding party came on board and declared the vessel a prize of war and the entire crew prisoners.

I joined the vessel 12 November 1916 as a cadet. This title did not mean very much. We had to work just as hard as anyone on board, plus attend navigation classes in our watch below. I have put the story together over the years, with much reference to notes, excerpts from letters, and stories told by the Norwegian second mate whom I met in Newport, Bristol Channel, England.

Ships waiting to load coal at Newcastle, New South Wales.

Why I chose to join a sailing vessel when they were already doomed to extinction is vague. At the very impressionable age of seventeen, I wanted to see over the horizon. My family lived on the outskirts of Sydney, Australia, and Dad was a veterinarian. He raised strong objections, but there are no halfway measures or flirtations with the sea—you either hate it or love it all your life. When notice was received from the Shipping Master that read, "You will report at 0800 hours to Captain Deeks of Barque *Burrowa* now loading at Pier 12," all obstacles were swept aside and I prepared to leave.

The Sydney waterfront is a complex arrangement. It was almost noon before I located the ship. Then instead of going on board, I stood on the pier and gazed at the towering masts, the mass of yardarms, and the forest of ropes, wires, and rigging. My reverie was shattered when a tough-looking giant of a man approached me and said, "Is your name Palmer?" I nodded an affirmative.

"Well," said this man, "get aboard fast, don't stand there gawking."

"Are you the captain?" I asked.

"Hell no, I'm the mate and when you address me say *sir*, understand?"

"Yes, sir," I replied.

"Now get aboard, take that fancy uniform off and get to work—*move*." I scrambled up the gangway, and the cadet on duty showed me a bunk in the half deck.

When I reappeared on deck suitably dressed for work, the mate was waiting for me. How old was I, what was my first name, what experience did I have, could I climb? "This A. B., you are not an A. B., shirt tail."

"Alfred Brian," I said.

"O'Brian. Another shanty Irishman, goddamned ship is full of them."

The bosun passed by. Without any formality, the mate said, "Take this skinny bastard and put him to work, Bosun, and I mean hard work." Thus began a way of life completely different from anything I had ever known.

The *Burrowa* was a steel vessel of 3,200 registered tonnage. She was barque-rigged, that is, square sails on three masts, and fore and aft sails on the aft, or jigger, mast. Her main mast was 195 feet from deck line to truck. She had 55,000 square feet of sail and the span of her main yardarm was 112 feet. She was 324 feet from stem to stern. This was the largest pure-sailing ship afloat. There were other sailing ships much larger, but they had auxiliary engines to assist them in and out of port, whereas the *Burrowa* depended entirely on the wind to get her anywhere. In those days, sailing ships carried no refrigeration, or even an icebox, to keep food fresh, and a radio set on board was unheard of.

The sailing barque *Burrowa*. This oil painting was created by John L. Crossdaile in 1944 from the author's description of the ship.

The *Burrowa* had a full complement of thirty-eight men: Captain, first and second mates, steward, cabin boy, four cadets in half deck, carpenter, sailmaker, boatswain (or bosun), bosun's mate, and cook amidships, twenty-four sailors in the forecastle, and a brand-new kitten. Long before the United Nations was even thought about, a miniature league of nations was on board. Every European race was represented and even one character from Iceland—in fact, there was nobody on board who wasn't a character.

The bosun was a Scot and far too busy to be bothered with me. To keep me out of harm's way, he stationed me on the top of the midship house with instructions to stay there until he ordered me down. It was just as well he did because the decks were cluttered, the crew busy aloft bending sails, and the stevedores were loading the last bags of a wheat cargo. All this hustle was fascinating to watch. I could not understand what the sailors aloft were saying (there is a whole language in this specialized field), but those below on deck readily answered, "Aye, aye," and sent aloft whatever was required.

The stowing of wheat cargo was a complicated process. It had to be separated from the steel sides of the ship by wood planks called dunnage, the stanchions wrapped in burlap, and box-type ventilation shafts built to carry fresh air throughout the entire cargo. Each bag weighed 200 pounds and the stevedores wore special headdresses that protected their heads, necks, and shoulders from the sharp points of wheat grain. The *Burrowa* was almost down to her Plimsoll mark when the last sacks were placed in the hatches and the carpenter, assisted by three men, began battening down for the long voyage ahead.

There were no set working hours on board while the ship was in port. When the job was finished or it became too dark to see, the order would be given, "All hands below." I was convinced the bosun had forgotten all about me when he finally showed up and ordered me below. My cabin mates plied me with questions and advanced information about themselves. Two were Welshmen from the Bristol Channel Pilot Service, the third a New Zealander and a greenhorn like myself. The cook, a Dutchman, came in to say "Hullo." Best of all, he brought a pot of strong coffee and some cookies.

"All hands on deck" was an order I would hear often, but it seemed I had just gotten to sleep when the bell rang and the bosun's mate started hollering. We tumbled on deck and started clearing away the debris, coiling up ropes, and sweeping surplus wheat through the scuppers. A tugboat came alongside and eased us away from the pier and down the harbor to Rose Bay, where we anchored until the ship was ready for sea. We were also awaiting the captain, who had gone ashore to get two seamen to replace two who had jumped ship.

The working boat was lowered over the side, and two cadets and I were ordered to touch up the paint work along the waterline. When I dropped the third paintbrush overboard, it was agreed that I had better quit painting and just keep the boat steady. This was OK and gave me the opportunity to examine the fancy rope work around the stern and the figurehead on the bow: a blue-eyed, flaxen-haired, full-breasted beauty dressed in a bright red-and-blue flowing gown. Figureheads date back to the Viking days, but they reached perfection on clipper ships, with such elaborately carved symbols as Amphitrite, the Greek goddess of the sea.

The few times we came on deck the activity resembled a disturbed anthill. Stores were being loaded from either side. The steward and cook were checking meat, flour, tea, bread, vegetables, eggs, and other edibles. The bosun and bosun's mate were checking rolls of canvas, kerosene, oil, tar, ropes, paint, wire, tarpaulins, and other ship supplies. As each item was checked off, it was taken away and stowed in the proper locker. The water barge was alongside pumping our tanks full of fresh water, and the carpenter was supervising the stowage of five tons of coal for the donkey boiler. We finished touching up, brought the work boat inboard, returned our paint and brushes, then lay aft to hear the mate expound on the importance of getting a ship ready for sea. He was very interesting and made us realize the necessity of checking and rechecking every item because, once you cast off and head out to sea, you are alone in the world, especially on a sailing ship that does not traverse the regular trade routes or shipping lanes.

The ship was ready. All sails had been bent to the yardarms; rigging examined; halyards, buntlines, topping lifts all tested; and the decks cleared of stores and debris. Rumor claimed we would sail at dawn, but the skipper never showed until early afternoon, then he came off in a hired launch with two men. The gangway was lowered and when Captain Deeks stepped on deck, he asked the mate, "Are you ready for sea?"

"Ready, sir, ready."

"Heave up the anchor, take the lines from the tug."

The two men he had brought off were still in the launch and not the least bit inclined to come on board, but three hefty sailors changed their ideas. Later, we learned the true story: these men were being shanghaied. The skipper had exhausted every avenue trying to get two extra men legitimately, then he called the jail. Did they have two seamen? Yes, they had two seamen. The skipper interviewed these two chaps, offered to pay their fines, put them on wages, and discharge them in Europe. Of course, the jailbirds jumped at the opportunity, but they were firemen, not real sailors, and had never even seen a sailing ship, let alone serve on one. It was pathetic to watch them looking everywhere for the nonexistent engine room. They were London cockneys and gave voice to their disapproval in no uncertain manner.

With the tugboat easing the weight on the anchor cable, sailors were racing around the capstan to heave in the chain. They were homeward bound for Europe, where most of them had originated. A Swede had an accordion, or squeeze box, and he led the gang with sea chanties. The Swede would start, "Come all ye young sailors, listen to me, while I sing you a song of the sea." The chorus would fill in, "Then blow ye winds westerly, westerly blow, we're bound to the southard and steady we go." Other favorites were "Homeward Bound," "Shenandoah," and "Blow the Man Down."

The pawls on the capstan clanked away as the big links came up the hawse pipe. The anchor was walked in without effort and brought on deck, where it was unshackled and secured. The cable was brought inboard, stowed in the chain locker, and the hawse pipe plugged.

The liner *Ventura* had followed us out through Sydney Heads. After the tugboat cast off our lines, she came in close to afford the passengers a rare opportunity of seeing a large sailing ship under full sail. This is something a sailor rarely sees, and I hope those on board appreciated it. The ship's band played "Goodby Sydney Town," and the ship's whistle blew a few toots as the ships got back onto their correct courses, the *Ventura* heading for San Francisco and the *Burrowa* heading south to pick up the Roaring Forties, the stormy latitudes between 40° and 50° S, that would take her to Cape Horn.

When the sails had been set to the satisfaction of the captain, buntlines overhauled, braces tightened, and every rope coiled up on its correct belaying pin, the order came, "All hands lay aft." The entire ship's company assembled at the break of the poop deck where the Old Man gave a short speech: "We are bound for Europe under sealed orders, the ship is well found and a fast sailer; you will be issued the regulation Board of Trade food allowance, plus a half pint of water per day per man. I want every one of you to obey orders, work with a will and make this a happy ship. Mr. Mate, select the watches."

The speech was over, and the mate took charge.

There are two watches on board sailing vessels, port and starboard. The port watch belongs to the mate and the starboard watch is technically the captain's, but in actual fact it belongs to the second mate. These two officers take turns in selecting their men. As the names are called, each man steps over to the port or starboard, depending on which officer selected him. The only people not involved in watch keeping are the steward, cabin boy, cook, sailmaker, and carpenter, although everyone is called in an emergency. Once selected for a watch, one stays in for the duration of the voyage or, as someone quoted, like Tennyson's brook, watches "go on and on forever."

Watches are four hours on and four hours off, with a changeover in the dogwatches, but the four hours off are frequently forgotten in bad weather. The first lesson we learn from the sea is a sense of proportion. Man is humbled to insignificance in the presence of this relentless force. Nonessentials are out of place. Ships and techniques change, but the sea remains the same.

I was chosen for starboard watch and began my lessons in sea commands and learning the ropes. The bosun decided he was going to make a sailor out of me or die in the effort. My first lesson was to climb the rigging correctly: always climb on the weather side and hold the shrouds, not the lanyards. I would be allowed to go up as far as the main yard, cross over and come down the lee side rigging; then the height was extended to the lower topsail and then to the upper topsail. The bosun timed me on the climb and either grunted approval or made me do it over again. I quickly caught on to this monkey business and within a week was able to scramble up to the royal or topmost sail. Then came yardarm work, balancing on footropes and coming down on deck, hand over hand via the backstays. I was not alone in this field of learning. One of the cockney firemen was in my watch, and he had to learn and practice on the foremast while I was on the mainmast. When I had climbed to

Learning the ropes on the deck of the *Burrowa*. Sketch by John L. Crossdaile, 1944.

the truck and down three or four times, the bosun questioned me on the various ropes. He went to the pinrail and asked, "What is this, what is that?" This learning the ropes is a serious business. Each rope is belayed on its own pin, and the ship can be worked on the darkest night by touch. Then there is the technique of knowing when to pull, how hard to pull, or how to slack. If a man makes a mistake or an ill-timed move, someone could be killed.

Ten days out from Sydney, our ship was well south of New Zealand and heading eastward at a fast clip, with the so-called Roaring Forties at our stern. The royals, upper topgallant sails, and mizzen sail had been taken in and stowed; lifelines had been set up and stretched from the poop deck to the forecastle. The suit of sails was No. 1 storm canvas, and our ship averaged 12 knots. This speed did not satisfy the Old Man, and we kept farther to the south in order to pick up stronger winds from the Howling Fifties. The prevailing winds in latitudes 40° and 50° completely circle the globe—there is no landmass to break the swell. Although it is logical for sailing ships to seek out and get down into these latitudes, life can be very uncomfortable for those on board.

The sailors had been busy during watch below, making or repairing their hard-weather clothing. Some of them had to make clothes from odd bits of canvas, and quite an array of coats, pants, and southwesters hung under the forecastle deck, all homemade. They mixed an oil and tar concoction to waterproof them. It was hard to tell the difference between a bought article and the local product.

The last of our fresh food had gone, and the harness casks that contained salt pork and beef were tapped. The cook baked fresh bread three times a week. The basic diet was salt pork or beef, preserved eggs, and preserved potatoes, supplemented by a batch of fresh bread (weather permitting). Ship's biscuit, or hardtack, was the alternative, and sailors had to have strong teeth to make even an impression on it. They grumbled about the chow constantly and rightly so, but the stomach is above prejudice in those latitudes with near-zero temperatures.

The pressure of wind had caused further reduction in sail. We were now under fore and main upper and lower topsails and a clewed-up foresail, but even with this drastic shortening our ship had increased speed to 14 knots. Steering a heavily laden ship with towering 70-foot graybeards racing up from astern required great skill. Two men were at the wheel constantly, and the officer of the watch kept close by. A slight error might start the ship yawing or broaching, and that would be amen in short order. At night when the weather was clear, it was safer to steer by the stars because the ship movement was relayed much quicker than by compass.

The decks were constantly underwater. It was unsafe to walk without holding the lifelines and watching the roll of the ship. I spent most of my watch on deck aloft. The mate never ceased to find an "Irish" pennant or a buntline that needed removing or overhauling, but I had learned my lessons well and could scramble up the rigging and hang on like a monkey. When the ship was rolling both rails under—on a 30- to 35-degree angle at a hundred feet up on the rigging—the arc of the roll lengthened greatly. The roll itself was not too bad, but when it stopped with a jerk, it would have been easy to get flipped overboard, with the chances of rescue being *nil*.

It was summer in the Antarctic, but this was hard to believe. Our decks were coated with ice, there was nowhere to dry out clothes, and the galley was often out of service. In these latitudes we turned in, all standing, not knowing the second we would hear, "All hands on deck." The only other signs of life, which seemed completely detached and oblivious to the hardships that we were suffering, were the albatross. These huge birds kept us company day and night. Gliding gracefully, each had a constant eye for any food scraps tossed overboard. There's a saying that you can always tell a hungry ship if these birds are not following it. I think the only reason they followed us was that no other vessel was around for hundreds of miles. We never saw one of these birds perch on the masts or yards, and there was no land for them to rest. Because of their odd markings, we could tell the same birds stayed with us for days on end—where did they sleep?

The temperature dropped and the gale force eased slightly, yet there was no appreciable change in wind direction. We had shortened sail to the two lower topsails fore and main, but now came the warning, "Watch out for ice." Lookouts were stationed in the fore topsail and the Old Man, obviously worried, was pacing the deck. He kept eyeing a peculiar cloud formation building up to the south. The Howling Fifties had an evil reputation to maintain, and it became evident that they would make no exception for us. The barometer had been falling steadily; visibility had been reduced by a low skud that invariably denoted trouble. Clouds ballooned up fast to the south. Their gray-white coloring and long streamers looked ominous. We shortened sail again to the fore lower topsail and passed extra gaskets. The lifeboats were lashed down, skylights covered and battened down, and everything made snug and secure. The wind suddenly veered to the south and set up a cross sea that made steering difficult. Tons of water filled the decks. The cook was ordered to serve supper early.

We had barely finished eating when this devil's brew hit us with full hurricane force. The ship keeled over under the impact at a deck angle of 35 degrees. The sleet and hail accompanying this unwelcome visitor were driven with such force that many of the men had their faces and hands cut open. In staggering blows, squall after squall howled through the rigging and left everything covered with icicles. Movement was not only hazardous but well nigh impossible. There was no watch below for anyone that night; those up forward remained there, and those aft sought any shelter they could find. With 4 to 5 feet of water constantly sloshing around the midship section, many tons of weight were added to an already heavily laden ship.

This hurricane compelled us to head farther south. We were close-hauled to the starboard tack and breasting the waves on the shoulder. The fore upper topsail ripped under the pressure. Before anyone could even look aloft, all the canvas had vanished to leeward, leaving only the bolt ropes as evidence. Mariners have related stories throughout the years about the notorious storms in these latitudes, and many ships posted at Lloyds as missing or overdue have foundered with all hands in this same area.

The hurricane eased up on the third day. Efforts were made to get the galley fire lit and survey the damage. The roping from the lower topsail was salvaged. A section of the port bulwark had buckled, one side of the mizzen pinrail had vanished, the workboat had shifted out of the chocks, and several planks had stove in against the forecastle skylight. A storm at sea is much more severe to its victims than one on land because a ship offers no protection whatsoever. To stand for hours in wet clothing and freezing weather, without any warm food, and listen to the wind howling through the shrouds makes many sailors wonder why they ever decided to leave home.

With the galley back in business, a hot meal was being prepared. To celebrate the occasion, the Old Man called all hands aft and made a rum issue. I was astonished, when the men mustered aft, to see the deep raw cuts and bruises some of them had sustained. Those at the wheel suffered most because they had no shelter, and the sleet and hailstones had pounded their faces and hands badly. Sailors complain about food, they complain if the captain carries too much canvas ("He will blow the sticks out of her," meaning the sail area is too much for the masts to carry), but injuries, no matter how serious, are treated lightly. The men knew they would not get any sympathy, and complaining would mean loss of their manliness in the eyes of their shipmates.

We had sailed so far southward that a new hazard presented itself: icebergs. The presence of these floating mountains was readily detected by a sudden drop in temperature. Extra lookouts were posted, and the first warning came from the man stationed in the foretop.

"Icebergs," he called down on deck.

"Where away?" asked the mate.

"Two degrees starboard," came the answer.

It was my first sight of these enormous floating hazards, and to get a better view I went aloft to the fore royal. From this vantage point, I sighted six of these monsters. We were heading straight into a cluster of them, which is unhealthy for steamers but suicide for a sailing vessel. I reported my findings to the officer on watch, and our course was altered slightly to the north. The icebergs, surrounded by an almost purple sea and with the sun glinting on their peaks, were a majestic sight. As the sea pounded on their massive sides, huge sections broke off amid thunderous noise.

Once we got clear of this floating ice, the Old Man spread more canvas. The weather was still cold, but the wind had eased enough to allow us to set the foresail, topsails, and topgallant sails on all three masts. The ship boiled along. Again, the old sailors started growling about the skipper cracking on. Rumor had it that he was trying to make a record passage to the Horn, despite the delays already experienced. Rumors play a big part in a sailor's life: the man at the wheel overhears the mate say . . . the steward hears the captain say . . . this and that. These rumors are magnified in the telling, and in no time the whole ship's company has a distorted idea about nothing. However, we were heading for the Horn and, at the rate of speed the old ship was making, maybe we would take a record.

The albatross were still keeping us company. Chippy, the carpenter, devised a steel triangle that was baited and towed astern. The lure had not reached the end of the line before one of the birds swooped down, grabbed the bait, and promptly got his long bill caught in the triangle. We hauled him inboard, to which he protested strongly, but once on deck he sat quietly and became seasick. While Chippy was busy making a leg tag with ship's name and date impressed into the metal, two sailors stretched the bird's wings and measured the span—12 feet 6 inches! The small kitten, actually a stowaway from Sydney, ventured along the deck and pranced around this giant bird. Hissing and making all kinds of cat oaths, it then made a tentative swipe with its forepaw. The albatross eyed this critter with disdain, but when the kitten got too brash and too near the bird snapped at it and that beak clapped together like a trip hammer. The kitten leapt high. Its legs were going long before it came back on deck, and one very scared pussy vanished aft into the cabin in record time. Chippy had two men hold a sack over the bird's head while he fastened the band around his leg. Then we threw the bird overboard and watched him float astern as he tried to figure out what was on his leg. Pretty soon he was airborne again and gracefully glided alongside, none the worse for wear.

The *Burrowa* sailed best with the wind on her quarter, and while we were having supper the wind shifted slightly toward the west. In the morning watch of the fifth day after the hurricane, the glass started to rise, visibility improved, and by noon the fore upper topsail and a reefed foresail were set. Once more, the old ship was "running the easting down." To celebrate the change and buoy up the spirits of all hands, the Old Man made another issue of rum.

One gets accustomed to most things and after listening to the high-pitched whine of a blizzard, the whistle of a moderate gale seemed puny by comparison. However, the ship was making good headway and murmurings were heard from the shellbacks, "Why doesn't the Old Man carry more sail?" The reason soon became clear when the lookout in the foretop shouted "Ice ahead." This dreaded cry quickly brought everyone from below, and soon we could see the berg from the deck. The Old Man had expected the sighting and three men were posted to lookout duty, one in the fore crosstree, one on the foretop, and one on the forecastle. It was not the icebergs that worried everyone—they could be seen afar off, but it was the low "growler" ice that showed little above the surface, yet was large enough to stove in the ship's plates. The first sighting was quickly followed by another and another. Fortunately, visibility was clear and from the fore crosstree six large icebergs were within view at one time, plus numerous smaller floes and growlers.

I was seeing plenty of *firsts* on this passage. I had never even seen snow or ice, and the spectacle of seeing real icebergs, some of them more than a mile long, was an undreamed-of experience. One sight never to be forgotten was witnessed by the watch on deck when a huge berg cracked wide open and disintegrated into three parts. The thunderous roar brought everybody out of their bunks on the double, and the tidal wave caused by the sudden displacement made the ship roll steeply. The watch on deck was kept busy bracing the yards as the captain conned his way through the ice floes, guided by the man on lookout. Even with this precaution and good visibility, several small growlers grazed along the ship's side, shaking her like a terrier shakes a rat. A growler might show only three or four feet above the surface but eight times that height is underwater. It can be compared with land about an acre in circumference and thirty feet unseen to get a rough idea of what a menace these ice floes can be, especially when the following sea is tumbling and confused.

The foresail was taken in during the second dogwatch. Again, the ship slowed down as the captain eased her along with the utmost caution. It was another night with all hands on standby. Plenty of pulley hauley, heave this, slack that, tighten up, ease away—damn the ice anyway. The situation improved toward morning. When reasonable visibility showed no ice anywhere in sight, sails were set again as the *Burrowa* squared away for the Horn.

The sun peeked out sufficiently for the skipper and mate to get a sight. They worked out the ship's position and, providing we maintained the same speed throughout the day and night, we would pass the Horn before noon the following day. She was carrying all topsails, fore and main topgallant sails, and the foresail; the wind was on the starboard quarter at moderate gale force. The decks were awash (they had not been dry for weeks), but the ice floes had gone and the galley was back in full operation. The idea of passing from the Pacific to the Atlantic was sufficient to brighten even a sourpuss.

The long passage across the Pacific had been solitary. Nothing had been seen since the ensign had been lowered as a farewell to the SS *Ventura* but, with the knowledge that Cape Stiff would soon be reached, sea chanties were heard again and a spirit of elation seemed everywhere. We still had a long way to go, and the old sailors knew better than to trust the elements in this region: "Imagine if you were beating against this gale." They would warn, "Look astern at those towering graybeards." Yes, we were in luck to have this gale abaft the beam and the Good Lord had even given us a wonderful break weatherwise. The captain set every stitch of canvas, even the royals, and it was with this spread of sail that we finally reached Cape Horn on the twenty-sixth day out from Sydney. It may not have been a record, but it was a fast passage in anyone's language. We had crossed 5,000 miles of the Pacific without sighting a single vessel. At least fourteen of those days were under short-ened sail and three of them under bare masts. We had encountered gales, hurricanes, a "Cape Horn snorter," icebergs, and growler ice floes, but aside from minor structural damage and the loss of one sail, we had come through unscathed.

Cape Horn is a forbidding headland. Named after a small town in Hol-land, it lies in latitude 56° south. Sailors refer to Cape Horn as Calamity Point, Cape Stiff, and several other (unprintable) names. It was hard to believe all the stories I had heard from old salts about this Cape Horn as we sailed peacefully by with everything set, but the demons of the Cape area were not letting us get away scot-free. The wind changed from northwest to southwest, the barometer was falling, and the cloud formation was building up for trouble. We started shortening sail during the dogwatches, but it was a piecemeal arrangement. Obviously, the Old Man wanted to crack on until the last moment and give the Cape a wide berth. His timing was wrong and, long before we had the topgallant sails furled, another snorter hit us. The carpenter, sailmaker, cook, and every available man worked like crazy to get the sails furled, but we lost three completely and the foresail was split wide open and had to be sent down for repairs. Once again, we were getting buf-feted with mountainous seas crashing aboard. One man busy coiling the braces atop the midship house was washed overboard, then on the second roll he was washed back on board. Nobody got below that night, and the galley was wrecked when the skylight stove in.

The wind eased toward morning. New sails were hustled out of the sail locker and made ready to bend. The bolt ropes from the missing sails were sent down, along with the tattered foresail. As soon as we had sufficient daylight, the big sails were shouldered, the ship eased off course to keep dry decks, and we marched forward with the new foresail. Getting this big hunk of canvas up and secured to the foreyard was no mean trick. We still had more wind than we could use and the roll of the ship, plus the wet slippery footropes, made the going rough. I often laugh at the theory of "one hand for the ship and one for yourself." Whoever dreamed up that idea never served in any sailing ship, of that I'm certain. When work had to be done aloft, a sailor somehow got a sixth sense for knowing when to hold and when not to hold. When bending a huge sail 110 feet long and 40 feet deep, in a gale in latitude 56° south, he used both hands or the man on the footrope beside him wondered what the hell was going on—he hung on by his belly button and prayed the man at the wheel knew what he was doing. That is fact, not theory.

It was almost noon before we had everything ready. Fortunately, the cook and steward had salvaged what was usable in the galley, started the fire, and prepared a hot meal. Eight bells struck as the last man came from aloft, and the Old Man made another rum issue. Laced with the firewater and a good meal, the world seemed a much better place.

Sir Francis Drake, the first European to sight Cape Horn, would have felt quite at home standing on our deck—the ship was bigger and the rigging different—but the sea and the tests of survival against the sea remained the same. I think the old boy would have liked our ship. She had nice lines, her equipment was the best money could buy, and the crew of many nationalities were excellent sailors. But he would have had a great deal of trouble understanding two of his own countrymen. The cockneys had a language of their own and never did absorb nautical terms: "Wot dya fink?" translated into "What do you think?" and "Gihas a duke on dis bleedin fing" translated into "Give us a hand with this thing"—a rope, or whatever it was they were trying to do. But they learned fast and became good sailors, capable of standing watch with anyone on board.

We had passed Cape Horn and were heading toward Europe. I was watch on deck and lookout duty. The normal place to stand watch was on the foretop, but I decided to go higher to the topgallant. As I scanned the horizon, I wondered how things were back home: the folks, the horses, and the old household pets. My position on the foremast gave me the feeling of complete detachment from everything.

A sailor can see land or other objects at sea far quicker than any landsman, and although I could hardly consider myself a sailor, my eyesight was excellent. Several times an object to the south looked like a sail, but then it might be a graybeard breaking over or possibly a small iceberg. However, it could be a sail and the best way to make certain was to report to the officer on deck. The mate questioned me as to what bearing, then, taking his binoculars, climbed to the mizzen top. He needed only a few seconds to determine it was a sail, and the cry "S-A-A-I-L" was heard. Everybody tumbled out on deck to see the stranger—after all, we hadn't seen any sign of life for over a month and this was a rare sight. The ship's numbers were hoisted on the jigger halyards and the ensign was whipping from the gaff, but to everyone's amazement the stranger showed no flag or made any effort to answer. The captain and his two officers were on the poop, their eyes glued to telescopes or binoculars. The questions were: Why don't they answer? Why were they heading up from the south? Could it be the mythical Flying Dutchman? Why this, why that? This could be the German *Seeadler*. . . .

"Let's go! Brace the yards, Mr. Mate. All hands make sail, step lively there." The urgency of the situation was infectious, gaskets were cut, yards hoisted, sheets hauled taut, braces sweated up. In gig time, every stitch of canvas was drawing. The wind was now on the port quarter. The ship, staggering under the terrific press of canvas, was laying over almost lee rail under. Braces were doubled, preventer stays set up, tacks handily billied down, and every possible safeguard made as the Old Girl raced like the thoroughbred she really was. The stranger kept right astern, but the distance gradually widened.

We had the faster ship, and the approaching darkness would help us. The sail spread was far in excess of good seamanship, and no builder or designer had allowed for the terrific pressure on her masts and yards. Yet, nothing broke or carried away as she raced northward. The sidelights were kept in the lamp locker that night, the galley fire doused, no bells struck, and smoking on deck prohibited. There was too much tension for anyone to go below. The men gathered in small groups, ever ready to obey a command. The Old Man kept every stitch of canvas on until midnight, when the course was altered and sails reduced to ease the strain on the ship. The reduction also eased the tension of those on board. We followed the Patagonian coastline north. At the crack of dawn, lookouts were sent aloft with powerful glasses to see if there was any sign of the stranger. If it had been the *Seeadler*, she had abandoned the chase or decided the *Burrowa* was too hot a potato to follow.

We had learned a lesson after almost sailing into a trap. The policy from now on was "stand off" and maintain our own council.

Breakfast was very special that morning. The cook had pilfered a side of bacon from the steward's pantry and, to help things along, had baked a batch of fresh biscuits. This food, together with hot coffee, was a luxury and made everyone feel good. The pride of accomplishment was much in evidence. No one man sails a seagoing vessel alone. It takes a team and, after our escape, the feeling of mutual dependence was strong. We had again passed the severe test of survival.

We were so accustomed to gale-force winds that the comparative light southeast breeze seemed inadequate. With all sails set, however, we moved along at a steady clip. The weather improved, all ice formations vanished, the sails became more pliable and the decks dry. The mate and two bosuns were busy aloft checking for any damage. They started forward and examined every item from bow to stern and truck to deck. The mate kept notes on work to be done and, during the dogwatch, announced that watch below during daylight hours would cease the following day. This meant all hands would work from sunrise to sunset and four hours duty during darkness. It's said that the life of a sailor is a healthy one—it must be the work, not sleep.

Punta Mogotes was to be our landfall, and the lookouts were on the alert. We anticipated the sighting during the morning watch, but the wind died away and we were becalmed most of the day, which seemed uncanny after such a boisterous trip. The ominous silence was broken occasionally by the creaking rigging or the bell being struck every half hour, but the Old Man was restless and paced the deck as he watched the sails flapping against the masts. That night, the sky was clear, with stars shining brightly and a few clouds hardly worthy of the name, but low in the southwest some lightning danced around and the wind shifted from southeast to southwest.

With the change, the cloud formation enlarged and the lightning became more frequent. The watch on deck was ordered to take in the royals and upper topgallant sails. This had just been done when the call for "all hands" went out. Taking in lower topgallant sails, fore and main courses, we realized the urgency of this precaution. A bank of low black clouds came driving toward us and whipped the sea into a frenzy. It burst upon our becalmed ship and sent her skudding. This sudden blast was accompanied by hailstones and rain, driven at such speed it was necessary to seek shelter. The hailstones splattered against the hull and deckhouses like rifle bullets, peeled off the paint work, and polished the steel plates. This is a phenomenon known as a *pamperos,* experienced only in this region. It comes straight off the pampas plains in Argentina and, unless a ship is prepared for its onslaught, it can spell disaster. Our ship actually benefited by the storm. Instead of following the coastline, we set our course northeast, which would take us toward the African Gold Coast where we could pick up the southwest trade winds.

Work began in earnest. The heavy weather sails, or No. 1 suit of canvas, were sent down and replaced by No. 3, a much lighter canvas. Many of the sails already had been used considerably. When each sail was lowered to the deck, it was spread out and thoroughly inspected by the sailmaker, who made notes on whatever repairs were necessary. The new set of lighter sails was hoisted aloft by a gantline and rove through a snatch block near the masthead. The sailors walked the sail up by walking either aft or forward, as the case required. When the sail reached the yard, the men aloft shouted, "Vast hauling." As the bunt was secured and the earing stretched out, the sail laced to the jackstay blocks was almost becalmed. Blocks were sent down and overhauled, gaskets spliced, sheaves examined and greased, new footropes added where necessary, and the standing rigging, parrels, braces, sheets, and every piece of equipment checked. We were due for fine weather, and the stress of our Antarctic sojourn was gone.

The daily routine in these latitudes began at 0600 (four bells). The first job was to wash down the decks, not merely wet the decks but scrub them. Each morning, a new section was marked off for holystone, a large brick of sandstone clamped into a steel frame with a handle attached. Using this stone helped keep the pitch of seams level and any deadwood was worn off. Those not washing or holystoning were polishing brass, drawing the rations of fresh water, or getting the equipment ready for the work to be done later. At 0730, seven bells was the call to breakfast, and eight bells (at 0800) was the signal for starting work. The bosun assigned five men on the foremast, five men mainmast, five men mizzenmast, two men on this, three men on that, and so it went—everybody busy until 1130 (seven bells), when lunch was served. At 1200 (eight bells), work started again and continued until sundown. Then the paint, marlinspikes, fids, tar, oil, and any other items used during the day were returned to the bosun's locker under the forecastle head. Supper was usually around 1830 (five bells). After supper, depending on the watch they were on, the sailors went below or stayed on deck.

This routine went on six days a week, with Sunday a day of rest. The washdown was done when the stools, mess tables, and odd chairs were brought out on deck and scrubbed and the forecastle deck scrubbed before breakfast. Sunday breakfast was usually special, maybe preserved eggs or something above the ordinary. Watch on deck required only one man at the wheel and one man on lookout. At 1100 (six bells), the Old Man mustered everyone aft and read a verse from the Bible. Sailors have a profound concept of religion. There is no pulpit, no incense burning, no organ playing, no preacher, but these tough-looking men are humble, devout, and feel God's presence very strongly. The midday meal on Sunday usually included a big plum pudding, known to sailors as duff. This creation would not suit Grandma and the recipe would shock a first-class chef, but it was something different. Sailors acquire the digestive processes of a goat, and nothing goes begging.

With the aid of the southeast trades, our ship tramped along steadily and hopes were high that we would make a record passage. Christmas was celebrated on board. The cook excelled himself, and the Old Man made another rum issue. Of course, we had nothing red or green, no tree, no holly, and no presents, but it was a Christmas holiday.

The desire to sight another vessel was strong. We had been at sea for forty-eight days. Aside from the mysterious stranger south of the Falkland Islands, we had seen no other sign of human life. The albatross had long since vanished, but whales had been sighted many times. Some of them actually came alongside the ship and scraped their hides on the steel plates. Schools of porpoises were plentiful, as were the inevitable sharks. We devised a homemade bomb from gunpowder, attached a slow-burning fuse, baited the whole contraption, and then lowered it gently over the side on a piece of wood. This floated aft and was quickly seized. When the powder blew up, one dead or very sick shark would thrash about, and his fellow sharks wasted no time tearing him apart. We killed five or six sharks with our bombs.

The weather remained good, the work went on uninterrupted, and all the yarns and stories were heard over and over again. The endless diet of salt pork and beef, plus close confinement, made everyone edgy. The cook did his best with the limited supplies on board, but the only variety we had for many weeks was a mess of fish when eight big snappers were caught one evening. Lime juice was issued daily—it kept down scurvy but did not improve dispositions.

The food problem was brought to the Old Man's attention rather dramatically when one of the cockneys took a pan of dry hash right aft into the captain's cabin. His approach or manner, or perhaps his brashness, displeased the Old Man, who promptly beat the beegeezers out of the poor guy, frogmarched him to the entrance, then booted him through the door. This incident was witnessed by one of the cadets who was cleaning lamps right beside the cabin entrance. He promptly dashed into the half deck and related the story to those present. His acting was superb, but when the kick turn came he emphasized just too much; his heavy slipper flew off and up through the skylight. Glass scattered over the deck beside the standard compass where the Old Man was standing. Wow!

"Clear the half deck, every damn one of you out on deck—Now!" came the voice of the skipper. The emphasis on the *now* left no doubt in our minds that he was good and mad. We scrambled out and very sheepishly stood to attention and listened to his tirade. The cost of repairing the skylight would be deducted from our pay. We were put to work cleaning the teakwood chart house with sand and canvas, a job that kept us busy until dark, then aloft to stow and reset the three royals. The curses heaped on the cockney, and also on the bearer of news about his ejection from the cabin, would not stand printing.

The horse latitudes of 30°–35°S treated us well. The average speed was reduced, but each day showed progress in the right direction and the torrential rains proved a boon to the freshwater supply. Our sailmaker made several large catchalls that were stretched across the deck to collect rainwater. Our tanks were refilled, and water rationing was discontinued. The heavy rains also afforded the luxury of a bath, something none of us had enjoyed for fifty days. It was amazing to see the changes soap and water wrought, especially in those who shaved off their straggly beards. Fresh water quickly healed the salt sores that plagued everyone and rid the ship of its salt coating.

The North Star climbed higher in the heavens as we neared the equator. The sailors began talking about what they would do when they were paid off. Some of their ideas stretched the imagination, and their stories were incredible. Few ever spoke of their wives or families, and all of them wanted to leave the sea. Of course, they never did and frequently found themselves outwardbound in another ship within a week of being discharged. One story reflects their thinking: "I'm going to carry an oar inland until someone asks, 'What is that thing you are carrying?' Then I'll know sailors don't live around there and that's where I'll stay."

The Doldrums at the equator were the complete opposite of the Howling Fifties. The ship was becalmed and the sea glassy smooth, as opposed to hurricane-force winds and mountainous seas, but the Doldrums were frustrating and the physical hardship severe. Fights started over the most trivial things, and despondency was ever present. It took great skill and much hard work getting a ship through these latitudes. The captain was hard-pressed and disagreeable to everyone, especially the man at the wheel. "You are off your course, damn it. Get her back, get her back." There was not enough wind to give the ship steerageway. The skipper knew this and so did the wheelman, but he caught hell anyway. The superstitions of centuries ago still worked their charm. Whistle to windward, get a broom and sweep the sky, spit over the side, shake a fist at the sun—all of them were ridiculous but practiced in good faith.

The irony of this region was seeing ripples on the water caused by a breeze and then watching the ripples pass astern or off to port, with hardly a breath of air coming near the ship. At night, the darkness was intense. It was impossible for us to see our hands before our eyes. Occasionally, the jack-o'-lantern, or Saint Elmo's fire, danced aloft. These lights appeared on the mast-head, then on a yardarm, or jumped to another yard or another mast, then disappeared only to reappear someplace else. This unworldly setting made the sailors talk in whispers, and relationships were very trying. Yet, through it all, the sails had to be worked and constant watch maintained so that the ship would not be caught aback or miss even the gentlest breeze.

Painting the ship was another all-hands chore. The masts, yards, deck-houses, and bulwarks all had to be painted. The workboat was lowered over the side and the men, armed with wire brooms, kept busy scrubbing marine growth off the ship side. When this was done, scrapers peeled off the rust and patched with red lead. I was on this detail and was surprised to see the deep scars along the waterline made by growler ice floes; some of them had almost cut clear through. The bow and the fancy figurehead were stripped bare of paint, and the stemplate buckled slightly to port. The Old Girl had taken a beating since leaving Sydney. Stages were rigged for painting the four masts. When the men were put over the side to repaint the hull, each one wore a life jacket plus a line secured inboard.

This activity attracted the sharks, and their dorsal fins gliding above the water looked like a miniature yacht race. There was one big stinker that kept position right under where the men were working. He was mean-looking and hungry, so plans were made to catch him. Chippy heated a crowbar and fashioned a hook with two barbs; he made a ring at one end of the shank and shackled on a length of chain with a 2-inch manila line. We baited the hook with a hunk of salt pork and tossed it overboard. The small pilot fish looked over the morsel carefully, then signaled the shark that it was OK. He closed in, snapped the bait, and started off, but he didn't get too far—the hook sank deep into his jaws and all hell broke loose for a while. We played him along-side and watched his antics as he tried to bite through the chain. Another line with a big noose was lowered over his head, worked back to his tail, and hauled taut; then with the aid of a topping lift, the monster was hauled out of the water. Chippy retrieved his hook, then cut the shark's head off with a saw. The carcass was lowered and about 3 feet of the section adjoining the tail cut off. The remainder was dropped back into the sea, where other sharks quickly tore it apart. The head was skinned, and the jawbone dried in the sun and mounted on the end of the bowsprit. The tail section was cleaned, cut into steaks, cooked and eaten—excellent taste.

We kept catching sharks whenever time permitted and followed the same routine in landing them. However, we confined the cutting to the tail section. The largest shark, from the tip of his snout to his tail, measured 28 feet. These cannibalistic monsters depend on their tails for guidance. When we dropped them back minus tails, they were still alive but unable to steer. Streaming blood, they raced off and were quickly devoured by their brothers. We saw a fight between two over a carcass; both sharks were wounded sufficiently to draw blood, and they in turn were eaten by their buddies. We tried another trick by tying an empty oil drum to the tail section, then let the shark go and watched the antics as he tried to get rid of the attachment.

We finally crossed the equator, but there was no jubilation. The trip had taken thirty-one days since passing Cape Horn, and the Old Man was fit to be tied. Anyone and everyone felt his wrath at one time or another. The only way to avoid being abused was to keep out of sight. The hatches had been partly opened to allow fresh air into the cargo, and this was the favorite spot to hide out.

The ship looked brand-new, with fresh paint sparkling from masts and spars, the backstays white leaded, the brasswork shining, the teakwood deck snow white, the fancy ropework around the counter reworked, and the figurehead restored with her blue eyes and flowing robe. The work still continued because a ship is always demanding.

We shook off the fickle weather of the Doldrums at last and picked up the northeast trades that would bring us toward the Azores. As the ship headed nearer the crew's homeland, dispositions improved and the sea chanties were heard again. With a rollicking rhythm, the Swede played chanties that dealt with sailors' activities ashore, as well as the old standbys, "Sally Brown," "Homeward Bound," "Southward Ho," and "Rio Grande." He managed to get some hefty verbal digs at the captain: "Here comes the Old Man looped to the gills, his hands in his pockets and a mouth full of pills, he's acussin' an hollerin' from dawn to dusk, get a move on, you ham-handed louts." Interpretation: the captain is drunk; the hands in the pockets signify he is tight with pay allowances; the pills are chewing tobacco that he rolls into small balls, and ham-handed is being awkward or careless.

Navigation classes were getting harder and mathematical equations impossible. The mate guided this phase of learning and set a different example for each cadet to work before the end of the dogwatches, 0800 or eight bells. He was strict and helpful over the rough spots, but the exam paper had to be neat and correct. Otherwise, a cadet stayed awake until he completed it and passed the exam.

It was winter in the Northern Hemisphere, and we still had a long way to go. The light sails had been sent below and replaced by the No. 2 set. Only the captain knew our destination. Nobody else on board had the slightest idea, although rumor had us in every port from Belfast to the Bosporus.

Lookout duty was my favorite. From my perch on the foretop, I could watch the big ship lift to the swell and glide noiselessly along. Such silent power is difficult for most people to comprehend. This vessel of 10,000 tons had traveled from one side of the world to the other without any aid whatsoever but wind on her sails. From my position, I could look down to the white deck and see the ship's outline lighted by the phosphorescent glow as the bow parted the water and the ship gracefully forged ahead.

2

MEETING THE WAR
HEAD ON

━━━ We had carried sidelights since leaving Sydney, with the exception of one night near the Falklands, but now we were entering the war zone and sailed in the darkness without showing any lights. One night, we were hailed by a man in a small ketch; he had sailed up from astern without being sighted and scared the liver out of the watch on deck with "Ahoy there, ahoy. What ship?" We identified ourselves. He was a Portuguese fisherman sailing out of Ponta Delgada, Azores. Unfortunately, his English was not good. We had almost every nationality on board and could have talked in any of a dozen languages—except Portuguese. He suggested we keep a better look-out, the ocean was full of submarines, the war was still being waged, and he was on his way to the fishing grounds. Adios.

The incident reminded me of a story: The very small ketch asked the big, deep waterman what ship. A strong voice answered, "This is the full-rigged ship *Nonsuch*, a hundred and five days out from Borneo, and pray who are you?" A high-pitched voice replied, "This is the *Susie Q* and we've been out all night."

We followed the fisherman's advice. Lookouts were increased, the galley fire was out by sunset, no smoking was allowed on deck, and the bell was muffled. The two main lifeboats, housed on skids abreast of the half deck, were given special attention and stocked with fresh water, biscuits, and chocolate bars. Sails, oars, lamps, distress signals, sea anchor, and other accessories were thoroughly examined. The boat falls were overhauled and drills held every day. We had lived alone in our peaceful world for two months, so the idea of war seemed incredible. Thanks to our friend from Portugal, we started preparations in the right direction.

Wool sweaters, seaboots, and hard-weather gear became fashionable again. The lifelines were set up; the decks were awash once more as we altered course for Europe. The trick of getting from aft to forward without getting wet became a ritual. A sailor learns when to make a move by watching the sea. This wave breaks—the ship will ride the next one—he makes a dash for the midship house and then waits for the next move. By knowing the tricks, he can go on watch with dry clothes. If he doesn't know when to move, he will most likely stand four hours in wet clothes. This know-how is even more important when bringing food from the galley. If he gets caught by a wave, he not only gets soaked but loses the food for himself and others in the half deck. This error can make a person quite unpopular.

The winds in the North Atlantic are liable to come from any point of the compass. There is nothing to compare with the trade winds, or the Forties and Fifties, where the wind blows steadily for weeks on end without much variation. Here we held a steady breeze from the southwest for a couple of days; then it changed to the north, veered to the northwest, and over to north-northwest. There was little time for any work other than handling the sails. The north-northwest wind was not favorable, and we had to tack constantly. Our ship was a wonderful sailer and as fast as they come, but she could not sail worth a damn close-hauled. If a submarine was trying to follow us, she would have gone crazy as we tacked back and forth every day against headwinds. This delay made the Old Man good and mad. His chances of breaking a record had been shot long ago, and now his chances of making even a good record were looking pretty bad. He was sore as a boil and even accused a school of black whales, cavorting playfully around the ship, of bringing fog. He resorted to changing the man at the wheel, changing the men on lookout, claiming there was a Jonah on board, and all sorts of crazy ideas to clear the fog and get us into port. "What's that damn cook doing throwing trash overboard to windward?"—there was not a breath of air moving, and smoke from the galley drifted straight up.

The fog cleared the evening of the second day. The breeze came away from the southwest and we inched along with all sails set. *Inch* is the correct term—we made 26 miles in twenty-four hours. Then fog descended again, and the black whales returned. The idea of floundering around in a submarine-infested ocean was bad enough, but when these huge black whales came alongside it was easy to imagine they were submarines. Everybody was as nervous as cats, and fights started for no reason. A big Russian clobbered me as I passed him on deck. "You are the goddamn Jonah," he said, and that was the reason for his clout. The fog lifted eventually, but the wind came from the north. Again, we started tacking.

The point of destination was finally disclosed. We were bound for Bordeaux in France and, according to dead reckoning, we should pick up the Cape Finistere light in the middle watch. The term *dead reckoning* is used loosely—the word should be "deduced," which abbreviates to "ded." A good seaman can chart a course by dead reckoning much better than others using the most modern methods.

Spanish fishermen sighted us long before we picked up the light. Two yawls came alongside to trade fresh fish for tobacco. We were pleased with the deal, and so were they. They politely bade us adios and returned to their fishing grounds. Our course was correct; just before midnight the lookout aloft reported the light, but our bad luck still dogged us. The wind veered around and came from the east, which was dead ahead. It was bitterly cold with the breeze coming straight off the French Alps, and we started to shuttle between Cape Finistere and Brest Lighthouse. We kept this up for ten days without gaining more than a few miles.

The wreckage of war was everywhere: upturned lifeboats, cases, sacks, gangways, hatches, and quite a few bodies. We saw one lifeboat with seven men in it, two still in the sitting position holding oars, but all frozen to death. We salvaged several sacks of flour, which may seem like an odd thing to do. Actually, the water had penetrated only a few inches through the sack, then formed a dough that sealed off the center, or core, which was perfectly good. Why we were not molested or sunk by submarines is a mystery. Here was this large vessel with a huge spread of white canvas sticking up 200 feet that could be seen for 20 miles. We can only surmise that the Germans who did sight her must have been sailing ship men.

The amount of tacking, or wearing ship, that we had to contend with made everybody an expert. Tacking takes place when a ship must suddenly change course, or "ready about." There is no running or fuss. Each man has a position to keep; when the order is given, he stands by his rope, sheet, brace winch, or whatever place he is assigned. The captain takes up his position on the weather side of the poop. The mate stations himself on the forecastle head and looks after the headsails and foremast. The bosun takes up his position at the main mast and the second mate the mizzen.

The Old Man watches the sea and at the precise moment orders, "Helm down."

The man at the wheel repeats, "Helm down, sir."

"Helms down" shouts the captain, and this is repeated right down the line. "Headsail sheets, let go." The ship pays off rapidly.

"Tacks and sheets" is the next order; the weather brace winch is spun out of gear and handles shipped on the lee winches. The royals and topgallant sails are hauled by hand, and if the timing is right (it better be right) all the yards swing together, the braces hauled taut, tacks hauled down and secured. Then come the affirmative calls: "Foresails trimmed and secure; mainsails trimmed and secure; mizzensails trimmed and secure."

Each call is repeated by the captain. He then makes a check: "Haul the main upper topsail, belay." "Ease the mizzen royal, belay." The whole operation is done with precision. Hundreds of tons of steel are swung around like a top and the ship is ramping along on her new course. When the captain considers everything snug and secure, he orders, "Relieve the deck," and whichever watch is on duty takes over and the others go below. When this operation is done well, it should not take more than eight minutes from the "helm down" to "relieve the deck" order, which represents eighteen yard-arms, twenty-four sails, and 10,000 tons of deadweight being spun around from north to south without an ounce of steam or electric power—only the wind and a well-trained crew. Should the timing be wrong, a rope foul in the block, or a man let go ahead of time, all hell breaks loose and the greatest snafu ever made piles up.

We finally beat our way to the roadstead of the Gironde River and reported to the signal station. A pilot was sent out with a tugboat. We hauled the pilot on board, none too gracefully, but he seemed to understand our anxiety. One of the crew, a Belgian, spoke French, and after these two yacked away we learned that it was most imperative that we get inside the boom defense. The submarines were as thick as fleas on a dog, and a ship had been sunk only two hours before our arrival. The tugboat skipper could not handle his craft and was scared to come in close enough for us to pass a line. The pilot berated him and was hysterical when effort after effort failed. The Old Man listened to this yackety-yack and displayed extreme patience. He eventually ordered the pilot below decks and signaled the tug to get out of the way. Without any knowledge of the port, he sailed right through the boom defense and into the Gironde River estuary, then asked the pilot where to anchor. The poor Frenchman could not speak a word of English, which was a saving grace because what the skipper called him, the tugboat skipper, and the whole French nation would have made his hair stand on end. Even his life expectancy was shortened.

The anchors had already been shackled on and readied with 50 fathoms of cable flaked out on deck, clear for running. When the order "Let go" sounded, the anchor was dropped and 30 fathoms of cable snaked out through the hawse pipe. Our ship came to rest after 110 days at sea.

The yardarms were swarming with men stowing sails, but for this occasion the stow had to be perfect, no loose ends, no bumps or uneven folds. Special aprons had been made for the bunts, and these were carefully laced into position. All chafing gear was cut down, loose ends removed, ropes hauled taut, yards trimmed, and the ship's colors displayed. When everything aloft had been approved by the mate, we started on the deck. All deckhouses were washed, any rust spots on the bulwarks touched up, and the decks washed until they shone. The workboat crew were touching up the hawse pipe and cable, while others were polishing the brass, so that the ship was spotless and ready to enter the port of Bordeaux, at that time the capital of France because of the German threat on Paris. There were several other sailing vessels at anchor nearby. No doubt, we were being closely studied. Sailors can tell a story about a ship without going on board. Their trained eyes know, from a mile away, whether or not a ship is well run.

When the work was completed to the satisfaction of the mate, he reported to Captain Deeks, "Ship ready for inspection, sir." The Old Man came on deck, walked forward on the starboard side, examining everything closely, up and across the forecastle, then back aft on the port side. He required a few changes. He then stopped by the galley to greet the cook and ordered fresh coffee for all hands. When this was brewed, another rum issue was made to spike it, then supper.

The watches were shortened and only four men required on deck for lookout duty. This was a luxury most of us had forgotten—to sleep a whole night without being disturbed. With the ship rolling ever so gently, we slept the sleep of the just. We had crossed the broad Pacific and Atlantic, battled gales and hurricanes off the Antarctic, raced the *Seeadler*, endured subzero weather and broiling heat, avoided submarines, and brought our precious cargo of wheat safely into port.

Three tugboats were alongside at the crack of dawn, ready to take us upriver to the unloading piers. The smaller tug with a propeller was given the head rope, while the two larger side-wheelers took up their positions on either side. These craft were antiques but powerful enough to buck the strong tide and move our ship slowly upstream. I sought out my favorite spot on the foremast and watched the scenery as we moved along the winding river. It was good to see the farms, vineyards, cattle, small homes, and friendly people waving, quite a contrast after seeing nothing but ocean. We had the urge to go ashore, meet people, eat fresh vegetables, look in store windows, see pretty girls, and maybe read a newspaper to learn what in the hell was going on in the world.

The trip from our anchorage to the piers occupied most of the day, but we eventually berthed immediately across the river from the center of the city. Preparations were being made to unload our cargo. The French authorities were worried about our motley crew and decided all of them should have an examination before being allowed ashore. The mate ordered everybody aft, and the order was read: "Nobody allowed on shore until examined and passport issued." Those Frenchmen should have known better—they placed a sentry on the gangway, but before he had taken up his position, some of the sailors had already left. The power of cheesecake was revealed when a madam appeared on the wharf with two girls wearing only fur coats, which they opened . . . and that was that.

None of the sailors went down the gangway and the sentry was never challenged, but it would have taken half the French army to keep those men on board. They had urgent business to look after and scrambled down the mooring lines. During the first two days in port, our crew shrank to seven men, and no shore leave had been granted. They started returning twenty-four hours later, but not for any reasons of loyalty or being rounded up by the law. The basic cause was a shortage of cash. They had spent the few dollars left over from Sydney and were flat broke.

The effects of their philanderings were much in evidence: black eyes, torn suits, skinned knuckles, and bandages that covered other problems never disclosed. All in all, they looked a sorry bunch. The French authorities belatedly decided to issue temporary passports to the crew, but even with official papers and some money in their pockets only a few returned to the bright lights. The French sentry was replaced on the gangway and his duties taken over by the cadets. We worked around the deck for six hours, then did a two-hour duty on the gangway, and every fourth day one of us had the all-night stint.

French manpower was at a low ebb, and stevedores were imported from Spain. Most of the Spaniards and their families lived in railroad cars alongside the ship. They were good workers but inexperienced in handling our type of cargo. Australians wore protection over their heads and shoulders when loading and unloading wheat, but the Spaniards did not know that the hard kernels could cut like a knife and disregarded warnings. They learned the hard way after several went to the hospital and others were so badly cut up they could not work. The mate showed them how to stack the 200-pound bags, so that the dead lift was avoided, and to build steps away from the cen-

ter of the hatch. All these tricks seemed elementary and to a regular stevedore very simple, but these people had been recruited from cities and farms.
Most had never seen a ship before, and the handling of cargo was a complete
mystery to them. They were experts at drinking wine from a bottle or con-
tainer—not the orthodox way but by holding the bottle at arm's length and
allowing a steady stream of wine to go right down their throats without swal-
lowing. It looked so easy until I tried and discovered how tricky it was. I had
wine in my hair, ears, eyes, nose, and down the front of my shirt, everywhere
but down my throat.

The wood used to protect the cargo from getting wet was surplus, and the
Spaniards pleaded to take bundles ashore for firewood. This was allowed
until we noticed many of the brass fixtures were disappearing. Solid brass
belaying pins, fife rail brass caps, some portholes, and, finally, the ship's bell
vanished. This tore the bag, and orders were issued that no wood was to be
taken ashore. I had the gangway duty that afternoon—as the men started
streaming ashore, I wanted them to leave their bundles of wood. The
Spaniards were hostile and threatened me with all kinds of dire punishment.
Quite a few produced knives and made feints at my throat, ears, and elsewhere. Of course, I didn't much appreciate this and was able to convince
them to leave peaceably.

Karl hailed from Finland, and often during the voyage he had shown me
how to splice rope, make all kinds of knots, and sew canvas. He had gone
ashore the moment our lines were secured and was loud in his praise for the
wonderful city of Bordeaux. He seemed very worldly to me, and I asked if he
would take me ashore when the captain gave us some money and time off.
Yes, he would be glad to show me around at any time. The fifth day in port
all cadets were summoned aft and the Old Man gave us each five dollars and
a French passport. I hurried forward to see Karl, and we agreed to go ashore
after work.

Passing the long line of boxcars where the Spanish families lived, we
walked over the bridge and into the city, but Karl followed along the waterfront and the area seemed to be getting pretty rough. Women predominated,
some scantily dressed for the winter weather. Fights broke out, and I was
knocked over when someone threw a chap out the front window of a cafe. I
asked Karl when we would come to the nice parts of the city. "This is the best
part of the city you are in now and we will reach my favorite bar soon."

We walked on. Suddenly Karl stopped and asked, "Did you bring your
knife?" When I told him no, he dismissed me as though I had the plague and
suggested I go back on board. Just in case anyone should rob me before
reaching the ship, he borrowed three of my five dollars.

I wandered back along the never-ending maze of dirty streets, narrow alleys, and dead ends. The area was full of dives, and the characters on the streets blended with their surroundings. I was hungry and finally entered a restaurant that seemed a shade better than anything I'd seen. The fancy cakes with chocolate and whipped cream were something I hadn't seen for a long, long time, but the madame in charge could not understand my language and indicated that I help myself. The French families inside the place had their small fry with them and no matter how old the kids were, they all drank wine. This amazed me, but I figured if they could drink the stuff so could I. The madame brought a bottle. With a half dozen pastries and red wine, I really had a ball.

Bordeaux had curfew laws. Only those with special passes were allowed on the streets after 2000 hours. The combination of cakes and wine wasn't making me feel too good, but I ventured forth into the night in hopes of making my way back to the ship. Two policemen stopped me before I got far and wanted to see my pass. I produced the fancy passport. It was thoroughly examined, questions were asked and not answered, arms waved, whistles blown, and the next thing I'm in the pokey—charged with breaking the curfew law and being a vagrant. It seemed nobody at the police station could speak a word of English.

I spent the rest of the cold night sitting on a wooden bench in the company of twenty other vagrants. The morning court was informal, and the judge handed out assorted sentences and fines. One girl yanked up her dress, pulled a wad of money from her stocking, paid the fine, and thumbed her nose at the judge. He slapped another fine on her right away, which she paid. Then, as she left the court, she lifted her skirt and patted her butt. One man unlaced his shoe and brought forth his fine from the toe of his sock.

My name must have been called, but I was fascinated by the judge's mustache, a scraggy arrangement badly in need of a wash and trim. Each time he spoke, this bristle stuck straight out like a miniature broom. The court interpreter was summoned. After the judge had talked a while, I was informed that my fine would be two hundred francs. My single dollar bill plus some small change was not sufficient. I was ordered to work rolling wine barrels over the cobblestones in the dock area until noon, when I was to return to my ship—"toot sweet," or something like that. Some of the stevedores loading the wine spoke English and directed me back to the bridge where I could see the ship across the river.

A very tired and sad cadet reported to the mate late that afternoon. It was foolish to expect any sympathy or understanding but maddening to get additional punishment, which I did. "You goddamned shanty Irishman, you think you can fool me with this cock-and-bull story. You will stay on board for the rest of our stay in this damn port and report to me every hour." Well, that's how it was, and at the time I didn't give a damn whether I ever saw Bordeaux again.

When the wheat cargo was discharged, we moved along the dock to load ballast. The ship had no double bottom or tanks; with the high masts and superstructure, she stood out of the water like a balloon. A good load of ballast was absolutely necessary. The stones and wet sand were delivered alongside by freight train and loaded by cranes with grabs. The crane drivers were unable to see up on deck and could only guess where the hatches were located. Consequently, many of the loads were dumped on deck. Who was chosen to shovel this heavy corruption off the sacred deck and into the hold—why, the shanty Irishman. The shovel idea was fine for about a dozen times, until it became heavy, very heavy. I waited until the mate went below. Then taking a can of plum jam from the galley to use as an incentive, I made overtures to the crane driver to lower his grab on deck, pick up the surplus, and dump it down the hatch where it should have been in the first place. All the details were worked out by signal, and for a while great progress was made. But for me to maneuver the heavy grab and signal the driver when to lower had complications. He dropped the gadget too soon, the edge caught on the hatch combings, and the steel corner gouged deep into the teakwood deck. This was sacrilege in the worst form, the mate's pride and joy. I had seen this deck scrubbed, holystoned, washed, and polished for months. Even when green seas were breaking on board, the deck had to be kept clean. Now I had managed to gash a 3-inch hole into two planks and right in plain view.

The thought of going ashore and deserting came to mind; maybe Chippy could dovetail a new section of wood into the spot; or possibly a few stones and wet sand smoothed off might fool the mate. I discharged the crane driver and continued to shovel, taking pains to leave odd patches of ballast around the damaged area, but this didn't fool the mate when he came on deck.

"What's the big idea? Sweep this junk up and wash the deck." I knew the gig was up before any water was applied. The mate sensed something was wrong and just stood there watching me sweep. I couldn't make that patch of sand look like wood no matter how smooth it was. The mate took his knife out and started to dig. The deeper he went down, the more cussing. "Two planks ruined, my beautiful deck a shambles." He raved on and on about the enormity of my crime, punctuated by profanity that included all my ancestors, past and present, as well as future descendants, and what had he done that the Lord had loaded him down with such a stupid, useless nincompoop as I. The punishment: climb the fore up starboard down port, then the main and mizzen, then stand to attention while supper was served.

My erstwhile Finnish buddy had returned on board much the worse for wear, with several knife cuts, both eyes blackened, and his suit torn to shreds. According to him, he had a wonderful time ashore. He waited until the mate went below decks, then smuggled a sandwich to me, plus my three dollars. "Tonight we go ashore and leave this lousy ship," he said. "I know where we can enlist in the air force. There is a new outfit being started, the Esquadrille, and they want men badly, good pay and food."

The idea tempted me. I went into the half deck, picked up a few treasured items from my sea chest and sneaked ashore with Karl, who had acquired extra money from some unknown source. He knew the streets and local bistros well. We had a good meal and much better wine than the vintage I had chosen, then headed for the recruiting office of the Lafayette Esquadrille. This was an air force branch of the Foreign Legion being created by assorted Americans, British, and French. They wore a cockeyed-type uniform, flew French Nieuports, and made quite a name for themselves. The recruiter accepted Karl and would have accepted me, but I needed my parents' consent because I was under 18. This, I explained, was impossible. Well, then, suppose you obtain the captain's permission—another impossibility. I bade Karl good-bye and rejoined the ship.

When the final load of ballast was dumped down the hold, the gangway was hoisted. With the aid of two tugboats, we eased away from the berth and headed downstream to the Gironde roadstead. Six men had left since our arrival, just two weeks before. One Dane and one Finn had joined the air force; one Norwegian was in the hospital; Pat, the Irishman, was killed in a fight; and one Swede and one Scotsman had disappeared over the French border into Spain. There was no possible chance of replacing these men. News leaked out that our next port of call would be Cardiff on the Bristol Channel. This brought great joy to our two pilot apprentices—Cardiff was their hometown.

The Gironde roadstead was crowded with sailing ships when we arrived. The wind had been westerly, and the U-boats were reported waiting outside. We anchored near a five-masted American schooner. In no time, the captain's gig was lowered, with the oars manned by four cadets in uniform, so that the captain could make a courtesy call to our neighbor. I was in disgrace and given the job of minding the boat while the others went on board and visited. The captain had taken the precaution of carrying a bottle of his own whiskey, but from all accounts this was not necessary. The schooner skipper had a regular bar and dispensed a variety of concoctions that knocked our Old Man for a loop. About midnight, they lowered him into the boat from the end of a boom. We brought him back alongside our ship, where he was heaved aboard in a cargo net. The other cadets brought back a supply of tobacco, which was in short supply on board. The next day, while the Old Man was sleeping off his hangover, the boat made regular trips back and forth, transferring much needed items from our ship to theirs and vice versa. The catch with much of the tobacco was that it was chewing tobacco loaded with molasses and useless for pipe smoking. Plugs of the stuff were lying around as surplus. I tasted a piece and found it sweet, something our diet lacked, and so in quick time I became a confirmed tobacco chewer.

More sailing vessels came downstream to join the armada already there. Probably the largest collection of sailing ships ever assembled in so-called modern times was anchored in the roadstead awaiting the "go" signal from the port authorities. The right combination was difficult—we had to have a reasonably fair wind to navigate the channel out to sea, there had to be some assurance that a U-boat was not waiting a few miles out to pick off each vessel as it emerged, and these two basic factors had to be coordinated with the French Navy, who planned to be our escort out to sea.

The majority of the anchored ships were French, and only Frenchmen served on their country's ships, which were considered a part of France. Their ships were nearly all painted white—the masts, yards, deckhouses and most of the superstructures—and some had imitation gun ports painted along the sides. Our captain thought he would like to pay a courtesy visit to a full-rigged ship anchored not far off. Again, the gig was manned by cadets in uniform and the captain was seated in the stern, which was covered with white cotton canvas—embroidered, frilled, and decorated with fancy knots. The boat was always kept spotless, the inside painted light gray, the oars sanded, the brass polished, lines coiled down in a flat, and everything spick-and-span.

The Frenchmen did not appreciate our visit, refused to take our line, and warned us away from the side. This friendly ally's hocus-pocus was starting to wear thin. If any of the Frenchmen on board understood what the Old Man had to say about them, their ears must have burned. "You bewhiskered bunch of frog bastards, we British are on the wrong side." He was fit to be tied when we returned to our own gangway. After the Old Man was rebuffed, he never made any further effort to befriend our neighbors; in fact, he was definitely at war with the whole nation and considered none of them worth a damn.

Every night at sundown, a French destroyer went through the boom defense, made a short patrol out to sea, and returned at sunrise. What was seen or accomplished was never divulged. The captain of the destroyer made

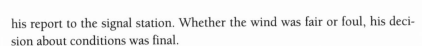

his report to the signal station. Whether the wind was fair or foul, his decision about conditions was final.

This waiting game developed into a routine, with everybody ready and eager to get going. Each morning, eyes were glued to the signal station, but invariably the red flag was hoisted. The mate would holler "Swab the decks, hands to breakfast," after which the ship's routine work was started. Trade with the American schooner flourished. We even gained an extra sailor when an Englishman on the schooner requested permission to join us. The skippers agreed, and the exchange was made for a small keg of rum.

The dawn of our twenty-second day at anchor brought significant signs of a change for the better. The old destroyer started blowing her siren as she came through the boom defense. The wind was fair but not strong, and the Old Man decided to shorten up on the cable long before any signal was displayed. When the "departe" flags were hoisted, the whole fleet of ships sprang to life. Every yardarm had men strung out loosening sail. A couple of antiquated tugs fussed around looking for work, and the destroyer tried vainly to organize the vessels into line. The French looked after their own, and priority to go through the boom gates went to the first Frenchmen under way. Our ship was almost twice the size of any ship there; with all sails set the Old Girl headed into position, with the American schooner right astern. Seventeen sailing ships with all sails set and their ensigns flying at the gaff were a very impressive sight. The flags represented France, Norway, Brazil, Britain, and Sweden.

Once outside, the fleet scattered. The Frenchmen huddled together, and the navy escort fussed around them like a clucky old hen. We headed toward the northeast and our schooner buddy, much more easily handled than a square rig, sailed almost alongside. With the crews shouting farewells, we dipped ensigns and headed back on course, the schooner for Boston and our ship for Cardiff. The schooner had left us only a few minutes before she struck a mine, which blew her bow completely off, and she started sinking. We swung around, backed the sails, and prepared to launch our lifeboats, but a French gunboat signaled us to proceed while she closed in to make the rescue. This was our first actual contact with the war and it was a good lesson to all aboard. The disregard shown to the menace was no longer evident, and an unusual alertness replaced the lethargy. This damn war was a serious business.

We sailed on out of the Bay of Biscay and up into the English Channel. The wind stayed fair but not strong enough to move the Old Girl, even as light as she was, more than 5 knots with all sails set. But the long voyage was nearing the end and "channel fever" was running high. The best suits of clothing were out airing, seabags were being packed, and treasured items purchased for relatives or friends were taken out of storage. Everybody hazarded a guess on our time of arrival, but the best anyone could hope for was to be well up the Bristol Channel the following night. The general feeling was that once we got past Lundy Island we were all set. If only we had a good westerly gale to push her along, everyone would feel more relaxed.

Eight bells had just struck in the afternoon watch when a screeching sound was heard passing overhead and a huge waterspout went up dead ahead. This was quickly followed by another screech, then another and another. We were under shell fire from astern, but from the deck nobody could see who was doing the shelling. The mate went aloft with his binoculars and reported a U-boat, right astern on the horizon, firing her forward gun and overtaking us fast. The only weapon on board was a small revolver and our chances of getting away were nil, so orders were given to abandon ship.

The mate's boat was the first one away and it had just cleared when a shell struck the jigger topmast and sent it crashing down on deck. It smashed the boat skids to matchwood, and buckled the davits like a pretzel. The haste to get the captain's boat swung out had proved unfortunate. One of the chocks was not down and the corner stove in several planks. The carpenter ran forward to his shop and brought some canvas strips and lead sheeting, with which he made hurried repairs, but when the boat was lowered into the water she leaked like a sieve. The ship was still sailing toward England with all sails set. The only things out of place were remnants of the jigger topmast draped over the side and the boat falls trailing in the water. Away astern were the U-boat, then the mate's boat, the captain's boat, and, sailing off alone, our gallant ship. One of the shells had ripped a hole in her port quarter, but she showed no signs of sinking or even the slightest hint of a list. It was pathetic to see this wonderful, proud vessel sailing off alone into the twilight to her doom. "Sail on, sail on, Oh Ship of State."

The submarine had closed with the mate's boat, taking everybody on board and towing the lifeboat astern, headed for us. We were ordered aboard, and our boat passed astern while the U-boat officers questioned the Captain. What name ship, where from, what cargo, what port of discharge? The captain's briefcase was passed to the conning tower and later returned with his master's ticket and his watch.

The captain, mate, second mate, and four cadets were separated from the rest of the crew and taken forward of the conning tower. "These SOBs are going to either shoot us or take us prisoner," said the captain. An alarm sounded and whatever plans the Germans had in mind were canceled. Everybody was ordered into one lifeboat as fast as possible. Unfortunately, the captain's boat was chosen. With all hands, it was overcrowded and had only 6 inches of freeboard; to add to this predicament, the boat leaked badly. The submarine cut us adrift and sheered off toward the west, towing the other lifeboat astern. The U-boat was in a hell of a hurry, but nobody knew the cause or reason. We had our own immediate problems to contend with before darkness. Efforts were made to stop the leak, and watches were set to bail out the water, a constant job. The nearest estimated position was 160 miles from Land's End, the cape at the southwesternmost point of England. Our chances of reaching there were fifty-fifty, providing the wind stayed fair. The Atlantic in winter was no place to be in an overcrowded lifeboat.

We were lucky to have everything inside the boat in excellent shape. The sail was hoisted and a course set by dead reckoning. The fresh water and ship's biscuits were okay and an issue was made. The first problem came from the cabin boy, who cried bitterly and claimed he was freezing to death. Extra clothing was given the lad, but he continued to cry and died early the following morning. A Russian sailor went berserk: he was a big powerful man and wanted to fight everyone. He was jumping up and making wild swings at anyone within reach. This was not appreciated and stern warnings were given him to pipe down. He seemed to understand for a while but jumped up once too often and damn near capsized the boat. Someone hit him on the head with a tomahawk that felled him like an ox. We threw him overboard, along with the cabin boy, and continued on our course.

During the day, we sighted smoke on the horizon. One vessel came within 2 miles but, despite our frantic waving, continued on her way without any signs of recognition. Another night closed in, the bailing kept the water under control, and a few feeble jokes were made about the sizzling steaks and hot coffee the cook was fixing. Sleep came easily in a sitting position; you couldn't fall over because you were wedged in. There was a degree of sadness over losing the ship.

Then a blimp came over. After circling us a few times, the chaps in the gondola waved and headed back toward land. We learned afterward that this dirigible was on regular patrol and coordinated with surface craft by radio. He contacted an armed trawler on patrol off Land's End. In the early afternoon, the trawler came alongside, picked us up, and, towing the lifeboat astern, took us to Penzance Harbor in Cornwall—and safety.

This terminated our voyage. Everybody reported to the shipping office, signed off the articles, and scattered every which way. My pay, less the deductions, even the damage to the ship's deck, was about fifty dollars, and that was my worldly wealth, plus the rather wet and dishevelled uniform.

What to do? I had no relatives in England and didn't know a soul. Obviously, Penzance was too small to offer any kind of work, so I decided to take a train to London.

3

ROYAL NAVY VESSELS—
WORLD WAR I

One of the porters in Paddington Station pointed out several nearby places where I could stay. The one chosen was, I imagine, a typical London boardinghouse, built of brick, three floors, quite ancient, and under the command of a sharp-tongued, heavy-bosomed lady, probably a direct descendant of those described by Charles Dickens. My room on the second floor contained a huge brass bedstead, a washstand with the prescribed basin and jug, a few towels, one badly worn chair, and a night table. The faded old wallpaper had been washed many times, and angels on the ceiling were blowing long trumpets. Pink dominated the color scheme. The only lighting was one unshaded bulb. The landlady, who smelled strongly of boiled cabbage, admonished me not to try smuggling women into my room—"This is a good place, this is." I was shown the bathroom, only one to each floor, located at the end of the hallway, quite a walk from my room. This introduction ended; the landlady departed.

I was dead tired and decided to hit the sack. I lay awake watching those pink angels with their horns and wondered whose idea they were and what they were supposed to convey. Soon I headed for the bathroom. When I returned, I had a feeling that somebody was there, and that scared me. My first thought was of a robber, but a gentle female voice assured me such was not the case. Of all places, the voice came from the bed. I asked who she was, what did she want, and several asinine questions, but eventually I was coaxed into bed. We talked in whispers so as not to arouse the landlady. My friend pleaded her cause—she was a munitions worker, no husband, no menfolk around, all at war, and all she needed was company and someone to help keep her warm.

I kept thinking about Mother's warning, "Never speak or get friendly with strange women." And here was something brand-new, a very friendly lady, eager to share my bed. Things began to happen. I was not sure whether I was seduced, or whether it could be classified as a technical rape, but along the way I lost my maidenhood, virtue, or whatever this first experience is called. We slept arm in arm, and her warm presence made me feel good. She left before morning, and another lonely dame took her place. Her technique was different—she was overanxious and so away we went. The old bed squeaked, and I wondered, expecting the landlady to arrive at any minute. The trouble I was having was not being able to see what type of woman she was—her features, age, or what have you. My only consolation was that these women were sex-starved, and in this respect I was helping the British war effort in a very nice manner.

My first time in London gave me the urge to see historic places—Trafalgar Square, Buckingham Palace, the Mall, and Piccadilly. By walking and riding the two-decker buses, I managed to cover many miles and see most of these places. My finances kept dwindling away, which caused me much concern. The result was my enlistment in the Royal Navy, where I hoped to become a midshipman but was trained as a gunner.

At this phase of the war, the need for merchant ships was urgent. My first assignment was on a cargo ship, the SS *Tyne,* carrying a 4.7-inch gun and three gunners. The chief was a French Canadian, who made sure I knew how to load, aim, unload, and identify various shells. The empty vessel was bound for the Bristol Channel to take on a load of coal and barrel oil for France.

The gunners' accommodation was right aft. Besides our regular watch, we had the job of making sure the ship was darkened. This patrol was made after being relieved with the gun watch. No lights—not even a match—were allowed to be seen. Every precaution was taken, as German U-boats were ever present.

We reached Penarth safely, where we took on a full load. The dust was thick from the antiquated method of loading. Every opportunity I could find I was ashore and away from that mess. When fully loaded, the ship joined others to form a convoy and, with two destroyers leading and armed trawlers covering the flanks, this group of twenty-odd ships steamed out of the Bristol Channel, around Land's End, and headed for Brest, France.

I had been relieved from the gun platform and was doing the inspection tour for any indiscretion about lights. Sure enough, a small chink showed occasionally on the forecastle alley. I went forward and discovered the offender to be the boatswain. He had a canvas curtain that moved with the roll of the ship, causing his light to show. I informed him about the error, and we visited awhile. He told me he was quite convinced we were going to be torpedoed and he could not sleep. As a precaution, he had his most treasured items wrapped up and placed near the door, ready to grab. I kidded him about the marvelous gunners now on board—no U-boat would dare to attack. Somehow my assurances did not make an impression. He gave me a magazine to read, and I bade him good night.

The time was about 0030. Walking slowly along the deck of the strange ship, I headed toward the midship section to complete inspection. I was rudely interrupted by a terrific explosion that shook the whole ship, sending oil barrels, hatch covers, lumps of coal, and other debris skyward. We had been torpedoed in the No. 3 hatch, and our ship was sinking fast. The crew had never had lifeboat drill, but the urgency, plus instinct, had them swinging out the boats and lowering them into the water. The chief mate took charge of the boat I scrambled into, and we pulled away from the sinking ship fast.

We now faced another serious danger—being run down by other ships in the convoy. Our ship had been leading the center line, with five other ships astern. Once they heard and saw the explosion, they had only one idea in mind: to get the hell out of the area. Of course, it was pitch dark, but from the water level we could see the silhouettes of other ships. It was scary to watch a huge bow bearing down at full speed. Those on the bridge had no way of seeing us, so we just stayed in place, ready to pull away or back up as the circumstances demanded. One might call it animated suspension, but whatever name applied, it was by no means a happy situation.

The mate had checked the time our ship was struck. From that instant until she was completely out of sight, seven minutes elapsed.

One of the armed trawlers came alongside. It had already picked up men from two other lifeboats. The mate checked to see who, if anyone, was missing. Yes, the third engineer and my chief gunner were unaccounted for. The engineer, no doubt, was caught below when the explosion occurred, and the chief gunner, who had relieved me, was probably blown overboard. I asked the boatswain if he had saved his treasures. "Hell no, I ran right past them."

The trawler was ordered to continue coverage of the convoy, but the ships had gained so much of a lead and were scattered every which way that the skipper had little or no chance of resuming his guardian position. He headed for Brest, the original destination.

It was dawn as we approached. Like many others, I went on the forecastle to look the place over. It was an artificial harbor, with long stone walls jutting out to break the swell, and afforded a safe roadstead. The French Navy had a comical warship at anchor. I say comical because it had six funnels. The idea evidently was to have independent engines in case one was put out of action. Someone suggested that the shipyard had a surplus and stuck them on this warship to reduce inventory. Whatever the reason, that vessel was really a sight and seemed to cheer everyone up.

I was cold and went aft to sit on the engine room casing to get warm. The trawler engineer came on deck carrying a big mug of hot chocolate. I guess I looked puny or cold, or both. He took pity on me and offered a swig, which I took with great gusto. The next thing I knew there was another explosion and I was in the water, my ears ringing and most of my clothing missing. The trawler had struck a mine right under the bow. Because she had no bulkhead or solid compartments, she filled with water and steamed right on down.

I couldn't see anybody floating and decided to head for the long breakwater. My early experience as a swimmer came in useful. I watched the breakers and timed myself to ride one in and clam onto the cement slope. A French sentry came running and held down his rifle for me to grab. Unfortunately, he gave me the bayonet end, but at least I had a grip on some degree of safety. The sentry was quickly joined by French sailors. I was taken to their barracks where several parts of the French uniform were given to me. I liked that fancy cap with a red pom-pom atop. The entire ship's company had been lost when the explosion occurred and that included my shipmates. One chap had tried to swim into the harbor but was run down by a launch sent out to see if it could find anybody to rescue. Alas, the only other survivor was killed.

The British Consul arranged for my return to England. When I reported to the duty officer in London, he thought he saw a ghost. "Why, Palmer, you just left here! What in God's name are you doing in that frog uniform?" After I related my experiences, I was given a new uniform and four days' leave. This gave me a chance for another look around my favorite London Town.

When I reported back, the duty officer informed me I would be assigned to the Grand Fleet in Scotland. Two days later, with orders to report to Rosyth Dockyard, I was en route to Scotland on the railroad that boasted the name "Flying Scotsman." This train had established a record for speed

SS *Princess Victoria*—sister ship of the *Princess Margaret*, which was converted to a minelayer during World War I.

against all comers. The majority of passengers on board were service people, with the navy predominating. The countryside was beautiful. I could understand why so many poems, essays, books, and speeches had been written about Scotland.

We crossed the Firth of Forth bridge and in view was much of the vast fleet known as the Grand Fleet. Battleships, cruisers, and destroyers were at anchor as far as the eye could see, all of them ready to head out to sea whenever the German fleet showed. The train stopped at North Queensferry. Most of those on board got off and headed for the dockyard where they would be assigned to the fleet.

My orders indicated that I was to join the HMS *Princess Margaret*, a ship formerly owned by the Canadian Pacific Railroad and converted to a minelayer. Along with the other merchant vessels, she was laying a huge mine field from Johnnet Roads on the Scottish coast to Archie Light on the Norwegian coast—a string of high-explosive mines stretching across the North Sea. The idea was to stop U-boats from reaching the Atlantic.

The mines, globular in shape and 5 feet in diameter, were each cradled in a metal box that served as the anchor. The depth at which the mine was to float was predetermined: if the mine was to float 3 feet under the surface at low tide, or 100 feet under the surface, or whatever depth necessary, the wire attachment was cut accordingly and stowed in the box contraption. Each mine had ten projecting horns made of lead, and inside the casing was a glass tube containing fulminate of mercury. The idea was that a submarine, or any vessel, striking the round mine would bend one of the lead horns and break the glass tube, which in turn would detonate the 100-odd tons of TNT, a very high explosive force that could sink the largest vessel.

These mines were loaded at Grangemouth and stowed on board below decks on small rails that ran the full length of the ship toward aft. They would be dropped into the sea from two large doors. Mine laying required skillful navigation. The vessel was under way all the time, busy laying these lethal eggs as fast as her crew could push them down the rails to the rear doors. The exact spot where each mine was dropped was recorded on the chart, and markers were left to show where the mine field started and ended. The Germans often moved these markers to louse up the best-laid plans.

HMS *Princess Margaret* had no armament worthy of the name; her defense was speed. She was under orders to stop all activities and race for home base should anything look like an enemy. When the last mine went out the rear door, we headed for Grangemouth, took on another load, then back we went to the mine field. The HMS *Angora* was in company with us. Whether it was imagination or a case of nerves, she flashed an alarm signal that an enemy destroyer was approaching. Off she went, belching smoke and racing to the base. We followed suit because it would be suicide to stay around with such a hot cargo. One lucky shot and whammo, finito, kaput, or whatever the hell you wish to call it.

I must have made six or seven trips to the mine field and got to know the ship and shipmates. It was far different from being on a sailing ship where close friendships existed. On a steamship, it appeared that everyone was for himself and you didn't get to know much about your own watch mates. During this time, the King visited the fleet on board HMS *Oak*, which steamed up one line and down the other.

The *Princess Margaret* was due for docking, and once again I was placed in a pool where men awaited new assignments. My draw was the collier *Ford Castle*, designed as a coal carrier. She earned her keep loading coal into various ships of the fleet; most of them were coal burners and required to maintain steam at all times. The *Ford Castle* went alongside a battleship, and the ship's crew scrambled on board and hoisted our cargo into their bunkers. Our deck officer kept watch for the signal to give another ship bunker coal and, when this loading was completed, we went on to the next ship until our holds were empty. We then reloaded and started all over again.

Because the *Ford Castle* had extra large hatches, she was pressed into service for boxing matches and theater shows. With a cruiser on either side, the forward hatch was decked in and bleacher seats made. Fancy flags and bunting were hung for decoration, and a band played. I liked this part of the activity and watched some wonderful fights—it broke the monotony.

While anchored one night, we had a visitor in the form of a zeppelin that passed overhead. The warships picked him up with their searchlights, but nobody took a shot. *Why?* There wasn't an antiaircraft gun in the whole damn fleet!

On the great day of 11 November 1918, when so-called peace was announced, every ship blew whistles or sirens, flags went up on all halyards, and great jubilation was everywhere. The terms of the peace agreement called for the surrender of the German fleet. I was very privileged to witness this ceremony—these mighty ships with their heavy guns pointed skyward, the crews lined along the decks, and the flags at half-mast. It must have been humiliating for those on board. Adm. David Beatty was our commander in chief and received the surrender of the once proud German Navy.

Winding down from an alert state of war to peacetime caused much disruption. Our ship had orders to fill the coal bunkers of every ship, and they would then be dispatched to various dockyards. There were also three American coal-burning battleships that had to be filled up for their long trip across the Atlantic. The *Ford Castle* was kept busy day and night in taking care of this mighty assembly. Along the way, I caught a bad dose of flu, which was raging at that time. I was put ashore and taken to the Rosyth Navy Hospital. Apparently, I was not given much chance for survival. One of the nurses told me later that the matron had told her, "Don't bother washing him, I don't think he will be with us in the morning."

Well, I fooled them all and made a sufficiently good recovery to be discharged from the hospital and sent to a convalescent home in Kent—the palatial home of a Mr. MacConachy, a fabulously wealthy meat packer. His home had been turned over to the navy and used as a halfway house.

Upon my release, I got into the bus and headed to London to report to my duty officer. While waiting to see him, I scanned the numerous notices, two of which made me laugh. "Join the minesweepers, earn three times standard pay, excitement and adventure." That was a joke. Adventure, yes, too damn much, but getting three times the pay collecting these lousy mines, when I had spent many cold and scary days laying them, seemed rather odd.

Another poster read, "General Wrangle wants you in Russia to stem the Red Army. The base of operations will be Archangel, N. Russia." Well, that went by the board. The general would have to get along without me.

"The Duty Officer will see you now," cooed a pretty Wren. The DO was an old friend by now, and he wanted to know if I had any desire to enlist for minesweeping or for chasing Red Russians.

"No, sir, I am disappointed in not hearing about my midshipman's exam—I am going to try reaching home and would love to arrive in my midshipman's uniform." Instead, I received an honorable discharge, a general service medal, and a victory medal, plus a solid silver lapel brooch bearing the words, "For King and Country." Holy Moses, I guess this should have impressed me but it did not. I was discouraged and frustrated, a very disillusioned civilian, and decided to go to the Australia House to join the Commonwealth Line.

4

TRAMP STEAMERS

The officials in Australia House were extremely kind and considerate. I was rather puny and skinny as a rail, after several months in the hospital, but they asked me a few questions and decided to send me out to Cardiff, Wales, to join an Australian ship. An official gave me travel vouchers and a note to report on board the SS *Carawa* and present myself to Captain Hyde. I found this ship to be a typical tramp type or three-islander, a medium-sized vessel of 3,530 tons gross, with forecastle, midship house, and poop (or aftercastle)—a coal burner with five hatches and cargo-handling gear.

I learned that the *Carawa* had been captured in October 1914 by the Australian government, headed at that time by Prime Minister William Hughes. Although he was much maligned, one of his foresighted endeavors was to create a fleet of ships. Named the Commonwealth Line, it consisted of ships captured in port when war was declared, plus a few ships that Hughes bought from a company having financial trouble. The Australian shipyards began building vessels, and the fleet grew and prospered. By the early 1920s, the line would have more than seventy vessels.

The marine superintendent of the Commonwealth Line was a Captain Innes, an excellent seaman. Under his guidance, the ships operated well,

46

"He stilled the storm to a whisper.
The waves were hushed . . . .
and he guided them to their desired haven"

Psalm: 109 vv. 29/30

"Morning Mist"

Reproduced from an original oil painting by Jack Rigg
Courtesy of Richmond & Rigg Photography, Hull.
01482 216914

were maintained in first-class condition, and carried cargo to all points of the compass. Innes made a practice of transferring officers around so that they spent time on all regular cargo vessels, colliers, and wheat freighters. The line later acquired five passenger ships.

The *Carawa* was formerly the *Tyrol* of Fiume, owned by the Austrian Lloyd Company. The name was changed to *Carawa* when she became a part of the Commonwealth Line's armada of wheat freighters in 1914. This type of vessel was the workhorse of the cargo fleet and also the money earner. The accommodation had been enlarged and modified to suit Australian regulations. The firemen lived forward, deck officers and engineers amidships, and sailors right aft. The entire crew were Australians except for one Scottish engineer. This was very unusual, but it was an outgrowth from the war days. After unloading a cargo of wheat in Europe, the *Carawa* had gone to the Bristol Channel port of Cardiff and was being readied for a coal cargo consigned to Egypt.

It took me several days to adjust to this new way of shipboard life, my previous experiences having been sailing ships and navy vessels. In contrast, this ship was very easygoing and what might be termed a happy ship. The method of loading seemed antiquated with much waste, but eventually we had a full cargo, took on a pilot, and headed down channel, hopefully back home. It had been almost three years.

The Egyptian Power Company in Alexandria was desperate for fuel, and double shifts were put to work unloading the cargo. I had never visited this ancient country and took every opportunity to sightsee and watch the dhows moving up and down the River Nile or one of the many estuaries of that great waterway. The natives were fascinating, in their funny hats and nightgown-type clothing, but evidently this mode of dress was satisfactory—it had been in use for centuries. Cargoes were scarce; the only thing offering was phosphate from Christmas Island to Fremantle in western Australia. It wasn't much, but Fremantle was at least on the way home.

I was seeing many firsts on this trip, and the trip through the Suez Canal was especially interesting. The priority scale was enforced, with one ship being tied up to the bank to allow another to pass. Mailboats came first, ammunition carriers next, troop ships third, and tramp vessels last. The *Carawa,* being empty and with only a tramp classification, had no status whatsoever. The canal pilot took two crewmen, plus a rowboat, for mooring to the bank. We tied up next to a refugee camp where Armenians were cooped up inside miles of barbed wire, a pathetic lot ousted from their homeland by the Turks and on the verge of starvation. We tried tossing food to them but were warned away by the Churka Troops guarding the camp. I understood that they had typhus in the camp.

We finally got clear of Egypt and headed for Christmas Island, a small speck just south of Java and owned by Britain. This island had been a bird sanctuary, and over the years the droppings had formed huge mounds. This material, used as fertilizer, was mined and shipped to Australia. It was an odorless white powder and exceedingly strong.

We had experienced a flu epidemic on board, and two men had died. Fortunately, the medic on the island had some concoction that cured those still ailing. When we left with a full cargo, everybody on board was supposedly in good health. Not so; two more took ill on the third day out. We were already shorthanded. Everybody had to extend their work load and help out wherever they were needed. I did several stints in the stoke-hold shoveling coal into the furnaces, but even with everybody straining we could only make 5 knots. The unkindest blow came when the radioman jumped overboard. This cut off our communication with any shipping or shore establishment to advise them of our predicament.

We eventually made Fremantle, seven days late. Several men came on board to help us get the ship into port for unloading and to give everyone a thorough medical checkup. Two more of the crew went into the hospital, and another died. The ship got to be known as the death ship, and that wasn't the nicest tab to carry. We anchored outside the harbor and were placed in quarantine. The ship was fumigated, nobody was allowed ashore, and, to compound the issue, my dreams of going home were shattered—no way.

The isolation ended, and the urgent cry for food could be heard from Europe. We loaded a full cargo of wheat bound for Germany via South Africa, a long haul.

I was the third officer on board this tramp steamer. The captain, known as the Old Man, observed me for several weeks without giving any approval or complimenting my ability. In his opinion, I was the lowest form of life—wet behind the ears—and he wondered how I ever got on board. I considered myself "in" when he occasionally asked for my opinion or thanked me for some trivial thing I did.

The routine we kept at sea was four hours on duty and eight hours off or below. The reference to eight hours, however, was purely technical. I was required to be on the bridge at noon to take a sight and work out the ship's position. Most often, I was the ship's medical officer, available and ready to treat any crewman for cuts, burns, or stomachache.

The *Carawa* also carried mail, not first-class mail, but just any type with a stamp. I had to know geography thoroughly and figure out just where to offload mailbags bound for out-of-the-way places. The cargo stowage was also my responsibility. I had to be sure that items were separated to avoid contamination. The ship's manifest gave complete details of the cargo carried and just where it was located; it had to be available to the head stevedore at the next port of call.

The watches on duty time followed this pattern: The chief officer took the 0400–0800 watch, which enabled him to work out a routine for maintaining the ship. The crew began work at 0600 with wash-down of all decks. The bosun visited the mate or chief officer on the bridge and received his orders for the day. Breakfast was 0800, then things began to unravel. The mate went below and often did not reappear until 1600 to take over his watch. The second mate worked out the noon position and kept the charts up to date. He was responsible for all the ship's instruments—compass, chronometers, and so forth. As third mate, I had only a second mate license, whereas all other officers held a master's license.

The watch from 1200–1600, known as the gravy-eye, was actually the captain's watch, but he was liable to appear at any time, day or night. He checked the compass and the ship's course, read any new entries in the log-book, and looked at the barometer, the ship's speed, the cloud formation, or any other item of interest. He sometimes condescended to ask a question or speak about some incident, but he was more likely to leave the bridge without saying a word. On the other hand, if anyone was off course or not paying attention to his job, look out. Brother, was that person in trouble!

In port, I was the captain's messenger. "Take this to the office." "Tell the Chief Officer I want to speak with him." "Show those gentlemen the cargo list in No. 6 hold." I performed all sorts of tasks and learned by doing. With good shipmates, everything was downhill. When the captain called me "Mister," I considered myself accepted.

Our voyage from Fremantle across the Indian Ocean was uneventful. We made a short stop at Mauritius to offload medical supplies, mail, and a new flu serum. This small island had been decimated by epidemic, and we rescued a lone jockey who had no horses to ride. The next stop, Durban, was for bunker coal. Although it was a lovely city, the people were not very friendly. Damned if I know what was wrong with them. We had on deck several prize merino sheep, one ram and six ewes. The Australian government had placed a ban on the export of these prize sheep; this was probably the cause of the unfriendly attitude. The bunker coal was not of good quality and our chief engineer was bitching, but apparently it was the only type of coal available.

We headed around the Cape and into the Atlantic, bound for Europe and, of all places, Germany. The chief paced the deck and looked worried. He finally announced that if the good weather held we could make Bremen, but if the Bay of Biscay acted up we would be out of fuel and floundering at the mercy of the waves. Charts were studied and, sure enough, right at the top northwest corner of Spain was Corcubian Bay bearing the mark of a coal port. This must have been someone's pipe dream, but we decided to investigate and steamed into a deep channel entrance with high hills on either side. There was no lighthouse or any navigational aids, but our soundings showed 20 fathoms or more.

After rounding a few bends, we sighted a small village with colorful houses clustered together, facing one street, and near the center a wooden pier or wharf. There was no sign of activity or people working, with one exception. A rowboat was being pulled by two men and, sitting right aft in the stern sheets, was a miniature elderly man dressed in a white uniform. When he came within hearing range, Captain Hyde asked who he was.

"I'm the pilot," was his reply.

"Well, I don't need any pilot, I'm already here . . . are you the harbor master?"

"Yes, I am."

"Can I anchor here?"

"Yes, you can—about 10 fathoms of water."

"Is there any doctor here?"

"No, do you need pratique? I'll give you pratique."

"I came in for coal, do you have any?"

"Yes, I'm the agent."

"Lower the gangway, we can't allow this character to leave," the captain ordered.

The agent proved to be as good as his word. We were to get our bunkers and . . . "Was there anything else?"

"No, thanks." He departed and we expected to see activity within the hour.

What we didn't take into account was the noonday siesta, or long lunch hour. The captain finally gave up and ordered me to take the workboat ashore and find this guy. I dressed in my white uniform and, with two good deckhands, shoved off and headed for the rickety jetty. After much searching, I located my miracle man fast asleep in a hammock. I aroused him none too gently. After much cussing in Spanish, he agreed to show me where the coal was stored. I stayed with him, just in case he rolled over for another forty winks.

The coal depot was truly a joke and consisted of an old barge loaded with black dust. It had been exposed to the elements for years and the locals had picked it over numerous times. It looked pure dust to me, without any substance. The miracle man promised to have it moved and alongside pronto, but I was still wondering where the stevedores or work gangs were coming from. I reported on board and, with the rest of our crew, waited for the coal. Sure enough, the barge appeared, being towed by an ancient launch that had about a dozen women on board—these were the stevedores! When the chief looked over the side and saw the heap of dust, he damn near fainted—what the hell, what the hell. The loading was pitiful, but we hoisted our booms and helped the ladies as best we could. Their numbers dwindled and, at times, work stopped completely—they were otherwise busy.

The captain requested (not ordered) that I go ashore to find out if there was any liquor for sale and to mail some letters. My two sailors had discovered that these people were in a bad way for foodstuff. It was a fishing village, and the men were out in the Atlantic. They would stay there while the fish were biting. Whatever catch was made, they took to Corunna, the railroad terminal, for shipment to Madrid. They would then return to the fishing grounds, sometimes staying several months on end and leaving their wives all alone. Other than the Catholic priest who came over the hills occasionally, a few old-timers, plus the miracle man, were the only males for miles around.

I reported back to the captain that the only hard liquor around was a local wine brandy made by the women, but there was a good supply of beer in storage that nobody liked. He gave orders for one third of the crew to go ashore for three hours and then return. I was to find the post office and mail the letters. My small crew had taken advantage of the local food shortage and were trading jellies, jams, ketchup, hardtack, biscuits, honey, mustard, and other assorted junk for the local wine and a few home comforts. I found the post office, which was actually the front room in the house of the postmistress, a very comely lass who seemed lonely as all get out. I never did find out whether the letters ever reached their destinations, but someday I'd like to revisit Corcubian Bay and look over the present population. I'm sure they must be an odd collection, with several redheads among them.

I think the chief was ready to shoot himself. We hove up anchor and headed out to sea with dusty bunkers, numerous hangovers, and many cases of local wine and beer. It had been a very nice visit. Now, across the bay to Bremen with our mercy cargo.

The German authorities could not believe their good fortune. I tagged along with the captain to the burgomaster, where the gift from the Australian people was formally presented to their recent enemies. The understanding was that the locals supply the labor force, our crew drive the winches, and unloading take place right away. We had to show the recruits how to hold a bag, how to stack them, and how to make up a sling. Much of the work was done by our crewmen; otherwise, we would have been there for weeks. Those young Germans knew the cadence of arms and how to goose-step on the parade ground, but stevedoring was alien and they were not worth a plugged nickel. The population seemed sullen. I got the feeling they thought we had shortchanged them. Our currency was worth a thousand times more than theirs. Every woman was available, and I recall one English pound bought a sextant, binoculars, and several other items, plus being bowed in and out the door with profuse thank-yous.

Germany was much better for our visit, at least I thought so, as we left for the Bristol Channel to load a coal cargo for the Azores. Everybody wanted food and fuel, which kept us busy. The loading methods were very antiquated, but eventually we had a full load and headed down channel. My old shipmate from the *Burrowa*, Bert Pead, was piloting another vessel ahead of us, and we exchanged greetings. Unfortunately, I never got to see Bert and a wave was poor consolation.

The *Carawa* was loaded to the lines. When we ran into an Atlantic storm, I thought it was the end of everything. She proved seaworthy, however, and aside from loose deck fittings and a few miserable days, we finally made Ponta Delgada in the Azores, a very old seaport steeped in history. Columbus had stopped there en route to the New World.

This was Portuguese territory, the people were friendly, and, although whaling was the chief industry, they made much wine. The arrangement was for the man to run the vineyard while his wife operated the store. Visitors were invited to taste the vintage free of charge, an item not overlooked by our sailors. The police force was paid a percentage of whatever fine was levied, and this created difficulties. I made a head count each morning and then headed for the pokey to bail out several sailors arrested for drunkenness or fighting. The fines also included meals bought or ordered from local restaurants, and the best on the menu was their favorite. We had one man drown in the harbor, which slowed down the activities and made our stay longer than usual. I bought a case of high-quality brandy and thereby joined the bootleggers. I sold it to a stevedore in Newport News, where we stopped for bunkers before going around the Florida Keys for Beaumont, Texas.

The huge Texas oil installation was well guarded—no smoking signs were prominent, and armed guards patrolled the whole area. The pilot ordered all fires extinguished. With just sufficient steam, we tied up at Port Arthur. We were reminded of a near casualty when the pilot asked what sort of a trip we had. Mention was made of the storm in the Atlantic, and it was disclosed that a huge French liner had foundered with seven hundred persons on board. I know we had received her distress call, although we could do nothing. In fact, we were thinking about sending SOS for our own miserable hides.

The cargo being loaded was mostly naphtha, gasoline, kerosene, and barrel oil. We had a consignment of steel rails for Russia below decks and the mate wanted to get them out before loading the case oil. The fear of sparks and untrained personnel prohibited their handling, however, and we just had to wait. The mechanical loading went fast. Any cases showing signs of leaking were hoisted out and repaired. Each case was handled carefully. The crew lived ashore, where meals were prepared. Because this was bad mosquito country, there was much spraying and we used nets. These varmints arrived from the Louisiana swamps and came over in clouds—they were mean.

When the cargo was loaded, a tugboat towed us downstream where the main boilers were fired up. With the galley stove sparking away, we headed for Panama. Another disaster almost caught us unaware when a tidal wave swept across the Gulf of Mexico near the Yucatan coast. Had it not been for the captain's prompt action, this wave would have rolled us over. It did quite a lot of damage and scared the beegeezers out of those of us below.

Cristobal on the Atlantic side had excellent coaling facilities. With our bunkers refilled and a pilot on board, we made passage through the Panama Canal, a fantastic engineering feat and great achievement made possible by American know-how.

We had left Balboa, heading out across the Pacific, when the man on lookout spotted a launch away on the horizon. Perched atop the roof was a man waving a shirt for help—almost a replica of the movies. We eased over to find out what was wrong. It appeared the launch had engine trouble and had been adrift for five days. The engineers tried to figure out the problem, but the smell and rapid movement of the launch made them sick and they abandoned the task. A conference was held to decide on the next move, and our shipmates had many views. There were four Indians, the owner, and one American on the launch. Take them back to Panama—no, that was ruled out. Ram the launch and take the people on board as survivors—no, that was ruled out. Cut their throats—no, also ruled out. Charts revealed a group of islands to the south known as the Galápagos. They were owned by Ecuador and had achieved some fame from the book written by Charles Darwin. We decided to take them there in tow and cast them adrift.

These poor people had been without water. Once they were given permission to board, they made a mad rush for the water pump. We had to beat them off and make them take a few sips at a time. The owner was notified of our plan and thought it best for all concerned. The towline was hooked up, three men were left on board to steer, and we got under way. The American chap was the news medium and interpreter. He was by trade a steeplejack and had been in Costa Rica working on a job for an oil company. His hobby was climbing tall buildings without the aid of ladders; he was known as the "human fly." He had numerous news clippings to verify this claim, and I recalled having read about him in various papers.

The basic objective of the launch's crew was to stake out a claim for gold in Colombia. The Indians had found a large deposit there. They were scared to notify the authorities because they knew that once the police learned of the location they would kill them and claim the gold for themselves. The Indians had crossed the gulf in a canoe, hoping to find an honest man to cultivate their valuable find. The honest man was the Costa Rican businessman who owned the launch. The expedition was poorly organized; in fact, it had no organization at all. The engineer knew only how to stop and start the engine. The compass was mounted on a metal seat one finds on a tractor. They had plenty of tools, very little water, and a limited food supply. Of course, the run across the water was only about 150 miles, but nobody had taken engine failure into account. Had we not sighted them, they would have surely died as they drifted westward across the Pacific.

The only island with any habitation in the Galápagos group was Chatham, and the residents were all convicts placed there for life. Their only communication was with a small schooner that came every three months. We approached Chatham Island with great caution. The launch crew was ordered back to their boat, and the towline was cast off. The operation took far too long, and a strong current caused us to drift toward the shore and onto a hidden reef. This was our undoing.

When the engines started up, two blades of the propeller snapped off and the rudder jumped the gudgeons. We were stuck, and the gentle surf kept pounding the unfortunate ship on the reef. We sent out radio distress signals, and a ship answered to ask if we were in any danger of our lives. We were not, and the ship then volunteered to pass on our name and position to the next vessel heading toward Panama.

Whether this happened, we will never know. Innocents abroad, we fancied ourselves being rescued within a day or so and casually made camp ashore. My tent was the lifeboat sail, and we gathered food from the ship, which was resting on the reef with her decks awash. This is where I spent my twenty-first birthday, 27 March 1920, and it seemed I never would reach my home in Sydney.

We scanned the horizon every day for any sign of smoke, but none appeared. Our days became routine. The convict settlement was in the hills, and our camp was on a stretch of sand. We had strung up tarpaulins, sails, blankets, and other gear in a haphazard manner, with everybody doing whatever they pleased. The engineers worked on the launch and finally got it going. It left for Colombia; hopefully, the crew found their pot of gold and made millions.

We spent our days swimming or just lazing around. Fresh water was at a premium, and most of us had left our things on board the wreck. When the ship broke up, the cargo drifted ashore. Wash day presented no problem. If you wanted to wash a shirt, you looked around for a can of naphtha, opened it up, dipped the shirt a few times, and—presto—it was clean as a whistle. Of course, this treatment eventually left only the buttons or maybe a pocket.

I ventured up the hill to inspect the settlement. The government had made a crude sugar mill where cane was crushed and the sugar made ready for shipment to the mainland when the trading schooner arrived. There were also bales of dried fish and hides from the few cattle killed for meat. Who suddenly appeared but an Englishman, a cockney who managed to speak a little English with occasional breaks into Spanish. He was a wizened old man, married to a huge black woman, and he held the rank of lighthouse keeper. His tale of survival could fill a book. He had been a cabin boy on a ship that was wrecked on these islands, and he was the only survivor. He managed to speak quite fluently after associating with us for a few days. He wanted several of us to take one of the lifeboats so he could guide us to a treasure cache on a nearby island. He did not trust any of the natives. When he related the crimes some of them had committed, I couldn't blame him.

He assured us the schooner was due any time, and his duties as lighthouse keeper called for him to hang an ordinary hurricane lamp in a tree. We watched this performance every night, but the mythical schooner never appeared. The dried fish bales were mustered near the jetty, the dried hides stacked up, and about thirty bags of raw sugar placed on stilts. This preparation at least convinced us that the schooner must be near. Sure enough, a diminutive ketch-rigged vessel of about 40 tons appeared on the horizon. Great jubilation spread around the island and the port of Porto Chico. The *Manuel J. Cobos* brought mail, tools, clothing, flour, and a few items that could not be grown on the island. These items were bartered in lieu of payment. While all the dickering was going on, our crewmen were busy loading the schooner. Within a few days, the vessel was loaded, including many cases of gasoline, kerosene, and a few barrels of oil salvaged from the ship. We bade adieu to the old *Carawa* falling apart on the reef. The lighthouse keeper got all dressed up for the occasion. The tents, tarpaulins, and odd items were parceled out, the sails hoisted, and off we went to Guayaquil, Ecuador,

The *Manuel J. Cobos*. Fifty-eight people traveled six hundred miles to the South American mainland from Porto Chico, Galápagos Islands, on this 53-foot fishing boat. The voyage took fifteen days, 20 April to 5 May 1920.

approximately 600 miles to the east. The trip took fifteen days; when we landed in Ecuador, a total of forty-five days had elapsed since the wreck off Chatham Island.

One can picture this small craft sailing toward South America—loaded down with sugar, hides, dried fish, three pigs, and a very fat cook, plus the original crew and our *Carawa* crew, about fifty-eight in all. The smell from the cargo and humans even scared the birds away. We slept wherever we could, the toilet was over the side, and meals were prepared whenever the cook felt disposed. Water was very limited and we had no exercise, but the *Manuel J. Cobos* finally tied up to a substantial wharf in Guayaquil.

The first stop was to see the consul, where we unfolded our trials and tribulations. The consul gave us some money and also a warning about unrest in the city. He suggested that we stay in our hotel. The one assigned was centrally located.

I had grown a full beard, nothing to be proud of. In fact, it was a very odd type with gray, red, and black hairs, plus curlicues, some growth upward and some downward, a regular mix-match. I headed for a barber shop first thing. It was very old-fashioned. By sign language I told the barber what I wanted, and he understood. First, the clippers, then a big broad open razor, and then a light razor prefaced by much lather, oils, and massage. He finally got finished and I departed onto the main street. The reaction of the folk seemed strange—most of them avoided me, one crossed the street in a run, and I wondered what the hell was so funny. My reflection in a small strip of mirror scared me, and I hurried back to the hotel. My face was truly a mess. The many days in the hot sunshine had browned the upper part, the whisker area was white, and the barber had nicked me several times, which showed red. Then to compound the whole mess, he had given me a liberal dabbing of talc. No wonder the mothers clutched their children and folks avoided me. Three or four days later, my face returned to normal and I ventured out to see the city.

The standard pattern of most South American cities centers around a square, with the church dominating several banks, city hall, and a few fashion shops. The square in Guayaquil had several statues, a big fountain, some shade trees, and benches. There was no such thing as air conditioning and not many fans, but the central square, with four roads leading into it, was cooler than most spots and a slight breeze helped out considerably. I was seated in the square when the people nearby started mumbling and most moved away to the distant corner.

A troop of cavalry approached from one of the roadways. The people began throwing stones, shouting at them, and several tried diverting the horses. It was not a very impressive troop, but the men stuck to their positions and paid no attention to all the shouting, cussing, and stone throwing. This only seemed to anger the crowds. After the troopers made the required turns and reached the continuation of the road on which they had arrived, the officer in charge gave a curt order. About six mounted men swung about, blocked off the roadway, loaded their rifles, and, without a word, fired right at the mob. Several men fell, and the others scattered, including me. I thought, to survive all my previous troubles and then get shot by a bunch of troopers would be ignominious, to say the least.

As I ran across the square, I had the company of a short, fat man wearing a straw hat. His legs were working like pistons, but when he reached the fountain he quit and dived into the pool, a rather shallow slimy puddle. His hat floated away as he skidded across the bottom and, despite the rifle fire, I just had to laugh at the spectacle. He was not amused.

The cause of unrest stemmed from an urgent call from the president's brother who lived in Guayaquil. The cavalry was housed on the opposite side of town, and this troop was being sent to rescue him. The shooting accounted for five deaths. I followed the consul's advice and stayed indoors for the next three days, when we were to sail to Panama. Hopefully, I could go home at last.

The old steamers trading along the South American coast were named after the various republics. The SS *Guatemala* was an old-timer flush deck with pocket hatches. She had seen better days and had none of the amenities of a modern passenger liner. Her main deck contained passenger cabins, dining room, lounge, and a small bar. The lower deck was designed to carry cattle. When I joined her, she had a full complement of humans and bovines.

This ship belonged to what was then known as the Pacific Steam Navigation Company, which was a subsidiary of the Royal Main Line. I do not know how many vessels were in this fleet, but their route was along the Pacific coast of South America, through the Panama Canal to New York. The cattle were from Peru—all prize steers consigned to the New York market and each animal had a stall. The cowboys attending them were responsible for their safe arrival, in good order and condition.

My cabin, which opened right onto the deck, was typical of all ships of that period. It had two bunks, one on either side of the cabin, with large drawers underneath, and in the center was a washstand that housed a basin, tumblers, towels, a fair-sized mirror, and a water pitcher. The regular door was hooked back while we were in the tropics, and a supplementary shutter-type door was used—somewhat like old bar doors that swung in and out. This provided maximum ventilation and some degree of privacy.

Carl Erskine, my roommate, was an engineer who had been working in Chile for three years on some project and was returning to New York to get married. He proved to be a worthy type and proudly showed me several items he had purchased for his bride. The most interesting, to my way of thinking, was an Indian bridal gown of red silk, very elaborately embroidered with feathers, jewels, gold buttons, and a few small mirrors, all woven into a pattern that made it really beautiful.

Our ship made calls along the Ecuadorian and Colombian coasts. Some of these stops were in regular ports, but others were simply in estuaries where we anchored and the freight was brought out in lighters or canoes. We were loading ivory nuts, a small hard nut with a white center from which shirt buttons were made. I noticed the crew members doing a brisk business on the side, trading clothing, knives, watches, and other items for monkeys and parrots. These were kept right aft in two huge cages that had obviously been used for storing fresh vegetables. The crew cared for them, fed and watered them, and cleaned the cages. This black market trade belonged to the ship's purser, who sold them to dealers in New York.

We had made our last stop in Colombia and were due to arrive in Panama by noon the following day. Carl and I had become good friends. I would be leaving the ship in Panama, so we decided a small celebration was in order. Right after dinner, we settled down to some steady drinking: to the bride . . . to her parents . . . to each other, and so on. We finally closed the joint around 0100, feeling no pain whatsoever, and headed for the sack.

I awakened around daylight to head for the bathroom, or that was my intent. When I opened my eyes to get my bearings, I noticed the red gown slowly moving toward the door. Vowing never to drink again, I took another look. Sure enough, there was a small monkey examining the pretty colors of the bridal gown and giving me the eye. I called Carl and was told to shut up, "There are no pink elephants around." I told him that was true, but a brown monkey was taking his prize gift out the door. He sat up, let out a yell that awakened the whole ship, and bounded over to the door so fast that the monkey dropped the gown and scampered away. The sight that met our eyes when we went on deck was unbelievable. The entire deck was cluttered with clothing, handbags, slippers, and assorted underwear while numerous monkeys examined every item, truly having a ball. Other sleepy, scantily clad passengers appeared, and it was a sight to behold them chasing monkeys around the deck for their possessions, including false teeth, eyeglasses, pipes, and shoes. Two monkeys were working over a two-way stretch girdle. One lady spotted her dentures being studied by a monkey sitting on the rail. She rushed at him, but all in vain, because he threw them overboard, hooked his tail to the railing, and swung below deck. He left a lady toothless but not speechless.

The crew were out in force trying to round up the monkeys, the parrots had flown ashore, and some degree of normalcy returned while the passengers sorted out their property. It was believed that the purser had failed to pay the crew for caring for the monkeys and so they released those little rascals, who sure raised hell for a few hours.

The most havoc was caused in the cattle deck area, where monkeys got below and scampered fore and aft on the backs of those steers. Of course, I heard all the rumpus and went below to inspect. The cowboys had rounded up most of the animals and were placing a halter on the last bull, when a monkey appeared out of nowhere. That bull lost all respect for man or rope; he lowered his head, charged, and away went the barricades. Cowboys scrambled for cover and here I was, right in the path of this crazy bull. Quickly looking for a place to hide, I got behind a small ventilator, a flimsy thing hardly six inches wide. The bull came thundering down and, as he passed me, he seemed to give me a look of recognition and then applied all four brakes. Fortunately, he had so much momentum as he was negotiating a turn that I was able to jump into the engine room and slam the door. My heart was pounding as though a main bearing had burned out. I left much later with a profound respect for bullfighters.

We docked in Panama, and I bade farewell to Carl, with the admonition to keep an eye open for striptease monkeys the rest of the voyage.

In Panama, I stayed at the YMCA, a very nice building, but aside from sleeping there was nothing to do. I visited the dockside and learned how the big locks operated, watched ships go through, and was surprised at the silence—no shouting and hardly a word spoken. The powerful electric mules on shore had lines attached fore and aft to keep the ship steady in the locks and prevent any error made from the bridge.

One day, I was approached by a doctor who had learned of my shipwreck experience and asked if I was looking for a job. He said it was right down my alley and filled me in on the details: skippering a small tugboat, the pay $250 a month, free accommodations, free breakfast, and three white uniforms. I quickly agreed—the pay seemed fabulous in those days.

The so-called tugboat was actually a small yacht with a West Indian deckhand and a Mexican engineer, twin screws, and the after cabin fitted up to carry four stretchers. The medicine cabinet was like a small drugstore, and the tiny galley could handle most things. The duty called for twenty-four hours a day. Although I was constantly on call, the few emergencies fortunately occurred during daylight hours. The main objectives for this luxury boat were transporting any crewmen injured while traversing the canal, helping any workers injured on the canal banks or locks, and, during slack periods, taking a senior pilot out to sound the bottom. The terrific pressure of the mountains on either side of the canal push up the bottom, and this is why soundings are made. I thought I had it made, as the saying goes.

The numerous ships traversing this famous waterway flew the ensigns of every country on earth. Lo and behold, an old tramp steamer came in one day flying the Australian ensign. The *Austral Range,* one of the Commonwealth Line, was empty. I thought it would be nice and friendly to visit and see whether I knew anybody. My launch (or tug) was moored alongside, and a sincere offer was made to take me back to Sydney, something that luck had denied me for many years. I decided to quit and travel homeward. The people at the hospital were hopping mad. I had been on the job for only three weeks! Who? What? Why? More pay? Are you sick? Can you get back soon? These and many other questions were fired at me, but the latent urge to visit my folks won out.

The *Austral Range* was nothing much. She was slow and uninspiring and not a happy ship. I sent a radio message when we were in range of Sydney and arranged for my parents to meet me on arrival. They came out to the anchorage, and we had a great reunion on board the small launch. I bade farewell to my old shipmates and went home after five years of wandering. The occasion called for parties; friends and relatives forgathered. Many of them had changed a great deal—my mother and father looked much older— but I was at long last home.

The entertainment and reception were all that could be desired. The local newspapers ran feature articles. Relatives and friends long since forgotten reappeared. They all seemed much older, and incidents of long ago were revived. The ladies seemed prettier but very dumb about geography. Mother's cooking that I had boasted about and dreamed about many times was even better. I listened to my father talking to three fishing friends as they tried to reach an agreement about which way to go, and each one had very good reasons for making his decision. As I expected, Joe, my father, didn't listen to any of them. He started up the motor, and off they went to some point he had already determined. Of course, they never caught any fish.

I was completely out of step—all of these social functions were a pain in the ——. Bayldon Navigational School had classes that I frequently attended. The students talked my language, and sometimes after class several of us would adjourn to a nearby pub and have a few drinks. There was a real biddy who kept tab on me. She reminded me of a vigilant submarine with the periscope always up, looking for some fresh juicy scandal. "What a pity your son drinks so much." Such disparaging remarks were not only annoying, but they caused unnecessary worry to my parents. They had not adjusted to a son who had left the nest five years ago—drinking was unheard of, sinful.

I found myself at the main railway depot and, to my surprise, spotted an old schoolmate, Gordon McDermott.

"Hi, Gordon. How the hell are you?"

He seemed taken aback and in a pathetic way said, "I heard you were killed."

"Hell no! I'm right here, let's go over and have a drink."

"Oh, no, I'm married and must catch the 5:50 train. My wife will expect me."

"Call her up and explain the delay," I said.

"Oh no, I couldn't do that. My wife is strict, but I'll see you again real soon."

Well, that was the brushoff. I never did see him again and had no desire to do so. I had reached a point of no return. The exciting tennis matches didn't mean anything, and the best sponge cake tasted awful.

I headed for the office and was given an assignment on the SS *Boonah* bound for Europe. After fond farewells with my family, I sailed over the horizon for another five years.

The *Boonah*, another war prize, was a tramp ship but entirely different from the *Carawa*. She was a very fine vessel designed to carry heavy cargoes and had huge booms on the foremast. The holds were free of stanchions and had large ringbolts secured on the hull for handling such items as locomotives, huge boilers, and big transformers. We even brought out from Europe a German long-range gun that had been used to shell Paris from 60 miles away. The ever-pressing need in Europe was for foodstuffs, and we loaded a cargo of wheat for England, as well as a few cases of serum for Dakar, French Senegal, on the west coast of Africa, where there was an epidemic of cholera.

We sailed around the Cape of Good Hope. Our first stop was Dakar, where the serum was discharged. Dakar was a very hot, miserable spot and few had any desire to go ashore. Two engineers did go for a walk and contracted high fevers. They were raising much noise and were delirious at times, so a "smart" guy, without any reference to the *Sea Captain's Medical Guide* or advice, decided to give them each a shot of brandy. The next morning they were dead, and our ship was going out to sea toward England.

The unloading at Hull was slow going. We again had to train the stevedores in the method of stacking a pyramid in the center of the hold and wearing empty sacks to protect their shoulders and necks. Australian wheat is hard, and the ends are quite pointed and sharp and can tear the skin quickly. When the wheat was out and the holds cleaned, we started loading copper plates, steel bars, special types of machinery and, of all things, special glass vats for making lager beer. The vats were somewhat similar to a vacuum bottle, but about 10 feet by 10 feet and at least 6 feet deep. We had four stowed in No. 2 hold, and the mate assigned me to take special care of them. The first thing was to get the carpenter to build a solid platform and then cut several hundred wedges.

The *Boonah* took on a full load of bunkers at Swansea, and we sailed nonstop to Australia in forty-six days. The glass vats were treated like babies.

The carpenter and I went below every day and, if there was any movement, simply pushed a wedge underneath. Every one of those precious vats was delivered to the Stroth Brewery intact. The company representatives told me it was the first shipment ever to reach them without breakage. I was invited to a meeting of the brewery's board members and given a nice check for my ever-loving, tender care. The carpenter also received a check, and several cases of good lager beer were shipped on board for the crew.

I was transferred from the *Boonah* to the *Gilgal* and promoted to chief officer. Previously the SS *Wildenfels*, the *Gilgal* was a large vessel of 5,512 tons gross but not a fast ship. Built in 1901, she was being outclassed by the new postwar ships for regular general cargo service. She was being sent to Genoa, where she would be transferred back to German ownership.

The new owners sent two engineers, two deck officers, and a shipwright to inspect the ship. We went out to sea and put the old girl through her paces: full ahead, full astern, hard a port, hard a starboard; drop the anchor, heave it up; check the loading gear, the lifeboats, and the radio equipment. The whole thing took five days before they decided that the ship was seaworthy and the price in order. The vessel was turned over to a brand-new crew. Our crew returned to Australia on a passenger vessel of the British India Service that was bound for Shanghai via Burma. We were amazed when news reached us that the *Gilgal* had foundered with all hands on her first voyage for the new owners.

Next, I helped take the *Australmead,* which had been bought in London in 1914, to England with a general cargo from Fremantle for London, Swansea, Liverpool, and Glasgow. On my return to Australia, I joined the crew of the *Ferndale,* the largest ship built in Australia up to that time. She was built expressly for the European service and could carry seven 6-inch guns. This was her first voyage to England, and she was loaded with frozen meat.

Back in Australia, I received a good object lesson in seamanship, one not recommended but part of the learning process. I was given temporary command of a small steamer that was, in fact, a fast ferry, complete with twin screws. She handled like a toy, could stop on a dime, and was a pleasure to command. This assignment lasted only five weeks, when the original captain returned after a bout in the hospital.

I was then given another ship, just the opposite type—an iron ore carrier, with single screw and poor accommodation. We entered port. I rang to stop the engines. Our berth was a good quarter mile away, but I realized that a heavy ship with 12,000 tons of ore would require some stopping. With engines stopped, she kept going, with no apparent slowing down. The pier started to loom large. I rang down for full astern, and that no-good SOB kept right on as though determined to hit something. Sure enough, she did. The stevedores ran. Planks flew skyward, along with sections of the railroad, before that damn ship stopped.

I was distraught. My first real ship command, and here I wreck the pier, plus buckle a few bow plates. My report to the superintendent was full of apologies. I had misjudged the stopping power of the engines and done thousands of dollars worth of damage to the pier. Very sorry, very sorry.

The reply was quite surprising. I was not reprimanded or relieved of command—only mildly warned to be more careful. I learned that several other captains had made similar mistakes. Apparently, the ship was underpowered.

The passenger vessels of the Commonwealth Line were named after prominent bays: *Largs Bay, Jervis Bay, Esperence Bay, Hobson's Bay,* and *Morton Bay.* These fine ships were actually designed with gun mountings, ammunition storage, and other facilities that could quickly change them from peaceful merchant ships into auxiliary cruisers mounting 6-inch guns. The accommodation for seven hundred passengers was also designed for troop carrying. Partitions could be dismantled; the galley had extra stoves, baking ovens, storage space, and refrigeration. And we had just gotten over a peace rally—no more war! I wondered why the extra and very expensive equipment was built into these vessels. They had no armor plating, and their speed was a modest 15 knots.

The cargo carried in the *Bay* liners consisted of frozen meat, butter, flour, and wool, mostly consigned to London. The new King George Docks gave us a handy berth, with excellent unloading and loading equipment. The Thames River was one of the busiest in the world. Besides the ships visiting the port, river barges and tugboats were everywhere. Every time we visited London, we steamed steadily for King George Docks, where we entered through lock-gates. When the pilot estimated he was near the gates, he used the loud hailer:

"Are you there, 'Arry?"

Out from the dense fog came the reply, "Right on, right on."

Or possibly, "Over to port a little."

Or whatever was required to get the ship straightened up for dock entry. I was always amazed at this performance. The Thames River pilot was, without doubt, one of the cleverest navigators in the world. He became outstanding when a fog descended. Known as pea-soup London fog, well named because it looked like pea soup, it was so dense you could barely see the forecastle-head. The pilot had an uncanny sense of timing and distance, and some of this was by echo. He blew the ship's whistle, held his watch, and lis-

The SS *Hobson's Bay,* a passenger vessel of the Commonwealth Line, in service between Australia and the United Kingdom.

tened for the echo. By experience, he knew exactly where he was by counting the seconds it took.

The usual stay in port was ten days. This gave me a wonderful chance to travel around Europe. I had worked out a system with fellow officers on board, whereby I would take their watches in other ports. I visited Holland, Belgium, France, Spain, Switzerland, and Italy. One memorable event was being in Paris on 21 May 1927, when Col. Charles Lindbergh arrived on his solo flight across the Atlantic. I watched him land and was later a guest at the reception for him.

While in Basel, Switzerland, I crossed the border into Germany. I was astounded at the change since my first visit to Bremen in 1919. It was an entirely different nation. The countryside was progressing nicely. Those to whom I spoke were quite confident about the future. By contrast, people in England and Australia were crying poor.

In 1928, things generally began to go sour, and an air of indifference permeated the world. The Commonwealth Line was dwindling fast. Competition became stronger. Older ships were being sold, with the Greeks and Japanese as chief buyers. Both of these countries entered the shipping business on the basis of what might be termed bargain basement. The vessels were ill-kept, the crews odd mixtures, and, as one would expect, they were frequently in trouble.

My seniority with the Commonwealth Line dated back to 1916, when I had joined the *Burrowa,* the large sailing ship that had been captured in Newcastle, New South Wales. My experience had spanned every type of ship in the fleet, and the routes taken usually were from Australia to Europe. But tramping brought me to many ports never visited by regular vessels, and this is what made tramping so interesting.

The bright bit of news about my seniority came as a pleasant surprise when more and more ships were being sold and the surplus of officers was rather large. By late 1928, I was the Commonwealth Line's senior chief officer, already with a record of command. I was, by all types of reckoning, next in line for permanent command. My thirteen-year seniority even included my service with the Navy. I had also made an interesting voyage on board HMS *Herald,* when we resurveyed the Great Barrier Reef off Australia.

My service with the Commonwealth Line was completed on the *Hobson's Bay* and *Jervis Bay.* These two vessels were running a ferry service between Australia and the United Kingdom.

My seniority and general way of life came to an abrupt end in 1929 when we returned to Sydney. The bad news came on board that an English company had bought the entire Commonwealth fleet. Two of the *Bay* liners had already sailed with English crews. A standby Limey crew was ready to take over the *Hobson's Bay.* My job as chief officer kept me busy—I couldn't just walk off a ship without making certain everything was left in order. The English officer to whom I entrusted keys and other items was a friendly guy, but my disposition had soured with the news.

I had received my pay from the purser, and a few of us adjourned to the bar for a farewell drink. Small debts were settled. There was much hand-shaking, and good wishes were expressed. In actual fact, none of us felt too happy about the sudden turn of events.

The first signs of a worldwide depression were starting to show. When my shipmates had gone ashore, the old ship seemed lonely. Being obliged to instruct the Englishman was akin to rubbing salt into a deep wound. When it came time for me to leave, I headed for the bank, only to find it closed.

The next day was "Bank Holiday." This was the start, or at least an early stage, of the big depression. I am usually blind when it comes to foresight, but on this occasion I took the precaution to rent a small apartment for three months. When I paid the landlord cash, he threw in a loaf of bread, a pint of milk, and the newspaper each day as a bonus. Apple carts were everywhere. People were selling pencils, and con men with three walnut shells, peddlers, photographers, and just plain bums were in evidence. Being idle grated my nerves, and I was ready to take on any job.

My first efforts were selling towel fixtures, then selling cars. Eventually, I landed the exalted position of bus driver. I got to know the regular passengers by their first names and entered into all sorts of deals with them: one long blast on the horn gave Jess sufficient time to swallow her coffee and be out front; two short blasts reminded Liz to get out of the sack; even Junior was left on the bus while Mother went shopping, and she picked him up on the return trip. One of the passengers came aboard one morning—bright-eyed and bushy-tailed and busting to impart some momentous news. It was peak period, and the poor guy made two round trips before he could give me the full details.

"Al, how would you like to go to China?"

"Hell, yes."

"Well, listen to this. Last night I was playing poker at the hotel and met a sea captain who intimated he was looking for a good second mate. I told him about you and have set up an appointment today. When do you get relieved?"

We set a time, and when my relief came I hustled home to get cleaned up. I headed downtown to meet my friend and the sea captain—Percy Angus, Master Mariner, Lloyd's surveyor, and poker player extraordinary.

Angus was the typical ship's captain one reads about in fiction but rarely meets in actual life. He was a fine figure of a man with bright blue eyes, white whiskers trimmed in Van Dyke style, a shock of unruly hair that always needed combing, and a permanent smile that hovered around his eyes and mouth. I knew the moment we met that the job was mine.

"What papers do you hold, Palmer?"

"Master Mariner, sir."

"When can you leave?"

"Right now, if necessary."

"Have you ever been in the Far East?"

"No, sir."

"That's good. I'll meet you at the shipping office tomorrow at noon. Bring your things along because I plan to get under way immediately after the Board of Trade surveyors have finished."

We shook hands on the agreement. I left to pack, give notice to my land-lord, and resign from the bus company. The next morning I took my old bus out as usual, with my replacement seated nearby. I greeted old friends and bade them farewell. At 1000, I climbed down, said good-bye to my conduc-tor, and headed for the shipping office to sign on articles. Angus arrived on time with his shipping papers.

I signed and started a completely new life.

5

EN ROUTE TO CHINA
ON THE SS *BALLS HEAD*

I was now a ship's officer bound for China via the Great Barrier Reef, Borneo, the Philippines, and points north. The ship I had joined in 1930 was SS *Balls Head,* a collier of ancient vintage that had been laid up, owing to the depression. She derived her name from a bluff headland adjacent to the yard where her cargo was stored. Captain Angus had purchased her on behalf of Chinese interests and had brought his crewmen from Shanghai in order to take delivery of the vessel. She was designed for carrying a coal cargo.

Her whole midship section was cargo space, with crew quarters forward and the bridge, engine room, and officers quarters aft. She had ample accommodation with room to spare, both fore and aft. The engines were complicated, with sleeve valves that gave her greater economy. They needed fine adjustment in order to function properly. The original chief engineer, known as "Bunny," had signed on for the voyage, a venture not exactly to his liking because, as he said, "I hate going to sea with a bunch of heathens."

He meant the Chinese crewmen. Bunny knew those engines and was indispensable to us on the voyage until his assistants learned how to make the adjustments.

Bunny had served for many years as chief on the missionary yacht *John Williams.* Quite a lot of Christian influence had rubbed off and stuck to the

68

old rascal. He had also served on the *Balls Head* as second and chief until she had been laid up. The second and third were both certified engineers, but they had to learn from Bunny. The deck department, headed up by Percy Angus, had an ex-British naval officer as mate. He was a nice guy, although top-heavy with his own importance, but he was a first-rate navigator.

The route we planned to take inside the Barrier Reef required a damn good navigator. I was the second mate, but I had not done any navigating for almost a year except to steer a bus through congested traffic.

The third mate was a man of parts, many parts. He was an excellent sailor, good shipmate, tough as they come, and had an abundance of that priceless possession—humor.

The cook and steward were Chinese, both first-class men, who occupied a room aft where most of their activity centered.

The radio operator had his accommodation alongside his equipment on the boat deck. That rounded out the after-guard. Forward, we had ten seamen and twelve firemen, making our total crew thirty-two. I was the last man to join. The vessel would be ready to sail after the Board of Trade survey for seaworthiness was completed.

The Board of Trade officers came on board early in the morning and started their survey. We already had steam up because part of the tests included power trials. They first examined our two lifeboats. One did not look very seaworthy, so the head surveyor ordered it to be swung out and lowered into the water. The Chinese crew sweated and struggled to get it free from the chocks. The davits squeaked like a frightened sea gull as they swung out. The blocks squeaked on another key when the falls were lowered. When the boat hit the water, it just kept on going and sank before our eyes. The surveyors got out their notebooks and started writing.

"Try the other boat."

"OK."

More struggles, more squeaks. Fortunately, this boat floated.

"Try the life rafts."

We tossed a few of them overboard and they floated OK. The surveyors seemed satisfied.

"Now we shall get under way and see how she handles. Let go fore and aft."

Three blasts on the whistle—well, we tried to blow the whistle, but a swallow or something had blocked the thing up. It did make a noise that, providing one had a good hearing aid turned up, might have been heard. The only thing very noticeable was a cascade of boiling water that poured onto the bridge. The Board of Trade men made more notes. Meanwhile, our ship was going astern, whistle or no whistle. Once clear of the dock, we swung around and headed down harbor.

"Hard a starboard. Midships. Hard a port. Midships."

She handled beautifully. Then came the windlass tests.

"Drop port anchor, heave up, drop starboard anchor, heave up. Drop both anchors. Slow astern, half astern, full astern."

The last order tore the bag. Our anchors held fine and the windlass was OK, but the vibration set up by going full astern in an empty ship proved too much for the old stack. Down it crashed on deck, stove in the good boat, buckled the davits, and showered the bridge with an accumulation of dust and soot inches thick.

Such treatment is not conducive to good relations. The surveyors wrote more notes. Several small craft came alongside to find out whether we needed aid. Down below in the engine room, old Bunny could be heard singing, "Jesus wants me for a sunbeam," while we limped back to the sanctuary of the dock. Needless to remark, our examination for seaworthiness failed. The surveyors prepared a long list of suggested changes and requirements, which they gave to Angus before going ashore.

Captain Angus looked over the list and his usual smile vanished. It meant considerable delay, much expense, and possible loss of freight for which he had already contracted. We needed two new lifeboats, new davits, funnel, whistle, and guy lines, plus steam pipes and other essentials.

The biggest item was the funnel. These things were handmade. We couldn't just go to a hardware store and buy a ship's funnel. We might have passed the exam with a few modifications had that stack remained in its original position. The delay changed our trip—changed it in such a manner that, instead of a routine voyage to China, we were in for a most unusual experience.

The scene now switches to Shanghai, where the office boy of a commercial firm was arrested for swiping the petty cash and brought to trial. His story and testimony revealed he had lost all his money at dog races and was forced to steal in order to live. Evidently the Chinese judge had also lost plenty of money at dog races and was in an indulgent mood because he handed this youth a very light sentence, much to the consternation of everyone in court.

The newspapers featured the case. A chain reaction started overnight. Everyone brought to trial for theft immediately claimed he had lost his money at the dog races. There was more newspaper ballyhoo. Finally, the Nanking government took up the problem as the noise gathered momentum, and dog racing was featured as a blight on society, temptation to youth, and a very undesirable sport.

The Nationalist government finally ruled against the tracks and requested the owners to close. Two tracks were in the International Settlement. One was in the French concession. American-British interests owned the settlement tracks. They complied with Nanking's request, but the French owners in the concession told Nanking to "go jump in the lake," or words to that effect.

This track, known as the Canidrome, kept right on operating and boosted the number of races to cope with the extra crowds. The owners' attitude did not please Nanking, which could not enforce the ruling. Nanking did the only thing possible by placing a ban on the importation of greyhounds.

China is not a good country for breeding animals. Imported strains must be brought in frequently. Canidrome officials were well aware of this fact. The litter from a first-class greyhound bitch would be undersized and their stamina doubtful. The pups might grow up and possess the speed and wind to race around the track, but it was pure conjecture. Ultimately, the official ban was going to close the Canidrome for want of capable dogs.

Now back to Sydney and the crippled *Balls Head,* languishing beside the dock as it awaited repairs. I was sent around the waterfront to see what was offering in used lifeboats. I visited every yard for miles and finally came across two fine boats that were reasonably priced. I relayed the details to Angus and was given the OK to close the deal. Next day, I took a couple of men to the yard where we set up the sails of one boat and took the other in tow for the passage back to our ship.

Angus was ashore much of the time. He had met, quite by accident, another Shanghailander, and these two entered into a fantastic deal. (In the light of later incidents, I wondered whether the meeting between these two had been accidental or actually well planned.) Two old China hands meeting in a strange country always scares up sufficient justification to celebrate. But this celebration was a prolonged affair—lunch together day after day, plus a series of get-togethers at night. I never attended any of these luncheons, but, as Angus related to me, the setup followed along these lines. First, the approach for a passage to China. Agreed. We had plenty of space on board. The next approach was:

"Do you mind if I bring along a couple of dogs?" Agreed.

Next luncheon: "Captain, I have a few more dogs."

Well, after several more lunches and several more repeats about dogs, Angus asked point-blank, "Just how many damn dogs do you have now?"

"Thirty-five, Captain."

The white whiskers stood out, and the smile faded.

"What the hell goes on? First you ask me for a trip to China. Then you want to bring along a dog, but now the idea has grown out of all proportion. The only agreement I'll make is to carry the dogs at the prevailing freight rate per head. You supply the handlers, food, and proper housing facilities for their passage."

This was obviously the anticipated move this chap wanted because the dog population increased rapidly. Lord only knows how many we would have had if the ship repairs had lasted much longer.

The dockyard had fitted the new funnel. The davits had been straightened. A new whistle was installed. The old ship looked spick-and-span. The Board of Trade was notified. A time was set for our exam, which we passed with flying colors. Our ship was declared seaworthy.

The dog cargo was the next item of business. Two huge iceboxes were shipped on deck. Then came truckloads of canned milk and special dog food. Each dog was to have its own kennel. These were lined up along the top of the main hatch. Two dog handlers reported on board, and we awaited the arrival of our live cargo of seventy-five greyhounds and their owner. They came on board about noon, and we sailed for Newcastle to load coal for Iloilo in the Philippines.

Greyhounds were not our only animal cargo. The third mate had brought a small pooch on board the night before. He swore the little mutt had smiled at him through a pet shop window and he couldn't resist buying it for a dollar. It was a bitch about two months old. The mother had obviously been Airedale and the father a leash violator. She was a cute little bundle of fuzz. Right away, we named her Mitzi. We also had an Australian cockatoo, a large white bird with a yellow plume that stood up like a question mark (?) whenever the bird was aroused. Nobody seemed to know how the bird came on board, and certainly nobody claimed it. Just an orphan of the feathered class.

When we reached Newcastle, all the dogs were placed ashore while loading operations were on. Mitzi and the cockatoo stayed on board. They were not listed as cargo.

The design of the ship was such that a full cargo was dumped aboard, trimmed, and stowed within a few hours. With the hatches battened down and decks washed, we were ready to receive our dogs again. We had 4,500 tons of coal, which placed the vessel well down in the water. The greyhounds walked on board and were placed in their kennels, which were already arranged in rows atop the hatches. A huge awning, supported by a fore and aft ridge wire, was spread across the top of this assembly. We were ready for sea.

We had quite a sendoff from the pier by dog lovers, dog fanciers, and greyhound breeders—more darn people around to give those long-nosed hounds a bon voyage than they were worth. Nobody even noticed the mutt Mitzi, yet she had more personality than all of them put together.

We cleared the breakwater, dropped our pilot, and were on our way. The funnel stayed in position, the whistle whistled, and I knew the boats floated. Come hell or high water, we would make the Philippines OK.

Our ship's name caused some embarrassment. We sighted a British warship next day. When she signaled, "What ship?" the officer on watch spelled out "balls," then paused to give the rest of the name. The pause was not appreciated. That warship swung around and came straight for us, evidently bent on correcting an insult. However, when she got near enough to read the name painted across our stern, she swung back on course and vanished over the horizon.

The very same thing happened with an Italian liner: "What ship?"

She got real uppity and refused to answer further signals or even radio messages explaining that was part of our real name—no humor.

Our little ship proved very seaworthy. Aside from occasional stops while Bunny made valve adjustments, we maintained a steady 10 knots toward Cape York, the most northern point of Australia.

Angus had chosen what is known as the inside passage, which meant the inside of the Great Barrier Reef. This is a hazardous route, but the risks are weighed against smooth water and less mileage. The mate proved his worth in navigation and could work out a position quicker than anyone I ever met. We passed by Sandy Cape. Our next landmark was Lady Elliot lighthouse, where the inside passage begins and the depth of water shallowed up to about 15 fathoms.

Those damn dogs on deck started off by being seasick but quickly became adjusted to their new mode of life. The handlers exercised every dog twice a day. The awning was rolled back so they could add basking in the sunshine to their life of luxury. They were served the best of food. This so-called "dog's life" was really one to be envied. Those hounds had one idiosyncrasy that worried all of us, especially watch-keeping officers. When the moon was up, they set up a howl that could be heard for miles around. We went on watch armed with potatoes. The first long-snouted hound to see the moon would let out two yowls, one when he spotted the moon and the other when a spud cracked him on the dome. It was a lost cause once they got in the groove because each one tried to out-howl his brother. The racket was gawd-awful. Imagine being on a ship's bridge steaming along through a tropical night, the sea a flat calm, no traffic, the only noise is the steady thump-thump of the engines and splash of the bow waves. Astern, as far as can be seen, is the broad wake of the ship, lighted by phosphorescence. Inside the wheelhouse, the dim light of the compass lights the quartermaster's face. Everything is peaceful. Down below on the deck, some long-snouted hound peeks out of his kennel and spots the moon. Wow! Watch out! That potato has to be delivered fast and accurately, or else the peace is shot and complete bedlam reigns. I sometimes wished those Board of Trade surveyors were with us. They would have readily agreed that the necessity for a new whistle was out.

The cockatoo led a very ordinary life and never seemed to bother about what went on around him. Much of his time was spent sleeping. He stuck his head under a wing and dozed for hours on end. The only apparent interest he showed was in tearing wood apart. I think the toothpick industry could save lots of money by using these birds in manufacturing. Just give them some pieces of 2 × 4 and, with those powerful beaks, they would chew the wood down to toothpick size within a day or so.

We had placed a hook in one of the passageways and the cockatoo's cage hung there most of the time. Several of us decided to break his habit of sleeping, plus make him talk or at least show an interest in his surroundings. The usual trick was to give his cage a flick with the thumbnail. This startled the hell out of the bird. Up went his yellow plume, accompanied by the meanest look. I think the look caused us to follow through with the remark:

"Get out, you old bastard."

Nobody claimed the bird. Regardless, he received plenty of attention and chow.

Mitzi was growing like a weed. She had trouble getting over the doorsill of my cabin, which she had claimed as her own. If anyone was around she got an assist, but, left on her own, she balanced on her tummy and rolled out on deck where she attended to her need, looked the ship over, and then scrambled back in and played with my shoes or chewed up a sock. The usual ship noises never bothered her. She had a wonderful disposition and was, without doubt, the best-liked pooch aboard. The nocturnal howls from her distant relatives worried her. If I happened to be in my bunk, she climbed in beside me, burrowed down under the covers, and trembled until her kith and kin quit their racket or the officer-of-the-watch had cussed loud enough to make them cease their mournful howls. Then Mitzi scrambled out of the bunk, very courageously let out a couple of feeble woofs, coiled up in her own box, and fell fast asleep.

Bunny announced it was time to stop awhile. He had more adjustments to make. Some steam pipes needed repacking, and a few tubes were leaking badly. Angus consulted the chart and decided the best and most suitable anchorage was Bird Island, one of the many small islands that dot the reef. We made this site before sundown. As we approached, the whole sky seemed crowded with birds, coming back from their day's fishing to roost. They were tern, gannet, and heron, plus a few other species that live and thrive on this fabulous reef. I don't know who named the island, but watching this aerial parade as we carefully inched in for anchorage certainly qualified the island for its name. When we dropped anchor, the splash and rattle of cable shattered the quietness. All the birds took off from their nests and wheeled overhead, chattering away as if to warn us not to make such a noise again. Then as the crescendo of their shrill squawks subsided, silence returned once more.

The anchorage was perfect and weather conditions good. Bunny drew the fires to allow the boilers to cool down. We lowered the lifeboat and, with a work party, went ashore to find fresh water. The island was typical of most Pacific isles—coral formation with a shady beach surrounding it. The water slowly changed from a deep blue to greenish blue, then light green until it met the beach and ended in a white spume as each wave lapped the beach line. The trees were coconut and mango, with small tundra patches. There were no large trees and no hills or rocks worthy of mention. The main population consisted of birds and small crabs. The latter greeted us on the beach when we landed, but they burrowed so fast it was impossible to catch them or get close enough to examine them. There was no sign of humans or any sign of their ever having been there. We loaded our water containers several times and ferried back to the ship, then stripped and went swimming.

I took Mitzi ashore and initiated her to solid earth, something the little girl had never known. She walked very gingerly, stopped to look at her paws, chased a crab, and set up a whine when it got away. Swimming was her best medium. She needed no coaxing but simply reveled in this new experience.

Darkness comes quickly in these regions. The sun sets and the heavens turn all the colors of a rainbow for only a few minutes, then dark, pitch dark.

We quit the beach and returned on board. The cook had prepared a nice supper of cold cuts and salad, which was served on deck along with a few bottles of beer. Mitzi, who had developed into a first-rate panhandler, was too pooped to participate. She was sound asleep and dreaming about that crab she just missed catching. We lounged around awhile. Somebody turned on the radio and was promptly slapped down for even trying to break this magic spell of peace. The hounds up forward were silent, and the troubled world was many miles away.

I went on watch at midnight. Old Bunny was down below futzing around, looking over his beloved engines and figuring out the work schedule for the morrow. Bunny had no voice worthy of the name but persisted in singing hymns. His personality clashed at times. On the one hand, he was an old rough and tough engineer. Later in life, he had associated with missionaries, who gave him a veneer of Christian teaching. This gave him a split or dual personality. I had watched him working. He sang hymns all the time, but, if for some reason the part didn't fit snug or the wrench slipped and he jammed a finger, the effect was like this:

"What a friend we have in Jesus. What a friend—goddamn the bloody thing. What the hell—we have indeed."

Next morning, we started to ferry water again until the tanks were filled. Then a few of us made up a party to explore the island. The birds had taken off at dawn for their fishing grounds. The only sign of movement was a huge eagle gliding overhead in the wind currents with apparent ease. He would suddenly swoop down on some unsuspecting prey for his breakfast. We gathered several large clams; a bucketful of bêche-de-mer, a sort of sea slug, that our cook claimed to be "velly good"; some coconuts; and a few wild flowers to brighten up the saloon.

These coral islands, or cays, differ from the volcanic islands in formation. The cays are simply created by residue lodged atop the coral reef, where it has pushed up above the high-water mark. Coconuts blown away from nearby islands drift ashore and ultimately take root. Birds bring other types of seed from grass and vines, and the sandy soil is tossed up by storms. Bird Island serves as an average type, the distance around being about 4 miles and the highest point about 60 feet, which would be the top of a coconut tree. The approach is dangerous because of the long reefs running in every direction. The reef ledges can be seen clearly in the daylight, however, and, by skillful navigation, a vessel can be conned into safe anchorage.

We spotted an eagle's nest while on the island. Someone suggested that I take a look and I climbed up the tree to investigate. The nest was a huge affair, made up of twigs, branches, and odd bits of driftwood. The center held seaweed, moss, and a collection of feathers. Three chicks were sitting there waiting for Mrs. to return. They hollered murder when my head appeared alongside their aerie. One of the parents kept swooping low to scare me off. I informed those below that the nest had three youngsters and, if they covered me with a rifle, I'd try to capture one of them. The nest was a good 6 feet across. The supporting branches were strong enough to hold the nest but hardly enough to support me. Mrs. Eagle swooped lower and lower. Although the fellows below fired three shots, I doubt whether she knew the significance of a rifle crack. The youngsters were not cooperative either, but somehow I managed to collect the largest of the bunch and get back down to earth.

When we came alongside, Captain Angus remarked, "What have you got there now? Hells bells, a cockatoo, a pup, greyhounds to spare, and now a bloody eagle. Do you chaps think I'm running a menagerie?"

The repairs to our motive power had been completed. Those who had remained on board had been fishing with considerable success, so our combined efforts helped to brighten the menu. The stopover gave new zest to the voyage. Everyone was ready to get going. We hove up anchor and slowly eased out from this fairyland toward the deep water and headed northward into the tropical night. The Pacific islands were portrayed by Robert Louis Stevenson as a Paradise, but they are not exactly as depicted. Although lovely in their isolation, they smell strong because of the moldy, decayed debris of earth and life.

The eaglet was nested down in a half-case with straw bedding and placed on one of the small bunker hatches. The name chosen, after much discussion, was Egbert. It somehow fitted the critter, who was at the awkward age of shedding pin feathers. Part of him was naked, but nature had fitted him out exceptionally well. His ejection system was really something. He would stand up and let fly with a straight trajectory of 10 feet. We soon learned the symptoms and, if Egbert was standing, turned around or got going fast. Mitzi, with her inquisitive nature, was caught off base on one occasion. That cured her. She never ventured near the area again. Eagles live on small fish, crabs, and sea snakes. We were fresh out of all three items, but one of the dog trainers took charge and fed him raw meat. He flourished on the new diet.

There is nothing in the whole wide world similar to the Barrier Reef in size, depth, or beauty. It is not a continuous chain but a series of sections studded with atolls and volcanic islands. Some of the islands are inhabited. Although I never visited any of these residents, I imagined that life was very pleasant. When the tide is low, the reef is exposed and stretches for miles in every direction. It is reasonably safe to walk on the reef and examine the coral formation and teeming marine life. But two danger points exist: the giant clams can snap off a leg without trouble, and the tides come in fast, at 2 to 3 knots, with a range of up to 10 feet.

The reef formation can be divided roughly into three lanes. The outer reef, which is coral formation, fronts onto the broad Pacific. This is the outer passage. The middle passage meanders among the volcanic islands, which are larger and much more substantial than the coral cays. These islands provide great beauty and variety to this fabulous region. Finally, the inner coral reef, with its numerous atolls, forms the inside passage. I marveled at the audacity of early navigators who brought their ships through this coral maze. Capt.

James Cook became the most famous when he discovered this phenomenon and charted much of the channel that is used today.

Restoration Island also featured Captain Bligh, who was made famous in *Mutiny on the Bounty*. We only occasionally caught a glimpse of the outer reef, where the long line of thundering surf reminded us of the sanctuary offered by this reef.

We were nearing the tip of Queensland and would soon be out into the open sea once more. It was typhoon season. The captain planned to skirt the New Guinea coast, then head up for Borneo and the Philippines. The radioman had picked up several weather forecasts indicating bad weather ahead, but in these latitudes luck plays an important part and everyone was optimistic. We passed a big Dutch liner during daylight hours, off the New Guinea coast, and spoke to her. She assured us that conditions to the north were good and made no wisecrack about the odd name of our vessel. The passengers on deck waved to us. As the two vessels passed, both dipped their ensigns as a token of goodwill. Damn good seamen, the Dutch.

The passage was uneventful until we reached the Straits of Zamboanga. The dogs kept howling at the moon. Mitzi could jump out of the cabin without any difficulty. The cockatoo still chewed lumber and slept most of the day. The eagle had grown all his feathers and looked very regal. What piercing eyes those damn birds have—mean-looking, too.

When we entered the Straits, several natives in their canoes were busy fishing. Ashore were a few native huts, half hidden under the dense foliage. The whole setting was peaceful, but repeated warnings of the approach of a typhoon made us wary. They are not to be fooled with, and warnings are respected. We kept watching the barometer, cloud formation, and the water for any signs presaging a storm. Sure enough, the wind suddenly shifted and a few rainsqualls whipped up out of nowhere. Another wind shift and the clouds looked threatening. Obviously, something was moving. The best precaution was to head out into the open sea and be ready to ride out whatever came.

We caught what is called the tail end of the typhoon, but that was plenty bad. The wind lashed the sea unmercifully, and spume driving horizontal to the surface could have cut our faces open; it was suicide to venture from behind cover. Walking was out of the question. We had taken precautions to lash down the large awning and lace a 2-inch manila crisscross to prevent it from bellying upward. We could have saved our time and energy. When the wind caught it, away it went like a postage stamp—lashings, lacings, ridge wire, the works, whoosh. The dogs, suddenly left in the open, whined from fright. The spume and spray whipped them terribly. Several kennels tore loose from the hatch and floated between the combings and bulwarks, where the water was several feet deep. Unfortunately, nobody could go to the rescue, and several dogs went overboard.

We recorded wind gusts at 85 mph. In typhoons, however, this velocity is not sustained for long periods, although it seems like hours. Our little ship rode the storm like a veteran. By keeping her head up into the wind and going full speed, we kept steerageway. When the wind had blown itself out, the rain came. To appreciate this deluge, one actually has to experience it firsthand. It is hard to breathe because this type of rain can penetrate anything. Everyone has to make up their minds that they are going to get soaked and like it. The good feature about this deluge was that it tamed the sea—it beat it flat in no time. Apart from a heavy swell, the sea was soon calm again.

When the wind eased up, I went below to see how things were going with the pets. Mitzi, coiled up in a wastepaper basket, was whining ever so softly. She knew that with all the water crashing aboard and the whipping of the wind, this was no safe place for her. The cockatoo was in his usual pose, head under a wing and asleep. Egbert was a casualty. The poor fellow had evidently suffocated. He was lying dead in his box. The only theory advanced was suffocation. It had been hard for humans to breathe behind shelter, but Egbert never made it.

What damage to the ship? The main awning had gone early in the fracas, and several smaller ones that had been stowed and lashed were torn to shreds. The starboard boat had been lifted out of its resting chocks and several planks stove in. The guardrails around the forecastle were twisted like a corkscrew, and some sections were missing. One sailor had been thrown out of his bunk and sustained a broken arm. The radio antenna had blown clear away and nobody had even seen it go. Four dogs had vanished overboard.

We heard later that the typhoon had whipped through the island we had seen before the storm and completely wrecked whole villages, with an estimated dead of two thousand. Eleven vessels, some of them canoes, were missing. With these figures as a guide, we reasoned that we had come through the ordeal exceptionally well.

The mate took a sight. We had been driven out to sea 23 miles from our original position. The decision to seek the open sea is a wise one when Mother Nature goes on the warpath. When we reached Iloilo, the pilot informed us that we had been listed as missing for some days. Owing to lack of communication, we could not advise anyone ashore where we were. The local newspapers made quite a fuss over our arrival. Hope was expressed that some of the other vessels would show, but up to the time we sailed no news had been received. The papers also mentioned our dog cargo, and dog fanciers from near and far streamed in to look over the collection of hounds. We had off-loaded them while our coal cargo was being discharged, so the curious had to go to the dog pound to see them.

About this time, Captain Angus was informed that his cargo of dogs was contraband. Holy Moses! Was he mad! Well he might be, stuck with a cargo and two thirds of the voyage over before he knew his freight was "hot"— rather embarrassing after he had accepted the cargo in good faith. The Canidrome officials had anticipated the captain's dilemma and were on hand to explain how the dogs were to be landed. The plans they presented did not meet with his approval, so the officials returned to Shanghai to find another avenue. In fact, the comings and goings resulted in a regular shuttle service.

Bunny intimated that his bunker coal needed replenishing. The prices quoted from dealers ashore were exorbitant. He forced himself to make a suggestion that, although brilliant, was downright thievery. His plan was to remove a small plate in the bulkhead separating the main cargo hold from the bunker. When the stevedores quit work for the day, we could go below and shovel about 50 tons through the hole, replace the plate, and nobody would be the wiser. There was one hitch in the proposal. Philippine customs maintained an officer on board twenty-four hours. To do this highjacking would be very risky. We called a conference, explained the problems, and then listened to suggestions.

"Throw him overboard."

"Cut his throat."

A few had gentle ideas, but it was interesting to listen to one's shipmates. The final plan accepted was to get him drunk. Angus was chosen to handle this situation. We investigated who was going to be on duty that night and learned that he was fond of bourbon and classical music. I went ashore and hired a record changer plus records and bought a couple of bottles of choice bourbon, so the materials were on hand. The stevedores quit work, Bunny opened the manhole in the bulkhead, shovels were passed through, and the plan was all set for the execution.

Angus missed his vocation. He really should have been a diplomat. He greeted the relief customs officer with all the flourish and courtliness of a Spanish grandee. The chef had bent over backward to prepare an exceptional meal. The officer was given the seat of honor at the table. Wine was served with every course, and no glass was allowed to remain empty, especially the visitor's. When dinner was over, he was escorted to the captain's cabin and the music set going. Angus intimated that some vital engine repairs were necessary, and he hoped the noise would not disturb their music festival. We all changed into old clothes and patiently awaited the signal to begin. The crew were eliminated from this chore. It was thought they might make too much noise and spoil the whole show. Bourbon flowed freely, and the music wove its magic spell. But that customs man certainly could hold his liquor. One bottle had been emptied, and the steward frequently hustled ice topside. Finally, the word came to begin. Eight of us went down into the hatch and started shoveling like mad. Bunny wanted 50 tons; we gave him 75. Coal simply cascaded into the bunker. We passed through the shovels and replaced the plate. All evidence of our raid was wiped clear. We came up on deck, showered, and were ready for the sack. I passed by the captain's cabin around midnight. "The Blue Danube" was playing. It was a toss-up as to which one could hold another drink. Brother, they were really plastered. No foolin'!

I had taken Mitzi ashore a few times for a walk. After wooden decks, the pads on her feet were too soft. She would romp around and chase anything that moved, imaginary or otherwise, but her sprightliness lasted only a short while before her feet got sore. Frequent lickings somehow never healed them. She would sit down, give me the most pitiful look, as if to say, "Hi, carry me, boss."

I was returning on board with Mitzi tucked under my arm when a well-dressed stranger approached and inquired if I wanted to sell the dog.

"It belongs to the third officer. I am merely exercising the animal. I doubt very much whether any thought has been given to a sale."

This character evidently wanted to buy Mitzi in the worst way.

"Price is no object."

When I told the third about the proposition, however, he shrugged it off with a "no interest" gesture. Mitzi had grown into quite a nice puppy. Although her ancestry was unknown, we all liked her for what she was.

The cargo had been discharged, but final details of our smuggling the greyhounds into China had not been straightened out to the captain's satisfaction. We moved our ship into a small river anchorage while the commuters came and went. I almost met my Waterloo with a water buffalo one afternoon. These big, ponderous animals looked docile enough. The small kids who were handling them in the fields had no trouble making them work or obey their commands. The pathway leading from where we landed ran alongside the river, past rice paddies where many water buffalo worked. I had passed by these animals fairly close several times, but they had paid no attention to me or even bothered to take a second look until this one critter let out a bellow and started off after me. Holy Moses! Which way to go? The river on one side and a waterlogged rice field on the other. My only escape was back along the pathway to where a canoe had landed me. There was no question about this buffalo being hostile. The distance separating us was a very few yards when the urgency of the situation finally penetrated my thick head. I took off. I doubt whether even an Olympic runner could have seen my dust. Fortunately, the canoe was only a short distance from the riverbank and the chap who had landed me saw me coming. He swung around and headed his boat into the shore again. I never waited for the canoe to even touch the bank but jumped aboard a few feet ahead of the buffalo, which skidded to a stop and bellowed his disapproval over my intrusion. I treated these animals with much more caution after that episode.

The chap after Mitzi was persistent. He had contacted the third mate with all sorts of offers but evidently had made little headway. He came on board Sunday morning and invited both the third and myself to go for a drive and visit his home. The ship was snug and we had nothing important to do, so we dressed up and accompanied him. His name was Madrigal, and he was the wealthiest man in Iloilo—he owned the power company and quite a lot of real estate. We were taken around some of the scenic spots and then to his home, a fabulous place set well back in spacious grounds studded with shade trees. The house was built for the tropics, with wide porches, screened patios, and big airy rooms that looked out onto well-kept lawns and gardens. He plied us with drinks, which caused me to remind the third of a certain customs officer we both knew well.

Lunch was served. Afterward, we were taken for a stroll around the grounds, which contained a small racetrack, stables for about ten horses, several small lakes, and the high point of the tour—dog kennels that were actually well-made brick houses. Each dog had its own exercise yard and a servant to take care of it. When we returned to the shade of the patio, the sales pitch got started. A very convincing pitch it was, too.

"Gentlemen, you can see what kind of a life your little dog would have in these surroundings. You know Shanghai is not a good place for dogs. Here, Mitzi could grow up with loving care, to play and run with other dogs. I'm sure you realize by now that I care for all my animals. Your dog would be no exception."

He aimed his remarks at me, even though I insisted the ownership was not mine and any decision would have to come from the third. He offered $75 for the dog and, as an added inducement, flashed the bills before our eyes. No dice. The third was adamant. No amount of convincing could sway either of us to part with the pooch. Madrigal seemed disappointed but realized the deal was off for that day. Anyhow, he called his chauffeur and ordered him to return us to the ship. He made one more try before we drove away. I'm certain he figured us both to be crazy sentimentalists.

We asked the driver to let us off in the downtown area so that we could take a last look at the city. The driver gave us a few pointers about the high spots and where to find cockfights, cabarets, honky-tonks, and numerous bars. We really had ourselves a time, but along the way our pockets were picked, leaving us with just enough small change to get back on board. We were supposed to sail the next morning, a fact neither of us appreciated. The laundryman came on board and we had to borrow a few bucks to pay him.

Our departure received another setback. One of the Canidrome executives wanted to sail with us and coordinate the transfer of the hounds. It was just as well because my head seemed several sizes too large and I couldn't stand the glare of the sun. The cook, with the wisdom of an Oriental, brought some coffee and toast to my cabin. He just walked in, put down the tray, opened the medicine cabinet, dumped two seltzer tablets in a glass of water, then departed without saying a word. The inference was there, nevertheless, so I downed the alkaline and light meal, which seemed to change the world completely. I figured I might live again.

The captain had sent the third ashore to get customs clearance. Before he left, he had mentioned in a halfhearted way that during the night he had been giving serious consideration to the sale of Mitzi—mumbling something about "being fair to the dog, better home for her, etc."

I paid scant attention to his ramblings, but obviously he had had a change of heart overnight. I was pondering his thinking when someone thumped on the door. It was Madrigal's chauffeur, who passed me a letter that read:

> Please don't sail away with Mitzi on board. I have probably been too forceful in my demands, and realize what that little pup really means to you. Let us forget our desires and think only of the dog's welfare. You know she will be happier here.
>
> Please let me have her, please.

The chauffeur handed me an envelope stuffed with greenbacks. Well, the resistance was low, so I told him to take the dog ashore but to wait until I could get down to the engine room before he made a move. I came back from my funk-hole an hour later. Mitzi had vanished. When the third came back on board, I told him about the deal and handed over the envelope. Damn funny to see that great big tough guy cry, but he did, for a long time. I wasn't feeling overjoyed about the transaction, either. I found myself looking at the doorway and expecting that pup to jump through it any second. We consoled each other with the fact that Shanghai was no place for a nice little dog. We could always come back and visit her. The envelope contained $95, which wasn't a bad investment for a $1 purchase from a pet store. Both of us were flat broke. The sudden change from rags to riches was an empty achievement. We wished our ship would sail. We had been in port over a week and a half. We had spent our time just waiting for these dog officials to get their problem ironed out.

The next morning there was another thump on my door. It was the same chauffeur, with another note: "Please give my chauffeur the dog's pedigree."

Well, this was a new slant. Mitzi had no pedigree and never had been represented as a purebred. I couldn't tell the driver that, so I stalled a while until I could scare up something that looked official. The answer came in the shape of a very impressive government form that had a huge crest embossed on the top, with a kangaroo and an emu plus a bunch of flowers, shields, and stars. I slipped this into the typewriter and created a pedigree for Mitzi that would classify her among the blue bloods of all dogdom. She belonged to the South Coast Kennel Club, and her lineage dated way back before the dogs' *Who's Who* was printed. I found a piece of red ribbon from a candy box, fish-tailed the ends, melted a big gob of sealing wax and pressed it with the top of a whiskey bottle cork, folded the pedigree neatly, and handed it to the chauffeur with a caution to be extremely careful getting it back home.

Where was that damn third? He had the happy knack of disappearing whenever a crisis arose. He was ashore again getting final corrections on our charts. We were at long last ready to sail. He returned before noon. We had the pilot on board already and got under way. I kept looking down the road for Madrigal's car chasing after us. The pedigree fooled the driver but wouldn't fool the boss for a minute. I often wondered what kind of puppies Mitzi had.

The details of handling our "hot" cargo had been finalized. We headed straight for Shanghai. The menagerie was somewhat depleted, but the end of our voyage was not too far off. I was on watch one afternoon when Bunny came up, looking as though he had seen a ghost. The poor guy was speechless. I looked astern, thinking someone might have fallen overboard, but he indicated such was not the case. I gave him some coffee. After a while, he seemed a little more composed and related his story.

He had come up from the engine room for a breather and noticed the cockatoo on the weather side. Occasionally, a spray would come inboard and wet the bird. Bunny thought a good gesture would be to move the cage over to the lee side. He had no sooner put the cage down when that perishing bird said, "Get out, you old bastard."

It was the first time anyone had ever heard the damn bird utter a cheep. Of all people, it would happen to poor old Bunny. The long lesson finally brought results. In fact, he "old bastarded" everyone. He was a slow starter, but, brother, did he make up for lost time and how!

Angus called a conference and explained the plan for off-loading the hounds. We would anchor at the Saddle Islands, a small group located about 30 miles off the estuary of the Yangtze River, where we would be met by Chinese junks. We would load our dogs aboard the junks, dump the kennels, and then head upriver with a completely empty vessel. The transfer was all arranged by the Chinese commander of the port. His soldiers would take charge from there. The plan sounded OK, and our chances of smuggling the cargo in were extremely good. In fact, the actual job was taken from us.

The Yangtze River is so large and the volume of water so great that the yellow discoloration of the ocean spreads for a good 25 miles from its mouth. The Saddle group lies just east of this yellow water. It is such a contrast, after coming in from the deep blue Pacific. We arrived at our appointed anchorage on time. Three junks quickly came alongside to off-load the hounds. Each junk carried almost twenty soldiers. With our crew hoisting the dogs from the hold, the transfer was completed in quick time. The junks hoisted sail; we hove up anchor and headed upstream. The kennels were jettisoned, decks washed down, and all evidence of the dog population erased, even the smell. We hoisted our flags, picked up the pilot, and headed for the estuary of the Whangpoo, a tributary of the Yangtze, on which the city of Shanghai stands.

This busy river and city were entirely different from what I had imagined. The traffic, variety of vessels, and stately buildings plus the terrific animation of the place left me somewhat bewildered. I had visited London, New York, Hamburg, Liverpool, and other great seaports, which were impressive but not to the extent of this Shanghai. The port traffic was so dense that, at times, I wondered how any vessel could get through. The freighters, liners, all types of junks, lighters, ferries, tugs, and powerboats crisscrossing the river gave the illusion of a disturbed anthill. We moved slowly past all this activity. The customs officers came on board and, aside from examining a few stores, the inspection was a routine affair. Our clearance was stamped.

The traffic eased up when we were abreast of the main section of the city. This area was known as Warship Row. Men-of-war from Britain, America, France, Italy, and Japan were all moored to buoys in midstream. The river is crescent-shaped at this point; the famous Bund, a beautifully landscaped, wide avenue, skirts the bank, with a facade of impressive buildings fronting the water. Our assigned berth was farther upstream. We passed large warehouses, docks, and shipyards before the pilot indicated that we had finally arrived at our buoy.

The Nanking government soon discovered that the greyhounds had been smuggled into China. In a court case lasting five days, evidence showed that one of the dog handlers had been drinking in a bar and started up a conversation with two strangers. The opportunity to boast about how customs had been outwitted was too good for him to miss. His companions were great listeners, and fresh drinks came readily. He learned too late that his companions were customs officers. Captain Angus was fined $70,000 (about $20,000 in U.S. currency); the ship was confiscated; and all dogs smuggled into Shanghai were to be shipped back to Australia at his expense. The Canidrome paid the fine, bought the ship, and gave it back to the captain. Of course, the dogs could not be found—they had been taken in a fleet of vans to the kennels where they rested, were given new names, and within a week were ready to race.

Thus ended the eventful voyage of the *Balls Head* to China.

6

CHINA INTERLUDE

Having lived most of my life according to Western standards, my initiation to China in 1930 was abrupt and full of surprises. Captain Angus invited me to stay at his home until I found suitable accommodation in Shanghai. His "guest quarters at his little house" turned out to be the entire third floor of his fifteen-room house, all beautifully furnished in modern Chinese style. A separate building for servants was located at the rear of the house. The captain's No. 1 boy decided he would look after me exclusively and completely ruined me with attention. This included a spotless white linen suit every day.

Each morning, I accompanied Angus to the office, where I assisted in the turnover of the *Balls Head* to Chinese interests. The strained relations between China and Japan were almost constant and were seriously affecting trade in this thriving community. Big liners, fast freighters, and regular cargo ships were avoiding Shanghai. The stranglehold of the Japanese on shipping prompted Chinese merchants to purchase their own ships. This turn of events made the Angus Company prosper, and I soon joined the firm. I was dispatched to buy ships and bring them back to China. The ideal return trip was to procure a cargo en route to help defray expenses. My first voyage was to Juneau, Alaska; then to Penarth, Wales, and Manila and Iloilo in the Philippines. I also made general surveys for Lloyd's of London, which took me into the interior of China and nearby countries—places I would never have seen otherwise.

When I was in Shanghai, I devoted evenings to learning the streets and general layout of the city. It was fascinating. Especially interesting were the street noises, not normal traffic noise but the sounds vendors made to announce their presence. Gongs, clappers, drums, whistles, and bells—each had its own meaning. The high-pitched gong indicated a blind man. A bell signaled the presence of a gray mare, whose milk was sold by the vendor (it was considered curative of all sorts of ailments). The drum meant that an animal or acrobatic troupe was about to perform. The clapper indicated a portable restaurant, a contraption made chiefly of bamboo and carried by a vendor on a pole across his shoulders. It was in two parts that were balanced for weight distribution. Within its framework was a charcoal fire, extra fuel, chopsticks, bowls, sauces, and a variety of food, including rice, noodles, patties, soup, and cookies. The total weight must have run into hundreds of pounds, yet a vendor carried this around until he found a suitable place to set up shop. It was commonplace to see half a dozen people standing around and eating at one of these mobile units.

Early in 1932, the Japanese launched a six-week aerial bombardment on the thickly populated Chinese section of Shanghai. On 26 August 1932, I joined the Shanghai Volunteer Corps, which was being mobilized to cope with unrest in the city and to help maintain order. When I replied in the affirmative to the question, "Do you ride, Palmer?" I was promptly put in charge of the stables, with five Chinese mafoos (horsemen) and 150 ponies. The bamboo structure was rather flimsy but capable of withstanding the elements quite well. Fresh ponies were led out each day for duty patrol. When they returned, we unsaddled, washed, fed, and bedded them down.

The ponies were rugged little chaps, rounded up each spring by Mongolian plainsmen, green broken, and then shipped to Shanghai for sale. Nature had given these critters special protection in order to survive the severe northern winters. Their hair was thick and closely matted, almost like wool. Their eyelashes were long and interlocking to protect their eyes from the glare of ice. On their fetlocks, long coarse hair grew almost to the thickness of string. This gave better traction on the ice because strands of hair would get beneath the hoofs and give them a grip on the ice. When they reached Shanghai, the Loong Fha stables sold them at public auction. After buying a pony, the purchaser had the long hair shorn off because nature had not intended that these little fellows withstand the heat of Shanghai. Naked, they looked like skinned rabbits. The troop ponies received special training to adjust them to street traffic, unruly mobs, and regular mounted drill. I saw these Mongolian ponies take off across rough country at a gallop and maintain their speed for hours. They are marvelous animals.

The city gradually settled down to normal living. The decision was made to demobilize the Shanghai Volunteer Corps, and I returned full time to the work of the Angus Company. Building programs resumed, and the influx of people continued until Shanghai exceeded the three million mark, the fifth largest city in the world. Shortly after the Angus family returned from a trip to Europe, I moved out and took up residence in the YMCA. It was quite a contrast to the luxury of a private home. No morning tea, I had to draw my own bath, and attend to my own laundry. After a short stay at the "Y," I bought a small but adequate house and obtained a houseboy with the help of the Angus cook.

On one of my return trips to Shanghai, after discharging a cargo of salt in Calcutta, we prepared for a short trip to Rangoon, Burma, to load rice for China. When entering the Irrawaddy River, I saw a collision between a ferry-boat and a large steel barge. The ferry was sinking, with numerous passengers being thrown into the fast-running river. I had the crew lower stages, ropes, ladders, and wood steps, which these unfortunates could grab and keep from being swept out to sea. We missed many of them but saved well over a hundred. Some time later, I was awarded the Royal Humane Society medal, distinctive and quite rare.

Many of my daytime hours in Shanghai were spent out on the Whangpoo River—making surveys, supervising the unloading of special items insured by Lloyd's, and making myself useful to the Angus Company. The Chinese junks that visited the port intrigued me from the first moment I laid eyes on them. They looked so ridiculous, with their high-charged hulls, cumbersome sails, squat lines, and curious decorations, that I wondered how such unwieldy craft could navigate at all. I asked numerous people, who had lived in China for many years and were either directly or indirectly connected with shipping, about their origin and construction, but they knew little and their answers were unsatisfactory. Eventually, I found a kindred spirit, Captain Jorgensen of the Yangtze Pilots Association, who had a wealth of information about junks and helped me considerably in my study of them. Jorge and I visited shipyards where these craft were built or repaired and found them to be a definite link to the distant past. When we viewed a nineteenth-century junk, we actually were looking at a mode of life from centuries past. As I began to understand the rig, construction, and design of these craft, my ridicule gave way to profound respect. I sailed on them and never ceased to be impressed by their design, ability, and seaworthiness. And the Chinese seafarers who handled them could be classified among the best sailors in the world.

I spent many years learning about Chinese junks. Several points were obvious: they were an important factor in the country's economy, there were many different types, and they carried the bulk of China's internal commerce. Delving deeper, I discovered many fascinating details.

Back in the fifth century A.D., a vessel capable of carrying a profitable cargo to such distant places as India, Mesopotamia, and Persia had evolved. It could house and sustain a crew for weeks on end. Sails to harness the motive power were of manageable size, and the rudder was capable of controlling the vessel in all weather. The Chinese had a good knowledge of navigation, primarily by sun and stars. They had invented the magnetic compass and had drawn charts as aids to navigation for centuries.

The first European to describe Chinese junks was Marco Polo, who lived in China for seventeen years at the end of the thirteenth century. Marco Polo's accounts of these fascinating craft led us to believe that the types he saw then were descendants of the trading ships that had voyaged in the Persian Gulf and the Red Sea many centuries earlier. His accounts are also amazingly descriptive of present-day junks. Many of these craft have obviously changed little in function, material, or appearance throughout seven centuries. When we look at Chinese junks today, we are seeing a little bit of life as it was lived fifteen hundred years ago in the Far East.

The characteristics and design of Chinese junks differ entirely from Western standards. The modern vessel, as we know it, has a sharp, high bow, with the stern usually lower and rounded. Masts are stepped along the centerline and might have a slight rake toward aft. In contrast, the Chinese junk has a low bow and a very high stern. The masts are never in the centerline and usually have a rake forward and outward.

There are many types, designs, and sizes of junks. One can identify regional types—river, canal, harbor, coastal, and ocean. They are known according to their function, as either traders or fishers. The characteristics of hull design differ, depending on the activity in which the vessels are employed and on the elements they must contend with, such as tides and shallows. Although diversified in form, color, sail plan, and artistic touches of the owner or builder, all junk designs follow three basic principles:

1. The hull is carvel-built on the bamboo pattern. Carvel-built refers to a smooth-sided hull with no overlapping planks, thus giving longitudinal strength. The bamboo pattern refers to the interior of the hull that is parti-

tioned off into separate watertight compartments by transverse bulkheads (the way a bamboo is divided into separate compartments). This type of hull construction protects the Chinese junk from the dangers of collision or stranding by localizing any structural damage and reducing it to a manageable proportion.

2. The junk is rigged on the controlled balanced lug sail. This enables the vessel to sail close to the wind and make good progress to windward.

3. A centerline rudder can be lowered into the water or raised clear. This system of steering is distinctive and functional, in that the rudder can be raised or lowered to suit the occasion. When sailing to windward, it acts as a deep keel; when beached, crossing a sand bar, or in shallow water, it can be raised to prevent damage, thus giving full control of the craft in deep or shallow water.

These three principles are fundamental in all types of junks, whether built to sail in the northern Gulf of Pechili or the southern Hainan Island. There are basically three distinct geographical types—the northern, or Antung; the central, or Foochow; and the southern, or Hong Kong.

The central, or Foochow, junk is one of the largest types and certainly the most colorful. Its approximate dimensions are length, 175 feet; beam, 25

These junks are southern, or Hong Kong, traders. They show a similarity in design yet differ greatly in size and detail.

The stern view of the Foochow junk in the top illustration shows the high oval-shaped stern, the fancy carving on the sternplate, the comparative height of the bow, and the rudder housing. The bow view in the bottom illustration shows the broad flat bowplate, the outward flare of the bulwarks, the position of the "eye," the masts stepped out of centerline, the bamboo battens for stiffening, and the common sheet and high peak.

feet; and depth amidships, 12 feet. Classified as an ocean type, it is used chiefly in the lumber industry. The bow of the Foochow junk has a backward-curved stem post and tapers as it emerges from the waterline into a broad wedge-shaped bow plate. The high bulwarks are fitted to the upper deck and flare out. Aft, the junk has an unusually high stern plate, carved with brightly painted birds, dragons, and flourishing lines. The bulwarks there merge into the deckhouse, which sweeps upward and might consist of two or three deckhouses superimposed in a series of steps. These deck-houses accommodate the master, crew, galley, and a joss house. Seen from astern, this junk has the appearance of a truncated oval. The hulls are painted white to the water's edge. The whole effect is very graceful.

The custom of painting eyes on Chinese junks reaches perfection in these central types. The eyes, or occuli, vary in size, shape, and position, according to the locality from which the craft originates. The Foochow junk carries a large eye on each bow. The eye is oval in shape, with a raised eyeball looking forward. When the craft is idle or laid up for repairs, the two eyes are covered over, indicating that the ship is at rest.

Although these unique sailing ships are now gradually being replaced by motor-driven craft, the basic principles developed by the Chinese are a rich legacy for shipbuilders the world over.

By early 1937, the Japanese were firmly established in northern China and began their full-scale invasion southward in July. Skirmishes occurred near Peking on July 7. Peking surrendered to the Japanese on July 28, followed by Tientsin on July 30. The Japanese attack on Shanghai began in August. The Chinese regular troops, the 4th Marines, Police Specials, and the Shanghai Volunteer Corps were mobilized, plus reinforcements from warships in the harbor. The Works Department of the Shanghai Council was busy stringing barbed wire and piling up sandbags; storefronts were barricaded; even banks had large sandbag emplacements. I was stationed, along with other Shanghai Volunteers, behind sandbags in front of the Shanghai Hong Kong Bank. One chap observed that when he finally got into the banking chamber, he was not sure whether he was a jackrabbit or a mole.

Real fighting started around North Station, a railway depot, but nearby was a Japanese Army barracks. The Chinese intended to capture this strate-gic post. They certainly would have done so had it not been for reinforce-ments from the *Idzuma*, a heavy Japanese cruiser moored near the Japanese Consulate. When the Chinese withdrew, they set fire to houses and other buildings. This became known as the "Scorched Earth." Many thousands of civilians were killed in the fighting or burned to death. The troops stacked their bodies about 8 feet high, in piles about 20 feet square, then threw gaso-

A Chinese junk under way near Pootung, a Shanghai suburb. He needs a new set of sails.

line over them and set the piles afire. The Chinese Air Force became active but proved of little use because of the close infighting on the ground.

I began jotting down a few of the tragic events during this time (some with dates, some without):

USS *Augusta* hit August 20, one sailor killed, eighteen wounded.
The Bund closed to pedestrian traffic August 21.
Hongkew in flames.

British Ulster Rifles arrive from Hong Kong.

American citizens without interests in China requested to evacuate.

Japanese land additional troops at Woosung, at mouth of Whangpoo River.

Nanking bombed.

Dollar liner *President Hoover* bombed in Yangtze River near Woosung; no direct hit, but seven crew members and three passengers injured; HMS *Cumberland* sped alongside and rendered medical aid.

Shanghai fell to the Japanese 12 November 1937. A few days later, Chiang Kai-shek moved his Nationalist government from Nanking to a new capital at Chungking, and, on December 13, Nanking fell. There followed the brutal "Rape of Nanking" with up to 200,000 Chinese civilians massacred on 5 February 1938.

There are always touches of humor in any crisis. One such episode was a small duel between a Chinese machine gunner and a Japanese destroyer that was entering the Whangpoo River and heading toward Shanghai. The machine gunner was concealed behind a stack of coal on the riverbank, and a rerun of David and Goliath was never more obvious. The Japanese destroyer steaming upriver, full of pomp and importance, was suddenly challenged by a single soldier with a machine gun who opened fire as the warship went by. The Japanese were so incensed by this affront that they dropped anchor, cleared the decks, and let go with their main battery. Trees, coal, fences, houses, and debris flew skyward, but when the smoke cleared pop, pop, pop goes the machine gun. Another broadside, more coal and dust. Once again, pop, pop, pop—the Chinese gunner is still there. Obviously embarrassed, the Japanese heaved up anchor and continued upstream.

The Japanese were steadily wiping out their own investments in China and destroying commercial opportunities in a land where wise and courteous treatment would have earned them respect for many years. After three months, the Chinese Army withdrew and things eased up quite a bit. The economic future of this city looked bleak. It was built on trade, and we had none. The river was blocked by a boom of sunken ships. The Chinese cities that had mushroomed around the settlement were completely gutted.

Angus was beginning to look awful. This war meant complete ruin; shipping bypassed the port as though it harbored the plague. Angus and I decided to close down the office, pay off the staff, and sell whatever was negotiable. The large launch was the biggest item, but file cabinets, typewriters, calculators, desks, and furniture were all sold at cheap rates. Angus finally went home to rest up, but he never did recover. He died—a war casualty—and I lost a great friend.

I sold my own house and moved into the Shanghai Club, which, after the sandbags were removed, looked as sharp as ever. The membership was down; quite a few had left for America or the United Kingdom, but the secretary was a financial whiz. He had salted away sufficient funds to rehabilitate the club, and the staff went along as of yore.

Meanwhile, war clouds were growing in Europe, and Hitler was stomping around.

7
ROYAL NAVY VESSELS—
WORLD WAR II

Shanghai, by the latter part of 1939, was again at peace with the world—as peaceful as a boisterous city ever can be. We had survived several minor wars and, in the process, buried several hundred thousand men, but casualties in the Orient are very ordinary. Life is cheap, food is scarce, and with no big public outcry, life resumes its normal pace.

The banks were flourishing, the stores were jammed, shipping was busy, and the Bund was crowded. At the Shanghai Club, reputed to have the longest bar in the world, eighteen bartenders, plus waiters on the floor, were kept busy. Members stood three deep at the bar. I was a steward at the club and was very contented with my lot. Things seemed too good to be true, and the telephone call was ominous: "Palmer, would you kindly present yourself at the Navy House in the consulate grounds about noon tomorrow?" Would I? What alternative did I have?

The interview revealed that I had a naval background and was single. His Majesty the King would appreciate my services. The question was urgent: "When can you leave? There is a state of war, and we are mobilizing ex-servicemen from around the world. We need you."

Thus began a merry-go-round—much excitement, too many casualties, ship sinkings, grand shipmates, numerous friends, wounds, and great honors—that lasted seven years.

I left Shanghai in September 1939, with half a dozen others, on the Jardine steamer *Ming Sang* bound for Hong Kong. We were all looking forward to naval service. I was probably the only man to hold commissions simultaneously in the American Troop of the Shanghai Volunteer Corps and the Royal Navy (my father being an American and my mother, an Australian).

The first step was to report to the HMS *Tamar,* anchored in Hong Kong harbor. She was an old vessel, half steam and half sail, but bearing the true naval tradition of spit and polish. The senior officer, Commodore Bertram, greeted us and explained the European situation: Hitler and his army were sweeping everything before them, and it was necessary to mobilize and be prepared while time was on our side.

We were required to serve in the Hong Kong Reserve, pass medical exams, give complete details of our previous service and qualifications, exercise, and learn all about the so-called "new Navy." My rank was sub-lieutenant, RNVR, and my gold stripe was wavy.

Things began moving fast. Two Yangtze River gunboats arrived in port. They were fitted up with extra deck supports, breakwaters, and other gear, ready for a trip to Singapore. These gunboats were designed and built by the British during World War I for the purpose of invading Europe via the Danube. They were extraordinarily powerful; their three engines were capable of forging ahead through turbulent current. They also had three rudders and triple screws. The armament was considerable—two 6-inch guns and much other secondary armament. The idea was to flood the ballast tanks located on either side, cant the deck to the desired angle, and, by this means, give the guns extra power to shell forts or headlands far out of reach under ordinary circumstances. The vessels had shallow draft, flat bottoms, and a 3-foot freeboard. They were excellent craft for their intended purpose. When World War I was over, they steamed out to China and formed what was called the Yangtze Flotilla. These vessels were named after insects—the *Moth, Cricket, Cockchafer, Ladybird,* and so on. The United States had a similar flotilla named after islands in the Philippines; one that caught public imagination was the USS *Panay,* which was sunk by Japanese aircraft in 1939.

I was appointed executive officer of the HMS *Cockchafer.* After moving my few belongings from the *Tamar,* I prepared for sea. The difficulty a reserve officer encounters when joining an active warship is a complete lack of knowledge of the ship, compounded by the caste system. A reserve officer wears different stripes from those of the regular navy officer; my stripes were crisscrossed. Of course, the regular enlisted men quickly recognize what might be termed a greenhorn or, as they say, a "Rocky," the inference being that the officer just came off the rocks. However, the biggest problem confronting me was the crew. They had been on the China Station where Chinese workers were allowed on board. For a few pennies plus food and handouts, they took over all the manual work—scrubbed decks, polished brass, ran errands. When the ship was placed on active list, all of these characters were put ashore and the regular bluejacket was confronted with a mop and told to get busy scrubbing decks. The skipper of this ship, Commodore Arthur Malcolm Peters, was not helpful. He apparently held the same views as the crew about Rockies, but I kept my council, rolled with the punches, kept watch, and stayed with the vessel to Singapore, with one stop at Saigon for fuel.

Our arrival in Singapore coincided with that of several other warships, among them the HMS *Medway*, a submarine parent ship, probably the largest ship in the whole Navy and, by comparison to the gunboats, a Goliath. My orders were to transfer to the *Medway*, and I left the *Cockchafer* with no regrets. It was not a happy ship.

My room aboard HMS *Medway* was sumptuous, and the officers I met were friendly guys. The commander was a regular sailor, meaning that he had risen from the ranks. In those days, that was a stupendous, almost impossible, task. The commander was constantly referring to security. This ship was irreplaceable: she originally cost 80 million pounds and, on war

The HMS *Medway*, a submarine parent and tender ship. Palmer was assistant navigator on the *Medway* in 1939.

A group of British officers on board HMS *Medway,* about 1940. From left are the torpedo officer, chief surgeon, commander, first lieutenant, and engineer officer.

standing, was worth 800 million, plus the crew of 3,800 men, many of them skilled workers.

This vessel made everything—below decks were blast furnaces, lathes, forges, cutters, and drills. For example, she remade the bow of a destroyer that had been in a collision, including casting hawse pipes, stem plates, anchors, and everything associated with reconstructing a brand-new bow plate, as would be done in a dockyard. She could straighten out a periscope from a submarine and build new boats, such as landing craft. The bakery alone made 12,000 loaves of bread each day, and the accommodations below could house and feed four complete submarine crews, in addition to the regulars. Thrown in were torpedoes and guns; carpentry; deep sea diving and rescue equipment; health department with a large dental surgery, a very large hospital with the latest equipment, and X-ray technicians; classrooms with professional teachers, a church, and perhaps more features that I have overlooked. A ship of 50,000 tons crammed with equipment is an extremely valuable item in case of war.

The first job assigned to me after being schooled and shown around was quarterdeck watch. This ship had a huge deck with gangways on either side, a telephone system, and alarm bells. The officer of the deck always had a quartermaster on duty with him, and I was fortunate in having a grand old guy—regular Navy, wise to the ways of all sailors, and a good companion. Watches were kept similar to those at sea, although we were tied to a pier with a huge gangway that had been used by all and sundry during the months *Medway* had been stationed in Singapore. My watch was 0800–1200 and 2000–2400. The duties required checking everybody coming on board, crewmen and civilians alike, including those from the huge British base in the city.

The quarterdeck had a desk on which rested the captain's standing orders, plus another huge document known as KR & AI, the King's Regulations and Admiralty Instructions. This is the Navy "Bible"; no matter what arises, the answer will be found in the book. It behooves the officer of the deck to familiarize himself with the captain's orders, and, being a Rocky, I studied this volume at every opportunity. One paragraph caught my eye: "Every civilian must have a valid pass." Holy Moses! We had a regular gang coming on board, and nobody even asked for a pass. I questioned my quartermaster. He observed that these people had been coming on board around 1130 for months, the big attractions being a free meal and a shot of gin costing twopence.

The quartermaster and I decided to change things around.

Dust clouds signaled the freeloaders' arrival because most of the roads were unpaved. They came from all corners, parked their cars near the gangway, and walked on board. Their usual routine was to raise their hats when stepping onto the quarterdeck, and the duty officer saluted and allowed them to pass. This day was different. The protests must have been heard for miles. The first chap, the gunnerymaster, was very polite. When I asked him for his pass, however, his attitude changed. He gave me every reason why he should be allowed on board, but I insisted that he produce his pass. Of course, he didn't have one, and I asked him to go ashore. This was repeated several times, and quite a number of disgruntled officials gathered onshore and glared at me. The dental surgeon came out on deck and berated me for being impolite; he had invited several of his group for lunch. He kept yacking away and annoying me, until I finally ordered him off the quarterdeck. Meanwhile, the telephone was ringing off the hook and lights were blinking—anyone would think a mutiny was in progress.

My relief failed to show on time. Ultimately, a messenger from the captain arrived on deck and requested that I accompany him to the captain's quarters. Capt. Keeble White, although not a well person, was as alert and sharp as they come.

"What is all the trouble on the quarterdeck, Palmer?"

I stuttered and fumbled but managed to quote verbatim his standing orders.

"That is correct," he said, "and I compliment you on carrying them out. This ship is becoming a hangout for derelicts, and the regular officers of the ship find it hard to get a seat or a drink. I commend you. You are dismissed."

I saluted and left his quarters, only to be greeted by the commander. He was full of praise for my stand. Nobody had had the guts to buck the enormous power of the dockyard hierarchy, who had garnered the equivalent of a dictatorship over the years.

Orders came for the *Medway* to proceed to Europe, accompanied by six submarines, and so we prepared to leave. Sailing day eventually arrived, and we eased away from the dock, assembled our brood of submarines, and headed for Ceylon. The daily routine on board was intensified with war games. The subs faked attacks, balloons were sent aloft to test out the antiaircraft batteries, the crew was repeatedly drilled, and rifle practice was frequent. The Germans, meanwhile, were overrunning most of Europe.

Our orders were to stop any ship belonging to France, Belgium, Holland, Denmark, and Norway. One can imagine the thoughts going through the mind of a captain steaming across the Indian Ocean, with a calm sea, blue sky, and everything going according to Hoyle. The officer on the bridge is probably dreaming about some dame miles away, when a huge battlewagon suddenly appears with six submarines! The captain goes chop! chop! in the opposite direction, just as fast as his engines can go! Every effort on our part to identify ourselves as friendly didn't mean a damn thing. That ship had business elsewhere and wanted no truck with us—no way. Finally, we had to abandon the idea of intercepting these ships; it was impossible.

Ceylon gave us a warm welcome, but we had no time to visit. After taking on fuel, stores, and fresh water, we were on our way. The captain reduced the scare tactics of having six submarines strung out, three on each side. They now followed in line astern and did not present such an awesome show of strength. Passing through the Suez Canal was again a great thrill to me, in spite of having gone through it well over twenty times and having helped to survey the Sinai Peninsula. Alexandria was our base of operations; when we had our assigned berth, things changed from seagoing to an ever-ready wartime footing.

Germany had overrun France by then, and Italy, sensing a good opportunity to be on a winning side, joined the Axis and was making all kinds of warlike gestures. The Italians bombed Malta every hour on the hour and helped to raid Albania, Yugoslavia, and Greece. Their army in Ethiopia was bogged down, but the huge Italian army in Libya was advancing and making sporadic raids on Sollum.

The *Medway,* as designated depot ship, was responsible for delivery of mail; we also attended to any illness on board other vessels, did minor repairs, acted as guard boat, patrolled the harbor, and watched loading and unloading of liberty men.

The guard boat was required to patrol the harbor and visit each ship at least twice a night. By this time, we had a big fleet of warships, cruisers, destroyers, auxiliary craft, aircraft carriers, ammunition ships, tugs, and other craft. We had about twenty midshipmen on board, straight from college, but they quickly caught on to the ways of the world—guard boat duty entitled the person to the next day off. The routine went something like this: boarding the launch at 2130 and paying a social call to each ship, sometimes flashing a light to alert the guard on duty—nothing subtle about this, just making sure that every vessel was notified and the visit recorded. The coxswain made no attempt to be quiet. Above the noise of the engine roaring full speed, the guard on a ship would challenge, "What ship?" The answer, "Guard boat," and it was off to the next ship. With any luck, the cadets could be back on board the *Medway* by about 0200 to write up the log, hit the sack, and goof off the next day.

The commander got wise to this caper and assigned me to straighten it out. Here again was a Rocky officer in charge of a gang of bluebloods. Some were actually aristocrats with lineages a mile long. Needless to relate, they resented me and, given half a chance, would have tossed me overboard. My first instructions when everyone was assembled on the deck were to shed white caps, cover up white shirt fronts, and wear sweaters and rubber shoes. The boat was covered with a black flag and the brasswork dulled. Instead of the big diesel launch capable of carrying one hundred men, we used a single engine with double mufflers. I then instructed them to be on board the following evening, and without exception—no absentees. Of course, they gave me the usual flimflam: Mother was very sick in hospital, Uncle made a special trip to visit me, and so on. None of these excuses impressed me. I was a "hard-hearted Hanna," and they sensed I was not fooling. The next evening at roll call, everyone was present—with dark caps, sweaters, rubber shoes, and a general air of excitement, even apprehension.

We boarded the launch and eased over to a large cruiser. The cruiser was at peace with the world, and nobody challenged us. We could see the quartermaster hanging around the gangway, but we came on board without being seen. I had had the carpenter shop make wooden blocks and paint on them "This is a bomb." I took two blocks of wood, opened the center gun and placed one in the breech block, then did the same to the second turret. We left without being seen. The next ship was a destroyer, and we really loused up her torpedo tubes.

The biggest fish was the aircraft carrier. Because I knew this vessel was well guarded, I chose to get the launch way up near the breakwater and, then at full speed, cut the engine and drift. We were lucky to find a rope ladder hanging over the side, but when one chap hooked it with a boat hook, the wood rungs banged and banged on the empty hull like a drum. I was sure a sentry would appear to find out what the hell was going on. We lay low, though, and nobody came, so I decided to climb on board. The ladder led into what we called an orlop, or open deck, and that led into a storage area full of engines, propellers, and intricate parts, but nobody was in attendance. Another canvas screen opened into the main hangar and here were dozens of fighter planes but, again, nobody in sight. The place was huge—I'd never seen anything like it. On the after end was a workbench that had evidence of recent occupancy—cigarettes still burning, coffee cups half empty, and a sense of someone being present. I was about to return but realized nobody would believe me about having been on board, so I took the inspection plate off the tail end of a fighter and headed for the open deck. Sure enough, my men were still there and nobody had challenged them. I handed down this rather large piece of plane, then went back into the parts department and took two propellers.

We eased away from the ship's side and headed for one of the battleships, presumably well guarded, but we managed to unhook two launches and the ship's nameplate. Next was an ammunition carrier. I went easy with her because she had a small crew and was not actually navy. However, her guard was very lax, so I took the logbook. We prowled around until almost dawn, boarded at least ten ships, and collected much evidence. The midshipmen, who originally had been reluctant to enter into the spirit of the adventure, all wanted to go again the next day. We wrote out the respective report, the loot was locked up in the cell block, and I took a shower and hit the sack.

It seemed only seconds before a messenger called me: "The captain wants to see you, sir!"

I was tired, needed a shave, and tried to stall for time, but no dice. The messenger returned. "Captain wants to see you, *forthwith,* sir!"

When you get the forthwith sign, you don't drag the tail. I appeared before the Captain in pajamas, hair disheveled, no shave, and feeling lousy. The loot was spread out on the deck, and it did seem like quite a lot. Guess I got carried away for a while.

"What have you done?" the captain wanted to know. "The aircraft carrier had twenty-nine sentries on duty and you climb on board and actually take parts of a fighter, plus other accessories, without being seen or challenged?"

He was hopping mad. Signals from other ships claimed I had never been on board, but when I referred to my notes—open the second turret breech and find a block of wood marked "Bomb"—they were quiet.

The *Medway*, it seemed, had everything possible, including a radio frequency panel. This is not the correct term, but it consisted of about ten or twelve men seated in a soundproof booth; with headsets, they constantly listened to the airwaves. I was called in late one night because a vessel in port was radioing in code and had to be stopped. A cross-bearing pinpointed the culprit to be a Spanish vessel, and with four trusty men I shoved off to see why.

The watchman was sound asleep. Our routine was to leave two men at the gangway to cover our retreat, as it were, then three of us would search the ship. First we checked the bridge, nobody there; officers' quarters, no luck. Then we went aft and got the scare of our lives. We were walking along a deserted deck, pitch dark, and some cumbersome movement was taking place right before us. We all had heard about Hitler's secret weapon, and I thought this must be it. The blood pressure returned to normal when one of the critters let out a "Moo." There were three cows asleep on deck, and we almost fell over them!

The after end brought pay dirt. We heard a high pitch coming from a ventilator and, with pistols drawn, two of us began opening doors—first one, nothing; another door, a blank. But the high pitch and purr of the motors grew stronger. When I opened a deck hatch, I was almost blinded by strong lights. Two men were operating, and one appeared to be coding. I was down the ladder and in the room without anyone even noticing, but what a surprised team they were, looking down the barrels of .45 revolvers. They cut off whatever message they were sending, raised their hands, and ascended the ladder, one by one. We handcuffed them, escorted them to the gangway, and took them to our ship for interrogation. It was a routine trip for me, but when I mentioned at breakfast about running into the sleeping cows I got the raspberry. Fortune was with me, though, for when the tugs moved the Spaniard from her original mooring, it so happened the move was reasonably close by. There on her deck stood the cows. This positive proof clearly vindicated me.

My reputation spread. Sentries were much more alert and liable to shoot first and ask afterward. The result of the big raid had spread, and almost every ship that had been boarded verified the report as bona fide. One cantankerous old Welsh skipper, the commander of the ammunition carrier, however, stubbornly refused to believe anybody had boarded his ship. I thought it best to teach this codger a lesson and picked one of the worst nights imaginable. I alerted my chief raider Rusty, and around 0200 we shoved off for the unwary carrier. Getting alongside was not easy with a modest sea running, but, watching the waves, we managed okay and started off to see what was available. The bridge yielded more logbooks and coded messages, plus the ensign. We passed up everything bulky or heavy but helped ourselves to the captain's rack of fancy pipes and also a plaque given to him by the Khedive Steamship Line. The night was miserable and, for Egypt, a bit cold. The watchman was sound asleep in the ward galley and strongly objected to being taken prisoner, but we took him anyway. We scrambled on board the boat and headed for base, a warm shower, and hot chocolate. I made up my report, had the captured sentry locked up, and, feeling very smug about the night's operations, retired. The ammunition carrier was signaled to send her boat to collect logbooks, coded messages, ensigns, assorted pipes, a fancy plaque, and one very frightened night watchman. No charges were made, but the skipper was warned about laxity on board and, supposedly, I was cussed in Welsh. My raid revealed how vulnerable the fleet was to sabotage. We could very easily have been blown up.

Much had changed on board *Medway*. The original skipper from China had been replaced, many of the officers were new, and our Chinese crew had been returned and now we had Maltese. Maybe the term *crew* is confusing. I actually mean the domestic staff—stewards, bartenders, and general houseboys. The new captain had also made changes in procedure. When I first joined, the custom was to dress formally for dinner. Everyone stood to attention for the commander or, on occasion, the captain, who stood at the head of the long table. Glasses were charged, usually with sherry, and a toast given to the King. Every night of the week, there was a different toast. The chaplain would then give grace and, on command, everyone was seated and the normal yackety-yack began. This was a nice custom, prevalent in the Navy for many years— rather formal but like many of our cherished traditions, now discontinued.

By now we had lost four of our submarines, enemy action had intensified, bomb raids became a nightly event, several French warships had joined the fleet, and it seemed that everyone at long last knew we were at war. I was overdue for leave and chose to visit the Holy Land, but it was soon time to return to reality.

The Italians had made an effort to advance along the Western Desert and were threatening Sollum (As Sallūm) on the seacoast in northwestern Egypt. Their objective was to seize the Suez Canal and thereby cut off supplies from

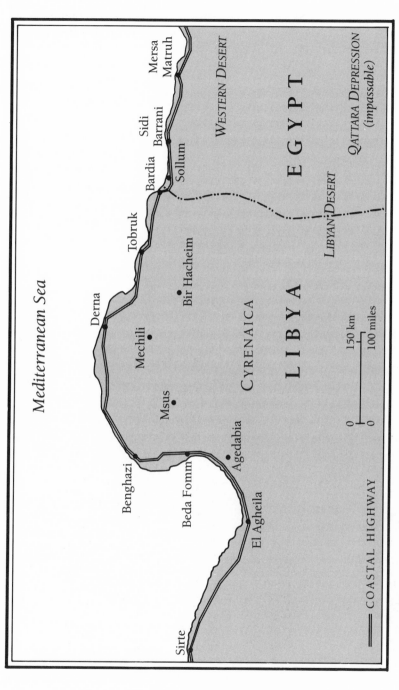

The British offensive in North Africa began on 9 December 1940, with a thrust from Mersa Matruh through an undefended gap in the coastal mountains, to take Bardia and Tobruk. The Italians were then in full flight. Rommel's first offensive began at El Agheila on 24 March 1941.

India, Australia, New Zealand, and other countries eastward. A British counterattack began with a thrust from Mersa Matruh (Marsā Matrūh), the base of operations for the British Western Desert Force.

The fleet was poorly equipped with small craft. We had battleships, cruisers, and destroyers but few, if any, of the disposable type. The Navy had built some barges—nobody seemed to know exactly why—but there they were. I was appointed to command one of these clunkers, the *X-39*, which was similar to those used in the Dardanelles in 1915. It had old-fashioned diesel engines that had to be warmed up three hours ahead of time. The steering was housed in a steel deckhouse and upfront was a steel gantry designed to lower or raise a platform for landing. The barges were the predecessors of the tank landing craft, which were to be very useful later on in Tobruk.

X-39 unloading on the beach at Sidi Barrani. A Chinese river gunboat, with her 6-inch guns, is behind *X-39*. Italians are assisting in the unloading. Courtesy Australian War Memorial.

My commission was to load this craft and take stores for the army that was preparing to hold back the Italians moving eastward out of Bardia (Bardiyah). Numerically they were quite a huge force, but one of Mussolini's many bluffs—not worth the powder to blow them to hell.

Submarine Flotilla General Information Circular No. 80 dated 16 December 1940 reads:

The Lighter X39 was towed to Mersa Matruh by ST. ISSEY loaded with Army stores. From Mersa Matruh she proceeded under her own power to Sidi Barrani, taking two days to do the seventy-mile trip. On arrival at Sidi Barrani she discharged between 1000 and 1830 the following Army stores:

Petrol	9400 gallons	*Ammunition:*	
Water	6000 gallons	Shells, 25 pdrs.	1092
Lub. Oil	200 drums	Breda	10 cases
Axle Grease	3 cases	.303	60 cases
Gelignite	3 cases	QF	10 cases
Fuses	1 case	Land Mines	17 cases
Detonators	3 boxes	Barbed Wire	45 rolls

Rations:	
Tinned Beef	95 cases
Biscuits	70 cases
Tea, sugar and figs	45 tins
Milk	25 cases
Pork Sausages	10 cases

X39 has certainly done her bit and is now at Mersa Matruh waiting more.

Sidi Barrani had been captured on 10 December 1940, with thirty-eight thousand prisoners taken. Bardia followed on 4 January 1941 and yielded another forty thousand prisoners. They were collected and marched across the desert three deep. It was a sight to behold this vast column of men several miles long being led by a British soldier, whose only weapon was a swagger stick, and along the lines a few soldiers armed with rifles. My warship had already unloaded its stores in Sidi Barrani. I was waiting for orders in Sollum when this army of prisoners arrived, with no food and no water. We had arrived at the battered Sollum jetty on Christmas Eve to assist the Sixth Australian Division, which was making its famous assault on Halfaya (Hellfire) Pass on the way to attacking Bardia.

Sollum waterfront. *X-39* is on the near side of the jetty, farthest out to sea. The road to Bardia is on the right, behind the buildings. Courtesy Australian War Memorial.

Sollum wasn't the nicest spot on earth. We had no guns and most of our cargo was gasoline. In addition to putting up with snipers, we got bombed constantly. The stevedores were recruits from Cyprus. What a scared bunch of jackrabbits they were—one shot or a small bomb and they took off. We lost a few crewmen to bombing fragments. Along with the attacks by torpedo and bomber planes, Sollum was experiencing fire from the howitzer guns at Bardia. The cliffs there were quite steep, and I don't recall hearing about big guns at Bardia.

We positioned Polish troops atop the escarpment. Their purpose was to signal the approach of bombers, but their reflexes were slow and they would signal at just about the same time as the bombers arrived. One day, before we could finish unloading *X-39*, the water lighter alongside received a direct hit. A number of soldiers and sailors were killed or wounded. One bomb hit us right on the bow and blew away half the topside. My signalman was killed, and *X-39* was slowly sinking. Two sailors were wounded and, bribing them with rum, I had to kid them into staying alive and on their feet until Red Cross help came. I caught a piece of shrapnel on the left hand and missed two fingers from the right hand—no big deal. We kept *X-39* afloat by stuffing bags, canvas, and any damn thing around until the entire cargo was off-loaded, and then we gently edged her to shallow water and let her sink.

Now I had a hungry crew and no ship.

8

HMS *MARIA GIOVANNI*— NORTH AFRICAN CAMPAIGN

The opposing forces in Africa continued to face each other on the frontier. By 22 January 1941, British forces had advanced well into Libya and captured Tobruk, an important convenient harbor seventy-five miles west of Bardia. The British then formed the Inshore Squadron, composed of little supply ships that plied to and fro between Alexandria, Mersa Matruh and Tobruk. Up and down that featureless, unlighted coast they ran the gauntlet of submarines, dive bombers, and torpedo-carrying aircraft through water-ways sown with mines. The petrol and ammunition carriers knew that one direct hit meant almost certain death for the crew. They made the perilous trip not once, but again and again without respite, because they were so few.

The Inshore Squadron consisted of the monitor *Terror* with two 15-inch guns, three river gunboats from the China Station (*Aphis, Ladybird,* and *Gnat,* to which was later added a fourth, the *Cricket*), two armed boarding vessels (*Chakla* and *Fiona*), and three Italian ships captured off the coast (the ketch *Zingarella,* the schooner *Maria Giovanni,* and the motor vessel *Tiberio*), plus minesweepers, patrol craft, and destroyers. The *Zingarella* later proved unequal to the wear and tear and was withdrawn early for an engine refit.

Official records reveal how these three Italian vessels had been captured. The Italians had also endeavored to use the inshore route to transport supplies, but with little success, and a number of their ships, small auxiliary schooners of around 150 tons, were destroyed or captured by destroyers of the Inshore Squadron.

At 0145 on 30 December 1940, the *Voyager* had intercepted the *Zingarella* (190 tons), which hove to when a shot was fired across her bow. The weather was too bad to go alongside or lower a boat. When the *Zingarella* was hailed, the Italians replied that they had English prisoners on board. At this moment, recorded the *Voyager's* captain, a "Sergeant of the Queen's Own" shouted that he had the situation in hand and that he and eight of his regiment had one hundred Italians battened down below. He was told to collect all mail, correspondence, and confidential papers and tell the captain to follow the *Voyager*. The sergeant replied, "We'll see to that." *Voyager* took *Zingarella,* which was armed with two .303 machine guns that were not manned at any time, into Sollum.

In the early hours of 1 January 1941, after a night patrol in the vicinity of Tobruk (her first with the Inshore Squadron) the destroyer HMS *Dainty* had begun to close the land to ascertain her position. Suddenly, a lookout reported a mast on the starboard beam, toward which *Dainty* immediately turned. The object was soon identified as an auxiliary schooner, the *Maria Giovanni*. She was flying the Italian naval ensign and trying to escape from Bardia harbor with Italian senior officers and Australian prisoners on board.

She at once hove to and, in a state of panic, the twelve-man crew frantically lowered a boat and began to abandon ship. A burst of 0.5-inch machine gun fire to make them desist only increased the panic; the entire crew threw themselves on their faces. As soon as the firing stopped, they leapt to their feet and started yelling. With their hands raised up to surrender, they then jumped overboard, some into the lifeboat, others into the sea. Finally, with the aid of an officer of the *Dainty* who could speak fluent Italian, they were prevailed upon to return on board their ship and to precede the British boarding party in case a booby trap had been laid. The white ensign was hoisted above the Italian. With a lieutenant from the *Dainty* in charge, the *Maria Giovanni* was ordered to proceed to Sollum.

Almost immediately afterward, and before her aircraft had returned, *Dainty* sighted another mast, which turned out to belong to the Italian motor vessel *Tiberio,* slightly smaller than the *Maria Giovanni.* She was captured under similar circumstances and also ordered to Sollum.

So, out in the harbor of Sollum were three captured vessels of Italian registry—the obvious thing to do would be to commandeer any one of them. I remonstrated with myself: Not so fast, Palmer, not so fast. Regulations had to be observed, and they were. The three vessels were not exactly liners, but they were useful craft and they were afloat. We needed this type of craft in the worst way. Once the Admiralty decided to acquire them, things began to happen. On 12 February, the *Maria Giovanni* was taken over by the Royal Navy and given the title of HMS, but the class of warship in which she belonged was a mystery. Because my *X-39* had been declared unseaworthy, orders came from Alexandria for me to transfer the crew and take command of the HMS *Maria Giovanni*.

This was a wonderful change. There had been no accommodation worthy of mention on the *X-39*, but we found reasonable quarters on the *Maria Giovanni*, plus fresh water, a commodity very scarce in the desert. My crew expanded from two men and an engineer to six men, an engineer, and a sub-lieutenant.

Maria Giovanni was an auxiliary 340-ton, three-masted schooner, 180 feet long. Prior to the war, she had been engaged in running between Italian ports and Africa. She had no weapons. Her diesel engine was capable of 8 knots, and she could carry more than 200 tons of cargo. Crew quarters were on the forward deck with officers and engine room right aft. Lifesaving equipment consisted of one boat that was carried on deck but hoisted out when cargo was being worked.

The vessel needed cleaning up badly. While the crew were busy, I checked her manifest and discovered a barrel of first-class brandy.

The *Maria Giovanni*, shortly after her capture from the Italians in January 1941. Palmer commanded this trim 180-foot schooner during the North African campaign.

The *Maria* had sweet lines and all the essentials. Although the accommodations left much to be desired, it was luxurious in comparison to *X-39*. I was fortunate in withholding two of the original engineers, and they explained the intricate mechanics of the diesel engine and the Italian markings for pumps, valves, and electric circuitry.

At first, we were kept busy ferrying stores from oceangoing ships anchored offshore to the pier at Sollum. When the Italian army surrendered and was marched from Bardia to Sollum, *Maria Giovanni* was pressed into service ferrying the POWs out to ships for transporting to Alexandria. On each pass, we crammed a few hundred into the hold and on deck, with standing room only. They were a pitiful lot—uniforms of poor quality and badly made, and their weapons must have come from the bottom of the barrel. On reaching the transports, they had to climb up rope ladders from our very low deck to the much higher deck, approximately 30 or 40 feet. Many were scared. Some even refused, but persuasion overcame this handicap. One prisoner, an officer, shot himself—an unfortunate incident that also brought up the question of how he managed to conceal a pistol while being searched. After depositing the POWs, we loaded stores to return to the pier. The bombing continued almost daily, and life was miserable.

As the advance continued, tens of thousands of Italians threw down their arms at the slightest provocation until the whole foreshore was thick with them. The transport of these prisoners to ships lying off the coast became one of *Maria Giovanni's* principal duties. We carried 750 on each trip and, on one day alone, transported more than 14,800. Return trips to the beach were not wasted; we loaded troops, mail, and stores.

Few of the prisoners seemed to have any heart in the war, and they were sometimes difficult to control. On one occasion, instructions were given for an entire load of 750 prisoners to be embarked in the *Knight of Malta*. For some reason, this ship failed to appear, and *Maria Giovanni* was left with these Italians on board for six hours. Eventually, we received orders to transfer 250 of them to a small Egyptian parquet, *Farouk,* but when we drew alongside there was a blackguardly rush to the guardrail as they all tried to swarm on board the *Farouk*. In vain, I shouted and the Egyptian captain gesticulated, but the situation was beyond control. When we finally cast off and returned to shore where it was possible to make a count, we discovered that more than 580 prisoners had embarked to the *Farouk*. The Egyptian captain was not pleased.

On one occasion en route from Sollum to Alexandria, we collided with the *Chakla,* a small, armed merchant cruiser commanded by Comdr. A. J. McHattie. He later wrote to me and described his version of the collision:

The *Chakla* and the *Maria Giovanni* collided bows on. It was blowing hard at the time and visibility was nil in a very bad khamseen sand storm. My forecastle lookout saw the *Maria Giovanni* about 50 yards dead ahead of *Chakla*, and we got hard-a-starboard on, and the *Maria Giovanni* bounced down our Port side, with no damage to either ship as far as I know. *Chakla* was from Alexandria to Sollum and *Maria Giovanni* from Sollum to Alexandria, and we were not far off the Western Desert Coast to the WNW of Mersa Matruh. I shouted "Happy New Year" to you from my port bridge wing.

I returned the "Happy New Year" to McHattie.

Within a few weeks, the *Maria Giovanni* sailed with a cargo of explosives for the Army, which had captured Tobruk. From then on, our schooner became a familiar figure up and down the coast. She was fitted with Italian Breda 20-mm cannon and machine guns that we had found stashed away in Bardia and promptly purloined. We installed them on our little ship. Together with ammunition, to which we could help ourselves at any one of a dozen points along the coast, we were able to get in much practice without any accounting.

On 31 January, I received a signal from Rear Admiral Rawlings, who was second in command, that asked would I come about at 1230, if convenient, and stay to lunch. Duly, I did so.

On 11 February 1941, the following signal was circulated to the officers of the Inshore Squadron by Commander-in-Chief, Mediterranean:

> The feat of the Army in clearing Egypt and occupying Cyrenaica in a period of eight weeks is an outstanding credit achievement to which the Inshore Squadron and the shore parties along the coast have contributed in no small measure. I am fully alive to the fact that this result has been made possible by an unbreakable determination to allow no obstacle to stand in the way of meeting all requirements. All Officers and men who took part in these operations may well feel proud as I do of their contribution to this victory.

My run now extended from Alexandria to Derna (Darnah), with occasional runs to Tobruk and Mersa Matruh. The bombing never eased up. Once, I employed an old ruse to escape a flock of bombers by running toward shore and seeking cover under the cloak of a *khamseen,* one of the frequent dust storms that plague the North African coast. The bombers knew where we were and dumped their cargo all around us. Fortunately, none hit its mark. I made figure eights and, provided the masts didn't stick up above the dust cloud, we were quite safe.

While the advance continued, the *Maria Giovanni* made a few trips back to Mersa Matruh for stores. The times spent there were regarded as red-letter days. The men got rest they had been forced to do without, and we had relief from the constant bombing.

We arranged to transport a little Fiat to Alexandria on our first trip to Tobruk when things were nice and quiet, with the enemy then in the Benghazi area. I remember one of the able seamen, Sput Peeling, collecting it from outside the town. We manhandled it on board, lashed it down on the after hatch cover for the trip east, and bluffed the Egyptian customs. The Fiat was quite a nice car, and I used it for about three months, then sold it for 40 pounds Egyptian. I also had two motorcycles and gave one to the chief engineer of *Medway*—I forget what happened to the other. One interesting souvenir was a sword with an ivory grip. I gave this to Captain Sam Raw of *Medway*. He had it on display at a naval museum when an American spotted it and asked details. The American did some in-depth research and found that it had originally belonged to a U.S. Marine lieutenant who was killed in Tripoli in 1862.

At the other end of the picture, we evacuated about twenty Italian whores. The Italian army always had a trailer that moved with the unit and supplied sexual comfort for the troops. When they retreated, it was typical of the Italians to leave behind the trailer and girlfriends to be captured. One woman had a pet dog. The dog arrived with the women when they came on board. When we transferred the women to a hospital ship, the dog was abandoned and stayed with us on the *Maria Giovanni*. He was a cute little dog. We named him Dusty because, when he shook, he stirred up enough dust to cause another *khamseen*. He was injured during a bombing raid and had a kink in his middle, which caused him to walk sideways. He was a male, but sat down to piddle, which I attributed to his never seeing a tree in his lifetime.

The army had advanced all the way to Benghazi, which was captured on 7 February 1941. This was very commendable but stretched our supply line quite thin. I had never visited this city before, and the engineer and I decided to take a walk. The big signs—LOOTERS WILL BE SHOT—didn't bother us, although sentries were posted at every street corner. We walked down what would have been a main street, but the city was a ruin. Aside from the sentries and a few dogs, the place was deserted. There were even some kids' toys on the front lawns, and clothes on the lines drying—rather a depressing sight. We turned down a cross street and here was a camera shop, without windows, and nobody around.

The lure of theft, or loot, lies dormant in all of us. My companion wanted to swipe a camera. Despite the numerous warnings, we scanned the area and, while I kept watch, he hopped in and ultimately came out with a fine-looking camera that could fit into his pocket. My one and only desire was to get a typewriter, and this shop had many brands and sizes. Again, we scanned the area and I ventured inside to look for my great treasure. A small, flat Olivetti portable was the obvious answer, and I stuffed it under my uniform, giving me a pregnant look. The return trip to our ship was a nightmare. There were sentries patrolling everywhere, and my fat appearance didn't help a damn bit. We passed one mean-looking sentry and, brother, did he scare the beegeezus out of me when he worked the bolt on his rifle. We managed to get on board, however, and I quickly shed my pregnancy, came back on deck, and started making noises to prepare for sea. The loot lay hidden under a drawer in my cabin, and I was thinking how damn smart I was to outwit the army.

When we cleared the breakwater, I turned over the watch to the lieutenant and went below to examine my prize. I took it out from its hiding place, inserted a sheet of paper, and started the usual sentence, "Now is the time for all good men and true to come to the aid of their country." Was I ever surprised! The type was in Arabic. Thou shalt not steal.

On 24 February, by a strange coincidence, *Maria Giovanni* was off Tobruk when the destroyer to whom she owed her existence under the white ensign met her end. Toward evening, *Dainty*, followed by *Hasty*, steamed out of Tobruk. Sudden flashes, explosions, and gunfire astern indicated an air raid. Darkness was falling, however, and this gave rise to a reasonable hope that the destroyers would be able to get away unobserved. But there was no such luck; the noise of aircraft was heard overhead, followed by the whine of a falling bomb that struck *Dainty* aft and penetrated into the captain's cabin, where it exploded.

The fuel oil in the tank immediately below caught fire, which spread so rapidly that the most strenuous efforts could not bring it under control. Ready-use ammunition on X run deck started to burst, and the after magazine was threatened. The situation was hopeless. The captain ordered every man to the forecastle, while the destroyer continued ahead and left a path of flames from burning fuel pouring into the sea. Then the torpedoes exploded, shaking the ship with a terrific concussion and sending up a great shower of torn metal and other debris to cause more casualties in *Hasty*'s whalers as they rescued men who had been blown into the sea.

For a few moments, *Hasty* swung her stern in under *Dainty*'s starboard bow. Some men jumped to safety but, as there were now several in the water, *Hasty* could not use her screws to keep herself in position. The bow of the stricken vessel rose higher and higher as her stern settled in the water. The remainder of the ship's company lowered themselves into the sea and got away before she made her final plunge. By this time other small craft, including *Maria Giovanni,* were on the scene to help pick up those men who had not been rescued by *Hasty.*

At the end of February, *Maria Giovanni* was ordered to Alexandria, where she was given her first thorough overhaul since her capture. The dockyard refurbished our accommodation, checked out the engine, installed the guns properly, made us seaworthy with extra floats, set up a small dinghy right aft, and enlarged the galley. The ship was docked and the bottom cleaned and painted. We were now ready for blockade running, and I was damn proud of my crew, who proved themselves purebreds on many occasions. This overhaul took a fortnight, at the end of which we sailed for Tobruk and thence to other places along the coast as we landed stores, embarked prisoners, and did a hundred other odd and useful jobs.

During the refit, I was given another, newer type of landing craft, *X-112.* We used this type to land commandos at airfields along the North African coast. On two occasions, the group raided the Italian mainland, at the port of Bari and a railroad tunnel north. In the group was a special type of lighter, built in the States, with a low profile. It had two Packard engines, port and starboard, a low-powered diesel amidships, a ramp on the bow, bunks for about twenty-five men, a toilet and galley, rifle racks, and, on deck, two small-caliber, general-use Breda guns. The only time I had any dealing with this craft was during the raid on Bari.

I was reputed to be an authority on everything. Such was not the case, but once I got that reputation, that was it—I was stuck. I'm not sure how many raids I participated in, but to convey an idea of what was involved, I'll relate the story of one such raid against an airport held by the Italians.

Aerial photographs showed quite a sizable concentration of bombers on a strip of high ground about midway between Benghazi and Derna. The people selected for these raids depended on which force was in command: if the Germans held the position, the raiders would be mainly German Jews; if the Italians held the post, the Senussi Arabs were chosen. The hatred these tribesmen had for the Italians was really something to behold—fanatical, one might say. We loaded on about twenty Senussi Arabs for this job.

Each man carried a very sharp knife, shaped like our Bowie knife, and four small bombs, about the size of a baseball. The base had a time mechanism that could be set for a ten-minute maximum, and a small coil of adhesive tape was atop. The method was to seek out the bomber farthest from the sea, set the timer for the full ten minutes, and place the bomb just where the wings join the fuselage. For a big bomber, a bomb could be placed on each side. Then the men were off to the next bomber and repeated the procedure. Each time, they were closer to the shore. The squad divided into two groups: two men set the bombs; two guarded and relieved after the bomb supply ran out. In the event a sentry appeared and made any kind of aggressive gesture, one of the guards would simply cut his throat—no noise with this method.

The pickup signal was a blue light concealed in a long telescopic frame. The landing craft eased inshore before departure time, and the raiders shone their blue light and came on board. When everyone was accounted for, we backed off and watched the fireworks. The bombs were already exploding before we embarked, and the flames from the gasoline lit up the sky. Strangely enough, not a soul came toward the sea—the Italians were in a panic and shooting each other. Two of the bombers did not get damaged because the bombs either were not placed correctly or were faulty in design. Air reconnaissance revealed eight large planes permanently damaged or on fire, and we brought back one half-caste prisoner who had a wealth of local information. I went to the bar for a drink.

Similar raids were constantly carried out—against bridges, trains, subways, ships at anchor. There was no discrimination.

When the dockyard in Alexandria had finished its job on the *Maria Giovanni*, I was ordered to take over and secure her to a buoy reserved for the fleet. It was late Saturday when we finally secured. Our little ship was filthy. I called the bosun aft and told him it would be necessary to work Sunday and get the ship cleaned up. We would start work at 0600. I assured him that I would give the crew another day off in lieu. Of course, this was no problem; everybody wanted a clean ship. The hoses were going bright and early Sunday and the paint was being prepared. Nobody was excused except the signalman.

I was going through my orders below decks when the signalman reported that he had a message from the flagship: "Refer you to KR & AI, pages 233 and 234, re painting ship on Sabbath."

Well! A cruiser nearby had already tipped me off, but the signal was sent by Admiral R, whom I mistook for Admiral Raw and I had to reply. After much thought and numerous changes, this was sent: "It is our belief that cleanliness is next to Godliness. We all prayed last Sunday."

Back came the reply: "You will report on board." I was unshaven, crummy and by no means ready to see anybody and I stalled for time. More signals signed "R" and to help the situation, he sent his pinnace, a really fancy outfit.

When I got on board, the gunnery officer, whom I knew, seemed as friendly as a black panther. I asked him what was wrong with Admiral Raw. "He is no longer on board. Admiral Rawlings is in command."

Well, that put another notch in the crime. His secretary arrived and announced that the admiral would see me right away. These things rarely happened, and I pictured myself walking the plank.

Rawlings was a fine specimen of a man and, dressed in white with numerous rows of decorations, he looked really large. "Palmer, what do you mean sending me a facetious signal like this?"

He held the offending document before me. By this time, rivulets of perspiration were running down my back and I was wondering why I was born. We stood in silence for a few seconds, then he broke out in a broad smile, reread the message, and asked if I would like a gin. Would I? Whew! He admonished me for not studying acoustics. Sound travels on water; the day was perfectly calm and during church service my loud-mouthed crew had interrupted the pastor, who was a sanctimonious character and had lodged a formal complaint. The admiral appreciated how I felt, however, and said he intended to frame this very special signal. We drank our gin, and I left. The gunnery officer expected me to be hung, drawn, and quartered, and damn near fainted when I blew my gin breath his way.

I remember a return trip from Derna, when we were intercepted by the *Voyager* and sent into Tobruk. Lt. Gen. Erwin Rommel had arrived with his Afrika Korps to turn the tide of war and was rolling everything before him along the coast road. The area stores manager was there on the Tobruk jetty and literally begged me not to land any supplies because of the possibility of having to evacuate. In retrospect, I realize how seriously he must have taken his job.

At Tobruk, we embarked our best-looking cargo. Sixty-four Australian nurses had to be evacuated, and *Maria Giovanni* was the only vessel available. This presented a big problem with her very limited accommodation, but the difficulties were overcome with good humor. The nurses boarded amid much wailing because they were leaving their husbands or boyfriends. Their behavior was excellent, very circumspect. All I did was to ferry them out to a hospital ship anchored offshore. That same ship had scared the beegeezus out of me on one occasion. We always steamed in total darkness and, suddenly, I sighted a ship lit up like a Christmas tree. I got out of her way, chop chop.

My ship became famous—or infamous—and was selected for a special tirade from William Joyce, an Irishman who broadcast from Berlin. A U.S. citizen by birth, his radio name was Lord Haw Haw. This bastard had a marvelous insight on troop movements, ship sailings, and their cargoes. He announced, "We will get you yet, Palmer." I also heard that the Italians had placed a price on my head. Who would dream that I would carry a price tag? Of course, none of this crap changed our modus operandi.

When the swift German advance took place and pushed back our force, depleted by the responsibilities we had assumed in Greece, the Germans bypassed Tobruk but cut the Bardia and Sollum roads. The *Maria Giovanni* was sent along the coast to Derna to pick up a trapped detachment of Indian troops. She was one of the last craft to remain at Derna, while the enemy's artillery hammered at the port. We loaded stores until the wharf itself actually came under the fire of hostile tanks that had appeared over the hill. After embarking the remains of the Indian regiment with its British officers, we headed out to sea, with shells falling round us, and formed the escort for the SS *Hanne,* also loaded with troops. The Indians had made a forced march from Mechili and had little or no rations, especially water. Together, the *Hanne* and *Maria Giovanni* proceeded to Tobruk, but the captain of the *Hanne* was somewhat concerned at having an inadequately armed schooner as his sole protection during this dangerous passage.

The Germans had now regained most of the territory toward the Western Desert, and, under General Rommel, the Afrika Korps was looking in the direction of Suez. The only dark spot clouding his victory was Tobruk—a very unlikely place without any natural cover or deterrent except tank traps, plus a very determined garrison under the leadership of General Leslie Morshead. The normal supply lines had been cut, and the enemy occupied the entire perimeter. The only supply route was by sea, which was mined, bombed, stalked by submarines, and shelled. The so-called harbor entrance was three hundred miles from Alexandria and the passage hazardous, to say the least. If anyone thought the open sea was risky, a survey of the harbor would quickly convince them otherwise. Thirty-one wrecks lay in the harbor, some visible but quite a number below the surface. We entered the harbor only at night. There were no lights, beacons, or navigational aids and little or no facilities for cargo handling. A German battery had been established down the coast. Depending on their mood, the Germans took potshots occasionally. The bombers, of course, were almost a daily occurrence but, despite the opposition, ships ran the blockade to bring food, ammunition and replacements and to take out the wounded.

The *Maria Giovanni* performed all of these services as she ran the blockade between Alexandria and Tobruk. We knew our way around the coast as well as, or better than, anyone else, so our schooner was one of the first ships to form the Tobruk Ferry Service that became so well-known.

We used sail to supplement the auxiliary engine. We took a chance on the shoals and minefields as we ran close inshore—we were often laden with unpleasant cargoes, such as detonators, acid, and gasoline. The trick of get-

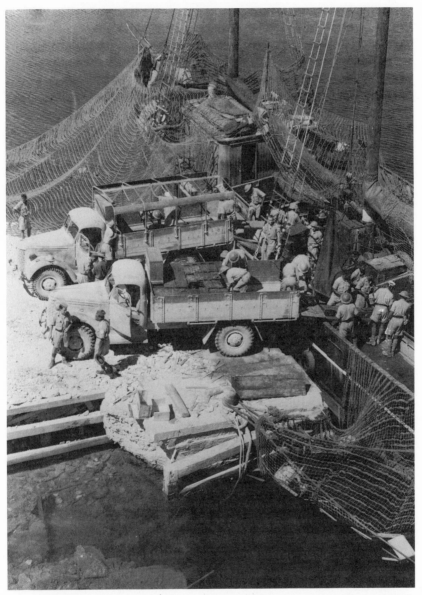

The *Maria Giovanni* tied up underneath a camouflage net at No. 1 jetty, Tobruk harbor. This photo was taken in 1941 from the large crane off the south end of the wharves. Courtesy Australian War Memorial.

ting into Tobruk harbor was to go in between bombing raids, unload as fast as possible, then get out and head for Alexandria lickety-split. It was necessary to outfox the submarines that lay in wait. They expected us to arrive from the east, so I fooled them by going around and approaching from the west. Their torpedoes exploded harmlessly on the foreshore. Then, on leaving, I headed due north. On one occasion, I had the fun of seeing an Italian submarine firing at a German submarine. I kept right on going, not wishing to get mixed up in that brotherly squabble.

On one occasion, a plane approaching *Maria Giovanni* from astern released four bombs. The ship seemed sluggish on the wheel, and two of these bombs looked as though they were going to hit. "Duck!" I yelled to a stoker of the fire party who was standing in rather a conspicuous position. Having mislaid his steel helmet, the stoker merely covered his head with an ordinary tin washbasin.

"That's about as much use as a pocket handkerchief," I laughed when the attack had passed (luckily the bombs had missed us). The stoker's expression was a study.

"Do you really think so, sir?" he said, and then automatically threw the precious basin overboard!

The hazardous voyages of the *Maria Giovanni* were described by John Devine in *The Rats of Tobruk* (Sydney: Angus and Robertson Ltd., 1943). Major Devine, a medical officer with the Australian 9th Division, was stationed in Tobruk during its siege by Rommel's Afrika Korps:

> The merchant ships that arrived at Tobruk in the early days must have contained cargoes of heroes as well as of stores. Many were sunk on the way up, and more were sunk in front of our eyes in the harbour of Tobruk. Yet . . . they set out lightheartedly up to us just the same.
>
> Most famous carrier of supplies to Tobruk was an Australian naval officer serving with the Royal Navy. He was in command of what was probably the only sailing ship in the British Navy. His tiny ship . . . would do about eight knots flat out, and it was said she did a few more knots with all sails set and the wind behind. . . . She took days and days to pass through the bombed and otherwise dangerous waters between the safety of Alexandria Harbour and the insecurity of Tobruk harbour. Again and again she was bombed and machine-gunned, yet she managed, with the aid of a few machine guns[,] to bring down three or four enemy bombers. The Captain made a score and many more trips, and always managed to get through. . . . It was a sight to see this skipper bringing his ship safe into the harbour of Tobruk. Royal Navy she might have been, but on casual inspection no one would have suspected it.

She looked like a paintless Greek cargo steamer, which indeed she was, carrying a crew of pirates. When she came near the wharf there was no mucking about. At the skipper's command. "Over you go!" a man would dive overboard and carry a rope ashore, and she was pulled straight alongside. Of ceremony there was none, yet again and again this little band made the perilous trip. (Pages 59–61)

The Australians made sure that there was no evacuation of Tobruk, but we spent two or three very unpleasant days moving from berth to berth to dodge the almost incessant blitz on the harbor and dock installations. Tobruk harbor was a complete mess, and it was very tricky navigating between the wrecks.

The *Maria Giovanni* next arrived at Tobruk on 27 April 1941 with 195 tons of stores, including 27 tons of amatol, an explosive. Unloading proceeded throughout the night, and the Army personnel worked extremely well at it. Next day, there were several raids on the harbor, one of which concentrated on small ships.

The following afternoon, 29 April, HMS *Chakla* entered the harbor and became the main target for an air raid. The Stukas had a weird gadget that howled as they descended in their dive attacks. This had a disturbing effect—stomach muscles contracted and everyone got scared—but the odd feature was that, once the first bomber had made his run, those being attacked recovered and the second line got a good shellacking. Many bombs were all round and under the *Chakla*. Only two men were injured, but the ship was left resting on the bottom with her upper deck awash. The *Maria Giovanni* had just completed the transfer of troops to the shore. We went alongside and picked up the crew and salvaged armament and any worthwhile stores. Within half an hour of her settling on the bottom, the crew of the *Ladybird,* then still afloat, boarded her and salvaged a heavy machine gun that they later used on *Ladybird.*

The *Chakla* had brought the Aldershot ovens to be used in the field bakery. These were safely unloaded by a team enlisted from the Yellow Express Carriers of Melbourne. By that night, the *Maria Giovanni* had also loaded military stores, consisting of empty shell cases and timber, plus thirty wounded Italian prisoners of war. We sailed for Alexandria at 0230 hours.

An outward telegram received about this time from Naval Commander-in-Chief, Alexandria, read:

The difficulty of working the port of Tobruk and the danger of sending ships to and from Tobruk without adequate fighter protection are fully realized by the Naval Commander-in-Chief and the Air Officer Commanding in Chief. Your squadron and the men in Tobruk are doing magnificent work and I trust that the present bleak period will soon be ended.

He mentioned salvaging big guns off the *Chakla,* and the *Maria Giovanni* was active in this effort. We went alongside, and a 4.7-inch gun was lowered onto the deck. That part was easy, but getting the damn thing off in Alexandria was a pistol or, as Churchill would have said: blood, sweat, and tears.

We continued to carry stores to the besieged garrison at Tobruk. With the establishment of an enemy battery along the coast that was able to command the entrance to the harbor, we could approach the port only after dark. This was not easy. Numerous wrecks, some showing above water but more just submerged, provided navigational hazards. In addition, a slow vessel, when approaching from seaward, might have been set off course a considerable distance by the uncertain current, which made an accurate landfall generally problematical.

Taking advantage of these difficulties, the Germans placed lights, similar to those used to mark Tobruk, further down the coast with the object of luring ships onto shore. The *Tiberio* nearly fell victim to the trick but was warned by the sound of surf, where no surf should have been, and promptly extinguished the light with gunfire. On another occasion, *Maria Giovanni* was led astray by these lights, but, fortunately, we also discovered the mistake in time. Infuriated by this deception, I swung the stern to the offending lights and opened fire on them at almost point-blank range with the 3-pounder. After the fourth round, the Germans replied with 6-inch shells, and matters began to look unhealthy. We escaped damage, however, and quite assured that the offending lights had been demolished we withdrew into the darkness.

The general evacuation from Crete was under way, and I was dispatched to round up as many craft as I could and tow them into port. The craft consisted of rowboats, Greek fishing boats, barges, landing ship tanks, in fact, anything that could float. During one of these rescue missions, a big German Heinkel made an attack with bombs and machine guns. Opening fire, we shot down the plane and brought in five crewmen as evidence. This piece of skulduggery was hailed, and Admiral Sir Andrew Cunningham, Commander-in-Chief, Mediterranean Fleet, gave me permission to fly the pirate flag: black with white skull and crossbones. I was invited on board and piped with full honors. Some of this glory was unusual and not deserved or, at least, so I thought. The admiral also invited me to dinner that evening on board his flagship, with 170 officers in attendance.

In a later letter to me, Bosun John Cundick recalled a similar incident:

There was the occasion when we embarked some 20 or 30 unfriendly Bedouin for Alexandria, much against your better judgment. The escort, as I remember, consisted of four or five Tommies with rifles and we had visions of waking up with our throats cut. That trip was certainly uneventful. We had an argument with two Stukas, shooting one down, or at least sending it with black smoke pouring from it and rapidly losing height in the direction of Sidi Barrani. Able Seaman Morgan was our only casualty but two of the Bedouin were killed and we dropped them over the side.

The climax of that trip was our arrival in Alexandria. The guard boat from HMS *Medway* met us outside the breakwater and tossed in a black flag with instructions from Captain Submarines to fly it coming into the harbor. The flag, as you will remember, carried the Skull and Crossbones and the outline of a Stuka. All hell broke loose after that, you had the crew wash, shave and change from crabby khaki into white shorts and shirts. I was used to steering the ship from the harbor entrance straight down the harbor to number six jetty—but not on this occasion. We sailed round by the coaling wharves past the battleships *Barham, Warspite* and other capital ships with whistles shrilling and bugles sounding—who produced that Bosun's Call? I did not know we had one on board. You enjoyed and deserved every minute of that little schooner's passage through the fleet with Ensign at the Mizzen, Skull and Crossbones at the Main and Pennants at the Fore.

John's letter brought back happy memories of that trip down battleship row with the pirate flag flying. I was all puffed on that day.

A telegram of 1 May 1941 from Naval Commander-in-Chief read:

The only solution appears to be for personnel ships to arrive about 2000, work for four hours and go to sea until the following night. Two nights should be sufficient to disembark and embark personnel, but ships must not carry stores nor kit which cannot be carried by its owner. Supplies should be sent in ships such as *Atid, Maria Giovanni, Tiberio, Nartemelee* (ex *Benghazi*) which should also arrive about 2000. During moonlight periods there will be considerable risk to personnel ships, but far less than during daylight.

On 8 May, the *Maria Giovanni* sailed from Alexandria with 165 tons of stores, consisting of 600 bags of mail, NAAFI stores, special detonators, and other items. We did not arrive in Tobruk until the 12th but were unloaded by 0600 on that day.

While we were in harbor, the *Ladybird* was subjected to a bombing attack. Commander McHattie later described this attack:

We had received warning that 100 plus aircraft were heading for the harbour. *Ladybird* had been unable to use her normal tactics that day, which was to move to different parts of the harbour after each enemy reconnaissance, because she was firmly aground. During the raid most of the aircraft made a dead set at her and left her battered and burning. There was a small harbour tug outboard of the *Maria Giovanni*, and both of us with others from the crew, jumped on board and helped to get the tug under way to pick up survivors.

Ladybird with her light draft had been performing invaluable service. Almost immediately the attack started, her stern received a direct hit, which wrecked her after pom-pom, killing the crew there. A second bomb burst in the boiler room, blowing out the sides of the ship. In spite of her damage and casualties, and the fact that an oil fire was raging from the foremast to the stern, her remaining guns continued to fire even when the vessel had settled on the bottom of the harbour. Not until the fire got so fierce that the magazine (the flooding valves were now inaccessible) threatened to blow up and the guns had been put out of action, was the ship abandoned, but her shooting had destroyed at least one of her attackers.

Maria Giovanni helped to rescue the gallant survivors.

On 27 May 1941, the *Maria Giovanni* sailed from Mersa Matruh, without escort, with 200 tons of ammunition and 240 crates of beer on board. While still northeast of Tobruk, we were attacked by two Heinkels. Probably thinking we were unarmed, both planes came in low and their first salvo of bombs straddled the ship. One plane returned for her next attack and was met by three pans of our 13.2 Breda ammunition. She lost height and crashed into the sea about 6 miles to the north. The second plane attacked four more times but, by quick maneuvering of the ship, we turned "probable hits" into "near misses." This plane dropped sixteen bombs, but most were above water. Two of the crew were wounded and the ship's side received holes in many places.

At 2030 on the 30th, we sailed for Mersa Matruh and Alexandria, with one hundred prisoners of war, ninety-nine Libyans and one German on board. We were escorted by *KOS 19* and accompanied by a tank landing craft, lighter *A2*. On reaching Mersa Matruh, the *Maria Giovanni* was making water faster than the pumps could handle. I stripped down the mainsail, made grommets, and passed them underneath the leaks. I put the crew and anyone else in sight to work, and we bailed out and kept the little ship afloat.

The *Maria Giovanni*, a veteran of many battles, docked at Mersa Matruh. The missing mast had been shot away. The schooner had fourteen guns. Her best gunner among the crew of twelve was the cook.

But there were other occasions when we were not so successful. Once, we received a severe hammering without doing any apparent damage ourselves. During a determined attack by two Heinkels, *Maria Giovanni* sustained seventy-nine holes from near bomb misses and cannon fire; twenty-six of these were below the water line. Three men were killed and five others wounded—a big proportion of our total ship's company of twelve. With 6 feet of water in the hold and another 8 feet in the engine room, we struggled to Mersa Matruh and then to Alexandria, where five plates were needed to replace those damaged.

Some of these attacks were not without their humor. The cockney cook manned the Italian Izzoti gun and, during one attack, he ran out of ammunition. Infuriated at being unable to reply to the enemy's fire, he took off his steel helmet and flung it at the Heinkel as it passed, spitting out machine gun bullets! This cook was very fond of dressing up in gay Italian uniforms whenever he got ashore along the coast. One day, to his great indignation, he was captured by some Australians. When asked at the point of a bayonet if he could speak English, his feelings were positively outraged. "Wot—me!— a bleedin' cockney," he screamed. Incidentally, the cook figured our runs were too risky and asked for a transfer to submarines. I granted the change with reluctance. My cook shipped over to a submarine that was lost on the first patrol—such a nice guy.

When the *Maria Giovanni* reached Alexandria, she went into dry dock for repairs, and the monotony of the ferry run was broken. It was very necessary to have the bomb damage repaired. While the ship was laid up, the Navy had me leading commando raids that were confined to airfields along the North African coast. On two occasions, the group raided mainland Italy. Back to the *X-112*!

After Crete fell, the scale of air attacks on ships making the run to Tobruk intensified. On 7 June, Admiral Cunningham, after consulting with the other commanders-in-chief, found it necessary to order a temporary suspension of all shipping except destroyers, which ran in supplies, off-loaded quickly, and made the return run the same night. The destroyers continued a nightly service until 15 June; it was suspended while Operation Battleaxe was fought out, and resumed on 18 June. At that time, the Inshore Squadron had four destroyers, three sloops, two gunboats, and a number of other small vessels, such as whalers, trawlers, minesweepers, auxiliary schooners, and A-lighters. For some time thereafter, the destroyers worked in pairs, two coming in on two nights out of every three.

One day in early summer at Alexandria, the commander-in-chief decided to pay *Maria Giovanni* a visit. The barge drew alongside the arsenal quay, where the schooner was lying at one of the wharves. A stoker in a dirty pair of shorts, with his cap on the back of his head, was the only man on deck.

"Is the captain on board?" Admiral Cunningham asked him.

The stoker scratched his head, not knowing who was addressing him, and said, "Yus, sir, I thinks so. Comin' aboard?"

The admiral climbed over the side.

"D'yer want me to fetch the Old Man?" inquired the stoker.

"No, not yet. I want to talk to you."

For a few minutes, the commander-in-chief chatted with members of the crew and then told the stoker to fetch his captain. On poking his head into my cabin, the stoker announced:

"There's an important sort of looking bloke on deck. From the way 'e's togged up, I think it's an admiral! You'd better come and have a look!"

Docking and refit of the *Maria Giovanni* were completed and on 13 July she was loaded with stores for Tobruk. She was to have sailed on 12 July but, before we could leave, we received orders to cancel the sailing. I was told to unload because the ship was to be converted into a petrol carrier and alterations would take five weeks to accomplish.

By 22 July, however, we were on our way to Tobruk. My moans at being turned into a petrol carrier had borne fruit. We were sent up with our customary cargo of ammunition (76 tons) and stores (80 tons).

The *Maria Giovanni* finally arrived at Tobruk just past midnight on 27 July. We had been machine-gunned by an Italian reconnaissance aircraft on the 26th as we held off to the northwest of Tobruk during daylight. An Italian Macchi suddenly appeared and cautiously approached in gradually decreasing circles. We held our fire until the enemy had plucked up sufficient courage to attack and then we let go with a hail of bullets from our four guns. The Macchi crashed, and we sustained no damage. Later in the day, we encountered another aircraft north of the normal shipping route, but it took no offensive action. *Tiberio* was also attacked, and she shot down one of the attackers.

The *Maria Giovanni* sailed for Alexandria at 2100 hours on the 27th after loading 32 tons of empty ammunition cases, 2 tons of ordnance, 6 tons of MFO, and also a number of Libyans who required evacuation. The senior naval officer did not like evacuating them in destroyers: "They are all lousy and it adds infection to affliction."

Three of my crew were awarded the Distinguished Service Medal as a result of attacks by enemy aircraft.

Announcement that I had received the Distinguished Service Cross appeared in the *London Gazette* of 29 July 1941 with the "usual" citation: "for courage, skill and devotion to duty in operations off the Libyan coast." I soon received congratulations from Capt. Sam Raw and many of my associates in the Inshore Squadron.

After an uneventful trip to Tobruk in early August, the *Maria Giovanni* left Mersa Matruh at 1500 on 15 August in heavy weather. We were carrying 211 tons of food, ammunition and ordnance, canteen supplies, and mail. By 1900, the vessel was rolling heavily. The main fuel tank sheered its moorings, and banged the ship's side badly, nearly going through it. All hands were employed in securing the tank and moving the ship's cargo. At midnight, the angry sea sent several good waves into the engine room, and all the cabins were flooded. Dawn brought little relief. The ship continued rolling, but the sky was clear. All hands were on the alert for an air attack. We sighted a Blenheim, a Royal Air Force plane, just before noon and we waved to each other. By midnight, my message went out: "All's well, heading toward the minefields and Tobruk."

A few hours before dawn, we reached the entrance to the swept channel at Tobruk. A pilot met us to guide the ship clear of the latest danger areas resulting from enemy mines. By 0600, we had secured alongside and were unloading. Air raids started at 0700 and kept up all day and hampered the discharging. There were nineteen raids that day, the smallest being two planes and the largest eighteen Stukas, supported by ten fighters, that made a dead set at the *Maria Giovanni*. One lighter was sunk alongside, the pier badly damaged, and several men killed. Although we escaped sinking, our port shrouds had been severed and carried away, and the ship's side was holed in several places, as were the deckhouses. The blast from a 1,000-pound bomb had carried away the after part of the wheelhouse, which contained the lavatory and the wireless rooms. At 2100, we sailed for Alexandria. The sea rose, and our course was altered to avoid the threat of a gale abaft the ship's quarter. Next day, the wind dropped and we had our first hot meal since leaving Mersa Matruh—very acceptable to all hands. That afternoon, we engaged an Italian Savoia 79. After a ten-minute action, during which a window in the schooner got broken, the Savoia realized it had caught a tartar and sheered off. I remembered putting a note in my log: "Consider we handed out more than we received. Pluto, our dog, sprained his ankle getting out of the way."

On 24 August and again on 2 September, we made trips to Tobruk to carry supplies needed during Operation Treacle. The Australian infantry division was being withdrawn and replaced with the Polish Independent Brigade. Our cargo on the second trip included twelve sheep for Indian troops at Tobruk, needed in their religious beliefs.

Operation Supercharge, which was the reinforcement of the Tobruk garrison by part of the 6th British Division from Syria and withdrawal of an Australian infantry brigade, took place in September. Stores, bulk petrol, and a number of tanks were to be landed. During the operation, the schooner supply service was to be maintained but, owing to various defects in the ships, this broke down completely. None of the five schooners succeeded in reaching Tobruk.

On 20 September, the *Maria Giovanni* and two other schooners were on their way to Tobruk. We were carrying 50 tons of ammunition, 115 tons of stores, as well as 2 tons of mail and twenty-four live sheep. The *Khaid el Dine* and *Hilmi* did not arrive as scheduled. They had met with a series of misfortunes and were back in Mersa Matruh. We also had to return to Mersa Matruh because of constant engine trouble that resulted from overheating and fuel of poor quality. Although we intended to sail again for Tobruk on 25 September, by the 28th we were returning to Alexandria, unable to make even 4 knots.

The Last Voyage of HMS *Maria Giovanni*	
Length	175 feet
Beam	35 feet
Tonnage	340
Speed	7 knots
Armament:	
Forward	20-mm Breda
Amidship	20-mm Isotta
Amidship	2 Lewis guns, shielded
	3 Strip Lewis guns
Aft	3 Pounder, 36 rounds
Captain	A. B. Palmer
Crew:	
1st Lieutenant	J. Lucas
E.R.A.	Murphy
Coxswain	H. Cundick
Stoker 1st Class	Schofield
Stoker 1st Class	F. W. McGowan
Signalman	G. M. Bartlett
Able Bodied Seamen	D. Lyn Ley, D. Shakespeare,
	A. C. Capp, F. Morris
Cooks	T. E. Wilkinson,
	R. A. F. Goodhand
Left Alexandria:	November 15, 1941
Left Mersa Matruh:	November 21, 1941
Sunk at Tobruk:	November 23, 1941

I was convinced that all the schooners were having engine trouble as a result of sabotage. Investigation revealed water in the oil and sand in the bearings. Perhaps Lord Haw Haw's prediction was coming true.

During the month of September, activities of the Inshore Squadron were almost at a standstill. In October, the Tobruk Supply Service was suspended during the full moon.

When the second battle of the Libyan Desert began in November 1941, the *Maria Giovanni* was on the job and carrying stores to Tobruk. We left Alexandria on 15 November and Mersa Matruh on 21 November, and went ashore west of Tobruk on 23 November. I knew the headlands and harbor entrance well but, on this occasion, I made a wide detour to avoid a surfaced

U-boat lying in wait for our arrival. I overshot the bearing and mistook a faint signal to be the correct entrance to Tobruk—a tragic error. To compound the mistake, the engine refused to restart. The little ship grounded on the reef and was quickly captured by the Italian army—an ignominious finish for a gallant ship.

We threw the guns overboard, along with our codebooks, but our effort to get the dinghy away with two men failed because of a heavy sea. We had been informed that most of our stores below decks were in preparation for an advance. Rather than destroy the ship and her cargo, I thought it prudent to leave her intact in the hope that the advancing army would find the supplies. We left the ship and surrendered to the Italian general. I learned later that most of the cargo was salvaged in good condition, but I never forgave myself for the manner in which the career of this gallant ship and her crew ended.

9

PRISONER OF WAR

The sudden break from being captain of a ship, with all the amenities, to being a prisoner of the Italians was a dramatic change, but none of my crew had been injured. We were all herded into a "cage," as it was called—about half an acre of barbed wire, no shelter, no toilet, no water, no facilities of any kind. To compound the situation, it was raining, the ground was clay and slippery, and we spent a very miserable night.

Next morning the rain stopped, but then came the interrogation. An assembly of Italian officers, in immaculate hand-tailored uniforms, appeared and asked very pertinent questions. I was separated from the rest and taken to a dugout in a nearby camp, where searching questions were asked about commando raids and my use of flags other than my lawful ensign—Italian, Albanian, German, and Greek—why, why, why? The subject of cruelty to Italian prisoners was highlighted, something I had never seen or condoned. The final decision was to execute me for deceptive practices, cruelty to prisoners, using Italian guns and ammunition, and no doubt causing them much trouble and frustration. I was taken out to an old ruin where, looking at the wall, I could see numerous pockmarks of rifle bullets. I knew about ten Italian soldiers were immediately behind me and three officers yacking away to the side.

135

When one approaches death, God is very close and very real. I expected at any moment to hear the order to fire but no, an officer came across, thanked me, and I was escorted back to the holding pen. When I turned up all in one piece, the crew gave me quite a welcome. Lacking an explanation for the change in plans, I thought of my past association with the son-in-law of Mussolini, Count Galeazzo Ciano, who had been one of my early morning riding companions in Shanghai. The count had invited me to come see him if ever I was in Italy—little did I know! The holding pen was small and obviously had been hurriedly erected for our exclusive accommodation, but more prisoners appeared, most of them South African soldiers. All of us had been captured just a few miles from the front lines.

Several of our chaps tried to beg food, but frontline troops have no surplus—they carry all they can but there are no giveaways. Water was our biggest need, but that was also in short supply. My guess is that we remained in that area three days before being put on trucks and taken along the dusty Derna road to Benghazi. We had a distinguished visitor before departing: General Rommel, riding in a weapon carrier. He was standing up there, with his salute. The German troops idolized him and, as it turned out, he was pretty damned good, too! The troops taking pictures of us were told to save film—"We will have the whole army before long."

Benghazi had supplies, and each man was given about one cup of water and a hard roll before boarding a destroyer, where we were crammed into the forecastle and the steel door locked. This was not a very pleasant thought. To add to our troubles, most of the soldiers became seasick—one hell of a mess when you consider we had about two hundred soldiers confined in a small forecastle while the destroyer headed through a storm for Tripoli. The guard finally opened the steel door to allow ten men at a time out on deck—at least that was the idea, but everybody went out at once! I tried to organize a group to take over the ship but was handicapped by the seasickness and a fifth-column captain in the South African army named MacQuarie, who ruined a perfect escape.

Tripoli had a regular camp, with very little food but with bunks, fresh water, and a few British POWs who had been picked up from raids or plane crashes. This was a welcome break, with much talk about conditions and how the war was going. One of the chaps belonged to what was known as the Long Range Desert Group, a fantastic bunch of fellows. He explained that four men, with supplies on board a medium truck, would start out from the Pyramids and travel across the Sahara, what they called the Sand Sea. There were no roads; direction was maintained by sextant and compass. The objective was to spy on troop movements along the coast road and report by radio on a special frequency. He told of several odd features about this area. When they stopped for chow, a swarm of flies would immediately arrive—not a sign of anything, no habitation or animal, for hundreds of miles. They found an Arab wandering in the desert and searched him. He had seven dates in his pockets—no oasis within hundreds of miles, and this skinny guy was alone, wandering the desert.

When the truck crew figured they were far enough west, they would turn north to observe the coast road, make their report, and head back toward the Sand Sea. Most of their travel was at the crack of dawn or by moonlit night because their trail and dust could be easily spotted by planes patrolling the back country. He told me of one chap who had gone closer to the road than usual to examine some heavy artillery. He spotted a group of Germans approaching and hid in the wreckage of a truck, but the Germans belonged to a salvage gang. In examining the truck remains, they turned it over and there was another prisoner to join the fold. Oddly enough, the chap had a brother also in the Long Range Desert Group, and he too was captured. They met for the first time in Italy.

The stay in Tripoli was far too short. We were loaded onto cargo planes and flown with fighter escorts to Sicily, where we landed at Castelvetrano, one of the few spots on this mountainous island where a plane could land. The housing for this occasion was a disused church, with boarded-up windows and a cathedral-type door. We had not eaten anything worthwhile for ten days. The commandant of the area was a fine gentleman with the rank of colonel, who made an eloquent speech of welcome that lasted ten minutes. When he finished, his interpreter, a roughneck who had lived in Brooklyn, condensed this flowery speech into a few words. He said that we would be fed soon and that the colonel didn't want any trouble and hoped the war would be over soon.

I was the senior officer and wanted some semblance of order for the meal. I tried to line up the troops in the aisle, with instructions for each man to take his turn, but it was not to be. When the smell of food came wafting in from the field kitchen, they broke ranks and charged. The church door that was designed to open inward was pushed outward, and the hungry prisoners rushed the field kitchen. There was complete chaos. The Italian cooks vanished, while prisoners swarmed over the boiling hot pans and fought each other. Among the prepared food was a thick concoction of macaroni and cheese, but it was almost boiling and many suffered mouth burns in their anxiety to swallow it. I was hollering bloody murder as I watched trained men behave like animals—a disgraceful spectacle. By the time the Italians returned the food had cooled and an orderly process began. The poor colonel felt bad about the turn of events and stated that he would be happy to see us go.

Several days later, we entrained for a trip across Sicily via Palermo to Messina. Sicily seemed to be all mountains, and the engineering required to build a railroad must have been fantastic. The train seemed to be hanging over the sea or going through tunnels much of the time. After the desert, it looked good, with clean little houses, some flowers, a few sheep or goats, and people going about their chores. Palermo was quite a seaport, and many naval vessels were in evidence.

As we approached Messina, we could clearly see Mt. Etna smoldering away. A change of guard occurred before we boarded a large ferry prior to crossing the straits to Reggio di Calabria on the Italian mainland. The cara-binieri dominated the military forces. Their uniform was all-black—pants, tunic, cap, shirt, and tie. The cap badge was a golden eagle and that, with the exception of campaign ribbons, was the only break in the uniform's color scheme. They were all-powerful; a junior officer could, and did, order a mil-itary person much senior in rank or age like a private. Some of these Fascists were overbearing and swaggering around with an "I'm the king of the walk" sort of attitude.

The northbound train followed the coastline. Despite the war, the electric trains were well operated and ran smoothly. We skirted Naples to Caserta and changed there for Capua, which, according to legend, was the campsite of Hannibal. Capua might have looked good to Hannibal, but it looked awful to me. Here again were miles of barbed wire, with one or two permanent buildings and rows of tents housing many thousands of prisoners. Drainage was poor, and the tents contained no straw, bed sheet, or a damned thing. The mess hall had electric lights, a jerry-built system with wire strung from nail to nail. When the lights failed during a meal, I was told they would be fixed *dumoni* (tomorrow)—this became the usual story all across Italy. We never did get the lights fixed and ate in the dark. The food was chiefly maca-roni, supplemented with several slices of bread.

I wanted to get away from Capua in the worst way. We became lousy with small white lice that irritated the hell out of everybody. I decided to report sick with middle ear trouble, which couldn't be traced very well. Because Capua had no medical facilities, patients were sent to nearby Caserta, which had a military/civilian hospital that was at one time part of the palace belong-ing to the Duke of Naples. I was escorted, along with others, to the hospital where a cursory examination was made by Roman Catholic nuns serving as the nursing staff. They wore huge headgear that shot out from the head about 2 feet—white and starched stiff, and the wearer could only see straight ahead. We quickly dubbed the nuns allotted to our wing with special names: Flossie Few Clothes, Lizzie Doolittle, and Sarah Seldom Slack.

I was placed in a ward with four other chaps, and a very interesting and comparatively happy period began. The Duke of Naples had arranged for a creek to be diverted and made into a waterfall, which cascaded over a series of steps, and nearby were some lovely gardens. We could see this display from our windows. The design of the hospital was different from anything I had ever seen. The rooms and corridors were all one, with partitions between the rooms but no doors. The Allies were bombing Naples heavily and on a few occasions the concussion of heavy bombs would shatter glass windows, causing the Mother Superior to run down the corridor, screaming, "Churchill will pay for this."

At the end of the corridor were toilet facilities in typical Italian style, which we called "wog squats." They were useful in most cases, but wounded and leg patients couldn't make it without somebody helping. A young Italian officer offered to get things for us on his trips to Naples, and our first request was for a toilet seat to fit an old unused regular toilet off in a corner. He obligingly brought one back, and we kept it in our room, hung on a nail. It was a sight to see a chap on crutches with a toilet seat around his neck as he headed for the bathroom. Shades of the old Roman Empire, where heroes were rewarded with laurel wreaths! Once we asked, in a joking way, for a *Baedecker Guide for Northern Italy* and, sure enough, the officer brought one back for us. Immediately, everyone began making tracings.

One day, I was ordered to get dressed and was ushered downstairs into an ancient cab drawn by a horse, with a priest as my guardian. We jogged along until we reached a brand-new hospital in Naples. This elegant building was one of the showplaces Mussolini had built for domestic consumption. I was taken upstairs and seated in an elaborate chair with many gadgets attached. A specialist arrived—a short scruffy person, unshaven, smoking a cigar, and his white coat had seen better days. Using a pair of scissors from the instrument tray, he cut off the end of his cigar and put the butt in his pocket. Then, without washing his hands, he began to examine my eyes. He must have gone through this testing six or seven times. At last, all was over and the headgear taken off. He looked angrily at me and, through an interpreter, accused me of being an imposter and many other things, that there was no shrapnel in my eye as I had claimed. I explained I was not the one with shrapnel, but the chap in the next bed! I was hurriedly returned to the prison section, but the poor guy with the shrapnel never did get treated.

While at Caserta, we were allowed to have dental examinations. The dentist was in Santa Maria, another small town nearby. A busload of about twenty left Caserta and, in about an hour, entered the fascinating old-world city of Santa Maria. Like numerous other old Italian towns, it had a claim to fame—it was the birthplace of a world-famous clown.

The dentist's office was in a secluded courtyard. Two rather large Italian soldiers were on duty or possibly acting as helpers. The first patient entered the surgery, and soon we heard groans. Within seconds, he reappeared— white as a sheet and spitting blood. This was sufficient for the rest of us to forget any tooth trouble, and we headed out the door. The poor guy explained to us later that the moment he got into the surgery, these two soldiers pinned him in the chair. The dentist made a quick examination and, without a "by your leave" or "may I?" pulled out a tooth—no novocaine or even running water. The guy had to fight his way out of the chair before several more teeth could be yanked out. It was good to be back in Caserta among friends.

I continued getting treatment for middle ear trouble, but somebody decided the treatment was getting involved. I was told to get packing and was brought back to Capua, about the last place to which I ever wished to return. The men were being treated for lice, but they were still evident and nobody seemed to be doing much about eradication.

The time came when everybody knew I was being transferred, but nobody knew for what reason or where. Final orders came early one morning; I was going to Sulmona. This camp was about a hundred miles directly east of Rome, high in the mountains.

I boarded a train heading north. Following the coastline, it entered the much publicized Pontine Marshes, which Mussolini had drained and cultivated, something that many previous generations had failed to accomplish. The train was a regular passenger type, a change from the cattle truck, and my three guards seemed composed and not trigger-happy. The air raids had been stepped up. Both Naples and Rome were catching plenty. In fact, we were stranded in the Pontine Marshes, while the rails were being blown up to the north and south. After languishing there five days, a decision was reached to head southeast for Foggia, an important railhead situated in the middle of a fertile land known as the breadbasket of Italy. The stationmaster of Foggia evidently was very proud of his command. There were numerous flowerpots, with everything spick-and-span, attendants in uniform, and the whole place giving off an air of efficiency. We did not stop there long but swung northward and followed the Adriatic Coast to Pescara, where I was separated from the rest of the chaps and entrained for Sulmona. We approached from the east instead of the west, as originally planned.

Within easy sight of Sulmona was Grand Sasso Mountain, called the Big Rock, the greatest in the chain of mountains that runs north and south in

Italy. It was wild country up there, snowcapped the year round. Even the dogs had big thick leather collars so the wolves wouldn't eat them.

Sulmona Camp No. 66, dating back to World War I, had been built by Austrian prisoners of war. It was built on the side of a mountain, maybe 7,000 or 8,000 feet up, and was terraced. The top section, known as Majori Block, contained five large huts and a mess hall and was reserved for senior officers. Then there was a high wall, with a no-man's land 10 or 15 feet wide between it and another high wall. On top of each wall was glass embedded in cement. The next section was occupied by noncommissioned officers. Their quarters were quite large and contained ten buildings, each accommodating about fifty people. Then another high wall, plus no-man's land, separated that section from the troops, who were divided into several ethnic groups, each one having a high wall with glass-encrusted topping. Finally, there were the camp's offices, guardhouses, stores, and barracks.

The surroundings of this walled camp were bleak. Two roads encircled the whole area, one for sentry walk and the other for trucking. Barbed wire was everywhere and attached to the strands were small bells, empty cans, bits of metal plates, and any device that could rattle. On the outer road, sentry boxes were spaced about 100 feet apart. Each one was fitted with three lights with separate switches, one left, one right, and one ahead. These boxes were manned twenty-four hours a day and, at each corner, there was a sentry tower. The guards were alert to the ever-present threat of escape, especially by way of a tunnel.

So this was Sulmona, with about twelve or thirteen thousand prisoners. Unknown to me when I first got there, the Australians, who dominated the camp, had started digging a tunnel. It was a masterpiece!

The pressing problem of food remained. The Red Cross—Canadian, British, American, and Swedish—were well aware of our dependency on their food supplements. In fact, their parcels kept us alive. The normal issue by the Italian government was a pitiful effort and equivalent to that for a nonworking civilian. In a Fascist country, this was damn small.

Quite a few incidents happened while we were in Sulmona, none of them very spectacular, but they relieved the tedium of our situation. The commandant decided that it would be safer if all prisoners wore bright red patches on their khaki uniforms. He ordered bolts of red material and had several soldiers, who previously had been tailors, do the work. Each chap lined up in the sewing hall and took off his tunic, and one tailor stitched a red patch on the back. He then moved to the next machine, where a patch was sewn on the front thigh section of his pants. We had a little theatrical group that decided this cloth was ideal for use in its shows. So, as a prisoner emerged, complete with bright patches front and rear, sharp knives quickly trimmed them off and the material was socked away for future use. In some cases, soldiers went through two or three times. This kept on for about a week. By then, the commandant figured everybody should be wearing bright red identity patches. He called for an inspection parade—what a mess. The chaps still wearing patches had painted the Union Jack, Stars and Stripes, the Hammer and Sickle, and even the Chinese flag on them. The commandant took a quick look, dismissed the parade, and canceled the idea.

One day when a group had been out for exercise and was returning to the camp section, a chap spotted a chicken pecking away next to the roadway. He watched his chance, stepped out, wrung the chicken's neck, and stowed it under his coat. It lay quietly until the chap was passing the sentry and then gave a final flutter. The chap was promptly put in the small pokey and informed the chicken he had killed belonged to the commandant. Why did he kill the bird? "It attacked me!" was his defense.

The tunnel being constructed was actually an engineering marvel. It began in a building removed from the wall, which seemed the obvious place to begin. The floor was black and white tile. Each tile was 18 inches square; four of them were cemented to a piece of wood for use as the cover for the tunnel opening—easily operated by one man. Next, the diggers went down approximately 10 feet, then lined up with a tree outside the barbed wire and next to a pathway used by the villagers who went up the mountain every morning to collect firewood. The engineers estimated that the dirt excavated could be spread evenly over the ceiling in a layer 3 inches deep. The tunnel was ventilated by suitcases used as a concertina to blow down fresh air and bring out stale air. The platform that held fire extinguishers had three iron struts. The engineers decided that two were ample to support the weight, and the third strut was removed to make an excellent pick. They made a small railway from the wooden frames of canvas deck chairs that were sold by the camp authorities. The wood slats were clamped end to end and slicked up with margarine. An inverted stool with its sides built up made a truck for hauling dirt from the work face back to the tunnel opening, where it was hauled up and passed to chaps in the room and ultimately spread over the ceiling.

John Fitzharding had designed the tunnel, and Col. "Spike" Marlin was in charge of the whole project. Marlin decided which men were to go, based on their ability to withstand the rigors of living off the country, their knowledge of Italian, and their worth as a soldier. I had brought the *Baedecker Guide* from Caserta, and it was worn thin.

Finally, the tunnel was completed. Everybody participating had their compressed food, chocolate bars, cigarettes, maps, and whatever else they could carry. The chap digging at the very end of the tunnel surfaced about

0300, and Spike called a halt to operations. The opening was boarded up and the tense waiting for the following night began. It rained heavily early that morning, but the villagers began making their pilgrimage up the mountain for wood. One of these old buggers had a diminutive donkey that led the way, and that damned donkey fell into the hole we had made.

The guy who owned the animal started hollering. Sentries came running, then the commandant and his staff. The jig was up. They swarmed into the camp looking for the opening, but couldn't find it, so a soldier was sent down to ferret the other end. When he pushed up the four tiles in the middle of the room, the old commandant threatened reprisals. He decided against any punishment, however, when someone explained that the tunnel had taken many months to make and the officials in Rome would want to know where the security had been.

It was at Camp Sulmona that I first met Eddy Ward, a well-known radio broadcaster from London BBC. Eddy had kept listeners informed about the war, especially the bombing of Benghazi. He was drinking at a bar in Cairo when a bomber pilot convinced him to take a ride and get first-hand experience. Eddy agreed and, so help me, the first bomber ever to be shot down was the one Eddy was on. While walking with him one day, I happened to mention knowing Count Ciano. Eddy's response was, "Let's write and ask him for a passport."

Well, that wasn't a bright idea, but kicking the thought around, we decided to ask for some books. There were none at all in the camp. A well-worded letter to Count Ciano was drafted and sent off. I immediately noticed special treatment, and sentries would point me out. I was relieved of attending parades, and some Italian officers even saluted me.

The urge to have a strong drink was prevalent. Potato peelings were saved, lighter fluid and raisins were thrown in, if available, and this concoction was allowed to ferment. The result was so potent that it caused several deaths, and the recipe was abandoned.

The next thing I knew, the Italians wanted to transfer me to Padula, where they said conditions were much nicer. My tenure at Sulmona had been about nine months, but now I packed a bag and marched to the railroad station between two sentries. Of course, I had no idea where Padula was located. The train checker handed tickets to my guards, and off we went due north. After thirty hours we arrived in Padua, away up near the border of Austria, only to be informed that the clerk had made a mistake—Padula was some hundreds of miles due south.

Meanwhile, an alarm had gone out that I had vanished with two sentries. When we reached Padula, the officials seemed thrilled to see us and no doubt relieved. The penalty for losing a prisoner was a transfer to the Russian front, which was akin to a death sentence. The short march to Padula was refreshing after being cooped up in that lousy train for four days. I found some of the prisoners there were well-known to me. It seemed we would get to know a group, then move and, weeks or months later, arrive at another camp and there would be the same group.

Padula had been built and used as a Trappist monastery, an order believing in perpetual silence. The monastery had been empty for a long time and was now being used mainly for navy prisoners. It was a marvelous structure nestled in a fertile valley with many acres of fallow ground. Its construction was fascinating—beautiful stonework, a cantilevered stairway, and carved statuary. The fountain basin in the center was cut from a single solid stone and measured 11 feet across. The floor of one chapel had once been inlaid with silver, but Napoleon's soldiers had torn it up, leaving only the earth floor.

The monastery had two stories, two churches, and covered walkways. The lower floor was divided into separate apartments, each consisting of a large living room, a study, and a bedroom, plus about a quarter of an acre of ground, and occupied by ten senior officers. Junior officers were on the upper floor, a drafty place without barriers or dividers. It had been used by the priests for exercise, and once around was equivalent to a quarter mile. Our parades were held there twice a day. Red Cross parcels were delivered to us on a regular basis, with extra food and small luxuries available through the black market.

There was an interesting mixture of people here—a couple of generals, a brigadier, all sorts of scientists, doctors, and even a character who spoke ten languages. One day, it was decided that we had some sick people among us, and a hospital train was sent to take us to Naples. We marched to the station, and here was a beautiful, luxurious train, one of Mussolini's showpieces. A group of society ladies came on board to distribute small presents—candy, fruit, and a few trinkets—and they rode the rails with us. To them, it was a great gesture. We thought it a nice idea, too. Several stops later, the ladies excitedly came through the train and grabbed everything they had given us. I'd already eaten my candy, and all I could give them was the wrapper. One poor guy had been given an apple and had taken one bite out of it. They took that, too!

We were told to get off the train fast. After we had waited a few hours, another train came through loaded with prisoners, most of them from the camp we had just left. We didn't know what was going on, but perhaps the tide of war had started to change and they felt we were too dangerous to have around in southern Italy. So off we went northward on an ordinary train, with guards swarming all over the place. Somebody managed to escape right in the middle of the Pontine Marshes. The train pulled off to a siding while the guards searched for him. A troop train of Italian soldiers came by, jeering and insulting us, and then passed on. The guards eventually gave up, without finding the escapee, and our train went on into the marshaling yards of Rome, where we learned that the troop train had been hit during a bombing raid and many hundreds killed. The delay created by the guy who escaped had been a Godsend for us.

The railroad was all cracked up and we couldn't go north, so we stayed there for a couple of days. Of course, food ran short, and the commandant decided we'd go the southern route. They turned the train around with the locomotive pushing, and we started for Foggia. On the Adriatic Coast, we came to Bari, which had been bombed but sustained comparatively little damage. I remembered Foggia as an immaculate place, but it was now a shambles. The fancy station was a ruin, with miles and miles of wrecked cars. One engine was standing on its end and an engineer hanging dead out of the cab window. We literally crept through the marshaling yard—stop and back up, go slow, stop and back up again. We were in the middle of this mess when the air raid siren started howling. Wherever we looked, people were scattering and running. I'll say this for our guards, they never quit and stuck to their duty, which was most unusual. We couldn't get out, anyway; the cars were all locked, and it would have been very dangerous to be loose in that mob of civilians, who were quite hostile.

We continued on, following the Adriatic coastline northward, until we reached Pescara, which was not far from Camp Sulmona. The civilians at Ancona were edgy and gave the impression of being ready to run at any second. After leaving Rimini, we headed northwest to Bologna, where a transfer was made; one group, mostly wounded and ex-Caserta folk, went on to Parma. There was nothing wrong with me, only sick and tired of train travel and eating from cans, constipated, and travel weary. Once a prisoner had been listed as wounded, however, he stayed in that category. Despite my protests, I was herded into the train bound for Parma with the wounded chaps.

Parma was not classified as a camp; for want of a better term, it could be called a hospital. We all had real beds and were limited to six people in a room. The building was laid out in a square, with three floors and huge entrance gates that fitted closely into an arched doorway and were secured by six old-fashioned locks, plus an armed sentry who patrolled the inside square. The staff consisted of two doctors and six nuns who substituted as nurses.

Supplies were short—sometimes only a box of aspirin or an old bandage seemed to be standard equipment. I prevailed on the commandant to let some of the badly wounded get out in the square so the sunshine could help cure them. I noticed that a young South African, whose wounds were septic, had no medication whatsoever. I got this chap and others out in the sunshine, washed their wounds, removed any pus, and let Ole Sol do the rest. To everybody's surprise, it worked. My South African recovered, and we corresponded for several years after the war.

It was here that a packing case from Count Ciano caught up with me. It was full of books, hundreds of dollars worth, beautiful red leather, gilt-edged books, one of Keats, others on science, geography, literature, and every conceivable subject, which worked out well for the chaps confined at Parma. The case was brought by a general, who questioned me about my associations with the count. I learned later that poor Ciano had been arrested and shot around the time the books arrived in Parma.

One of the doctors at Parma, Claudio Dardanie, was a great guy who could be trusted. I sounded him out about escaping and heading for Margherta. He thought the whole idea of no value but gave me two files and a water bottle. A storage room down the hall from our dormitory had a window with small steel bars; just below the sill was a tin roof covering a henhouse. From there a walkway led to the street, and this was to be our escape route. My partners in this project were Paddy Walters from Salisbury, Rhodesia, and a Swedish air force chap named Strom. Dr. Dardanie told us where sentries were posted and about the road leading west out of the city. We got busy cutting the bars, and the files were super. The fresh cuts into the ironwork were sealed with a combination of butter and cigarette ash or just plain dirt. Sometimes a soldier walked through each floor, so we made dummies to put in our beds the evening we departed.

The three of us were ready. We removed the bars and gently lowered ourselves down to the roof. The chickens had already gone to roost, but an occasional cackle made us very careful. The front gate squeaked badly, and a light went on inside the house but nobody showed. Once outside on the road, we kept apart, but with each other in view, as we followed the leader. Parma was not a large city. Long before dawn, we were out in the country and looking for a suitable hideout because our absence would be discovered sometime that day. We kept a low profile, studied our maps, and began moving westward at dusk.

We had chosen Margherta for several good reasons. It had been a favorite resort for American and British tourists. The bulk of the populace had served in hotels, restaurants, and stores patronized by these people and spoke English quite well. The Fascists had killed the tourist trade, which the local people resented, and it seemed the ideal place to get a boat to France. We alternated as leader and were making good time. From some hilltops, we could see the sea. The countryside seemed quite normal. Apparently, no search had been launched. Our legs were starting to object and we all needed a wash and shave, but our spirits were greatly spurred by sight of the sea, and it was nice to be free.

I was in the lead and had just crossed a wide roadway after stopping to look for traffic or sentries. On the other side, I ran into five or six soldiers from a patrol who were resting just off the roadway. They jumped up and got their rifles ready. None of them spoke English. They searched me and took my maps, food, and water bottle. For a while they gave me a rough time. In fact, they were giving me the once-over when Walters arrived, and he got the same treatment. Then came the Swede. The Italians thought he was German and gave him the red carpet treatment. Thinking more of us would show, they kept alert. After an hour, they relaxed and marched us out on the road; within a mile, we came to a police station that had two-way radio equipment. A naval patrol arrived to take us into custody—nobody to blame, although Dardanie might have told us that the main naval base at La Spezia was almost next door to our destination, a very sensitive area and well guarded. Lengthy interrogation by two naval lieutenants proved we were harmless, but a decision was made to break up our trio. I was handed over to the carabinieri and, with what seemed like a fantastic escort of seven people, I entrained for Florence.

The track followed the coastline, and the countryside was badly scarred by marble quarries. This was the center of Carrara marble, a lovely white hard stone that has been used over the centuries in decorating palaces, government buildings, and whatever the pocketbook could stand. At one stop, I could clearly see the Leaning Tower of Pisa. My carabiniere officer took me to a small refreshment room that was crowded, but one word from him and the crowd parted. We ordered black coffee and cognac, no payment due, which revealed the power of the Fascists.

Our arrival in Florence was anticipated. When we reached the main gate of the barracks, an officer and escort awaited us. I was quickly handed over to their tender care. My Fascist lieutenant shook my hand and saluted before leaving, and this gesture raised the eyebrows of the new escort. I was taken to a small room sparsely furnished, but a soldier brought some food shortly after, also some good-tasting wine.

Two or three days later, the commandant sent for me to inquire whether I was being well treated and whether I needed anything. Yes, sir, could I have a washup and a shave? Of course, and he called in a sentry to escort me to the barber shop, which turned out to be a crummy place with straight-back chairs, poor equipment, and two very ancient barbers. Both chairs were occupied, and my sentry grew tired, stacked his rifle, and strayed outside. He came back into the shop on occasion, and there I sat patiently. One chair became vacant. After the barber had finished with me, I fully expected to see my sentry walk in, but no way—he was impressing two young impressionable girls who were wide-eyed and lapping up his stories. I noticed a bus stop right near so, edging over, I got behind a fat lady and climbed aboard, and off we went. It was pretty obvious before we had traveled many miles that a general alarm had been issued because there was a group of uniforms on every street corner. The bus driver finally intimated that we had reached the end of the line, and two policemen were there to help me dismount. A telephone call announced my capture and, shortly afterward, two truckloads of soldiers, several motorcycles, and, of course, the carabinieri swarmed around like bees.

When we reached the barrack gates, there was no welcome committee. They marked my record "Molto Bellicose," which labeled me for quite a while. The prisoner records always followed the person. I received no food or wine issue that night. Guards stayed in my room, and more guards patrolled outside. The commandant, who had been so friendly, wanted to get rid of me as fast as possible, and I was soon on a train heading for Bologna, due north.

Camp Bologna No. 34 was big, and the new brick buildings were the best Italy had to offer. The grounds had been taken over by the Fascist government from the famous Medici banking family, and a descendant still lived in a palatial home adjoining the camp. My entry was hailed by quite a number of former campmates. I was also welcomed for the maps I carried—tracings from the *Baedecker Guide*. The chaps wanted to know all about my experiences, and my lecture gave them hope and some cheer. The unfortunate side of my frequent moves was the almost complete elimination of my supplemental food supply from the Red Cross. In fact, I was getting damn thin but felt fine.

Rumors were rife that the Allies were advancing north. Prisoners were still escaping, and there were dire threats from the commandant. The north-south railroad passed about half a mile from the camp, and the Germans were rushing troops south day and night.

It was at Bologna that we heard Italy had capitulated. The sentries were running all over the place and had abandoned their stations. Colonel Mountain, our senior officer, requested the commandant to turn over the camp to him, but he refused. We learned later that one of the Italian officers (we believed the commandant) informed the Germans that we were all armed. The German SS showed at the gates at 0400 on 10 September 1943 and, in regular combat pattern, began taking over the camp. Lieutenant Gooseveldt, who was in charge, was quite young, probably twenty-seven or maybe thirty, and his troops numbered less than one hundred men, plus three tanks, as opposed to a thousand men in the camp. The prevailing disorder gave some of us an opportunity to escape.

It was pitch dark, and I managed to get out the side gate onto a road bordered by a hedge (it seemed all the roads in Europe had hedges). I climbed over it and came to a very high fence. I was quite busy climbing up when I discovered it was the backdrop for a tennis court. The Germans were firing like crazy to deter anyone escaping. They had a fixed line of fire along the railroad tracks, and about every third shot was a tracer. I decided to stay on the camp side of the tracks and began looking for a suitable hideout. I knocked on the front door of the big house and a small emaciated guy answered. I told him I was trying to escape and would he allow me in the house. It was a stupid question, and I regretted asking it. He explained that he had three women in the house; if he was caught, the Germans would execute them all. I knew this for a fact and moved away into what appeared to be extensive grounds.

Dawn was breaking, the rifle fire had diminished, and I spotted what looked like the ideal hideout. A blackberry bush had grown under a pine tree with low limbs, and there was an opening that could have been used by a fox. For the immediate present, it was my foxhole. The Germans began searching, and a harsh "Raus, Raus," followed by a hand grenade, was convincing proof they were not fooling. One guard shouted "Raus, Raus" at my tree. I use the term *my* tree because I thought I was alone, but not so. Two other chaps had crawled under the low boughs, but their feet were sticking out. They surrendered quickly.

I played possum until a hand grenade burst and blew away my cover. There, with his rifle at the ready, a German guard beckoned me to come out. A thorn caught my cap and revealed my bald head.

"You are old?" said the German. "Yes, I'm old and how about forgetting you ever saw me?" He smiled and motioned me to head for an open space, where about twenty others had assembled. These guys were making a real windfall—getting chaps from every tree, capturing several hundred prisoners. One thing I noticed about the Germans: the ordinary soldier had the power of life and death in his hands; if he said go and you didn't, he'd shoot you, and that was it!

When we got into camp, we found the Germans had enlisted Italian soldiers and constructed a new holding pen of two rows of barbed wire about 10 feet apart. As the escapees were rounded up, they were placed in the pen. German soldiers were setting up machine-gun mounts, and it looked like another mass execution.

Gooseveldt, the young German CO, took up a position at the end of this enclosure. He had all the documents of prisoners and, with the aid of two privates, was sorting out names. It seemed to me that my name came up fairly early. I was marched to the desk where this guy sat and studied the report. Mine was not exactly one of the best.

He addressed me: "Palmer, you are a troublemaker. Ya, and the Italians have given you the title of 'Molto Bellicose' for obvious reasons. Let me tell you while I'm in command here, I don't want any further trouble from you or escape—if you do, I'll cut your throat."

I thought this over and told him I would consider that a very unfriendly act. To my surprise, when the Nuremberg trials were on, who should be up for trial but Gooseveldt. The charge was cutting prisoners' throats! I frequently think of that guy when I'm shaving.

For a while, I thought Gooseveldt was kidding. Anyhow, I was dismissed and put back with the others. As they rounded us up, a big train loaded with empty cattle cars pulled in. We were herded into them, but, at the last minute, about thirty of us were separated from the rest because we were on the sick list.

The Germans were hard-pressed for transport. With the surrender of Italy, many thousands of prisoners had to be transported into Germany. The logistics were impossible, but the Germans had been shuttling people around for years. In fact, they had moved half of Europe. Confined to barracks, we watched the Italian soldiers trying to be buddies with the German soldiers but it didn't work. The Germans slapped them around at every opportunity. The commandant, who had lied to us and betrayed us, got special care. I watched him being chased by a German soldier with a fixed bayonet just a few inches from his rear. He was hollering bloody murder, but he kept running and, unfortunately, saved his miserable life.

The one persistent rumor was that our troops had taken over Brenner Pass, and this somehow clinched the idea that none of us would ever leave Italy—how wrong could we have been? We were aroused early one morning, hustled into army trucks, and taken to Modena, where a long line of freight cars awaited our arrival. Our optimistic spirits sank way, way low, as fifty men were assigned to each car. We placed the few items we carried in the center and sat with our backs to the wall. Even that arrangement was uncomfortable, but we heard the Italians were packed in seventy-five to a car. Of course, there were no toilet facilities and damn poor ventilation. The cars were designed to carry freight or cattle—not humans.

The train was made up of three types of cars: steel cars with wooden floors, all-steel cars with wood slats for the floor, and old-style wooden cars. Much depended on what type of car you were assigned—mine was all-steel. At the rear of this rather long train was a flat car where two motorcyclists, plus several sharpshooters, were stationed. They had no accommodations, but in the adjoining car were food and bunks, with duty changes every four hours.

Our chaps quickly discovered that the locks on some cars could be easily picked, and others sawed away on the wood floorboards. When opportunity presented itself, chaps jumped out and headed for Switzerland and freedom. We had a near-miss when the train stopped for water. The officer in charge noticed a door open and only about twenty men remaining. Livid with anger, he pranced around, ranted and raved, and threatened to shoot those remaining. Colonel Mountain came to the rescue just in time and our old buddy, the radio broadcaster Eddy Ward, who spoke German, saved the day, but it took a couple of hours for that officer to calm down.

We were truly shocked to find that all the rumors about Brenner Pass were so much eyewash. There wasn't a soul in sight—no blockage, heavy guns, commandos, or anyone else. We sailed right through this strategic pass to Innsbruck. Our only compensation was seeing the beautiful country in the Austrian Alps—nice white buildings, neat homes with geraniums growing in window boxes. Of course, our magnificent view was made possible only by standing on a box and looking through the small window, maybe 2 feet by 1 foot, high up near the roof and covered with barbed wire.

We kept right on going to Bavaria, a lovely part of the world. It was damn hard to reconcile the fact that the birthplace of that infamous bastard Hitler was Braunau, on the border between Austria and Bavaria. It was, as well, the location of Dachau, the extermination center for Jews; also, one of the largest prison camps; and a few other choice pockmarks.

We headed north-northwest from Innsbruck toward Munich and ultimately arrived in Moosburg, the fantastic Prisoner-of-War Camp No. 7. It was actually a small city with a population of well over 100,000 men from all nations, and inside the outer perimeter were numerous smaller sections divided by barbed wire. The prison was patrolled by motorcycle.

The camp section assigned to us was alongside the Russians, and that was educational. A young man, without any rank or insignia, came up to the barbed wire where our chaps were trying to make conversation. He indicated that they needed food, of which we had absolutely none, but one of our chaps spoke Russian and informed him we would have extra food within a few days. We agreed to share it with our Russian friends. We ultimately received our Red Cross parcels and divided them up with the Russians, which they enjoyed. But these parcels were nothing compared with a large meal that came to us by mistake, and we passed it on to the Russians. There were three big aluminum tins, about 4 feet long, 6 inches deep, and maybe 2 feet wide, filled with nothing but squares of bacon fat. We didn't like it, but they eagerly grabbed it and ate it like candy bars. The young chap with authority reappeared and, in perfect English, thanked us for the food. We became friends from then on. The Russians could scramble over the 10-foot barbed wire fence as if it were an ordinary garden hedge. Sentries patrolling the road were ordered to shoot them, but that didn't mean a thing. They came over anyway and offered to do menial tasks for a few cigarettes.

I never actually saw this, but it has much truth: the Germans were afraid of the Russians and would not go into their compound unless fully armed and in groups of two or three. They let loose two fierce dogs into the Russian compound, and the dogs did not reappear. Sometime later, the skins and a few bones were tossed over, plus a note, "Here are your dogs." An estimated 50,000 Russians were in the compound next to us and more were scattered about the vast camp, all prisoners from the Russian front.

We had a surprise visit in our compound from about ten well-dressed Italians, complete with baggage. They belonged to the Berlin Embassy and were on their way to Rome, when the Germans shoved them into an ordinary prison camp. This gave the escape group plenty of good clothes, and one chap grabbed a smart briefcase, which came in very handy at a later date.

A black market was run by Arab prisoners, who seemed to have the Germans in the palms of their hands. These chaps had enlisted for outside work, mostly on farms. Of course, they would bring back all types of goodies that had been traded away for cigarettes, coffee, and chocolate items that the Germans had not seen in years. The Arabs were not supposed to bring items back to the camp, but for a religious occasion they actually brought back a live sheep. Their methods of hoodwinking the German sentries were worthy of Houdini. They traded in many things besides food. The choice wines that Hitler had so generously given his troops from the wineries of France filtered down to the Arabs, and they peddled bottles in the market square. They also had pistols, ammunition, commando knives, and hand grenades. When I looked at the motley group surrounding us, my one dream was to be long gone when the war was over. I never heard about what happened, but it was probably a blood bath, for sure.

The Germans rounded up all prisoners with escape records. One morning, a rumor went around that we were going to be moved from Moosburg to another more permanent camp in Germany. The rumor proved to be true: we were assembled, searched, and marched out the main gate toward another mystery destination. It was a very fortunate day to leave because a north wind brought a stench hard to describe. I learned later it was the smell of humans being burned at Dachau. We had seen long trains going by fairly often with cargoes of Jews from Romania and the Baltic States. Many thousands died in that awful camp but, despite the close proximity, we had no idea what was going on. My nostrils held that nauseating smell for months afterwards.

We left Moosburg and marched down the road to where a train stood waiting. The South Africans were with us, making a total of nearly two thousand POWs. When a group of fifty prisoners arrived beside a car, they were halted and ordered inside. At first, the car I found myself in looked like all the others, but when the Germans slammed the door shut we found ourselves in total darkness. Not the smallest beam of light filtered in from outside. In a few seconds, we realized that there wasn't a window in the car, and not even a crack to let in fresh air. It was a rotten feeling for fifty men to be shut up tightly in so small a space.

We set up a terrific howl, but the guards paid no attention to us. After half an hour, my bosom companion, Guy Cuthbertson, and I decided to stage a fit. We gagged, choked, and moaned, and at last the Germans opened the door. Every man jumped to the ground despite the threats of the guards, and we refused to get back in. Colonel Mountain came along just then and, after a long argument with a German officer, they agreed that the door of the car could be left open and a guard posted with us. At that, we piled in again. Without further delay, the train pulled away.

In the morning of the third day, we crossed the Rhine River into France and entered the city of Strasbourg. As we came over a hill, we saw a massive old stone fort built into the side of the hill. Fort Bismark was to be our home for ten days, and never was morale lower. The fort was ancient—very ancient—and formidable to the extreme. The young officer in charge greeted us and explained that the reason for our being there was that Fort Bismark was escape proof: "Nobody escapes from here." This was a stupid observation to make in front of three hundred men who had escape records. I'd liken it to a challenge or throwing down the gauntlet. The general opinion among those listening—well, we would see!

Describing the fort is difficult. It was part of the defense line between Germany and France, who had been at war since time began. The whole unit was underground, and quite large trees were growing on top of the second floor. It was built of hand-hewn stone with walls 6 feet thick, and to give some idea of age—it had the remains of a moat. The section to which we were assigned fronted the only straight part of the moat, which was 20 feet wide. Of course, the water had been drained and grass was growing; the earth that had been removed to build this ditch was heaped up behind a retaining wall about 8 feet high and sloped at a 30-degree angle to a pathway where sentries patrolled. There was a slightly recessed space where the ancient drawbridge had fitted into the retaining wall. A permanent wooden structure replaced the drawbridge.

On our fifth day in Fort Bismark, Colonel Mountain made a desperate plea for help, and the Red Cross managed to get a shipment of food parcels to us. These happened to be almost entirely Scotch parcels, so most of them contained a tin of compressed oats. We decided to pool the oats and make a communal pot each morning. Some of us still had several tins left from the trip from Italy, and these were added to the pool to make an impressive pile of eighteen tins altogether.

This porridge was to be the big meal of the day, since we had so little food for so long. Volunteers got up early to light the fire and get the jam and a tin bucket full of boiling water. I took on the cooking chore and used six tins of oats each morning. When the porridge was ready I bellowed a cheerful "Come and get it."

Because the stove was burning in the morning, we ate most of our food then and went hungry for the rest of the day. The black bread tasted better when toasted, so I usually did the toasting while watching the porridge— tossing the finished toast to the right owner, then catching fresh pieces from other chaps. Occasionally, we warmed up a tin of bully and, to top off the repast, also had a brew of tea or cocoa.

It was depressing at Fort Bismark, especially when the lights went out and we lay on the uncomfortable board beds trying to sleep. We took turns telling bedtime stories in order to fall asleep. Sometimes the salty language used was too much for the padre, but he was voted down by popular demand.

To take head counts, a bugle blew three times a day and everybody assembled in the moat, usually in groups of fifty men. Then, in columns of three, they marched up a slope to the bridge and moved across to the entrance gate. Two sentries counted from one end, and two more sentries counted from the other. When their tallies agreed, the columns could go inside and disperse. Then the next columns followed.

One must keep in mind that escaping is a team effort, and nowhere was a better team organized. What one person could see, another could amplify, and a jigsaw puzzle was fitted into place. The people selected for escaping were a special breed, physically and mentally; they were well-trained and preferably had some knowledge of the language. The escape committee was simply marvelous and, through devious means, had acquired money, tickets, identification papers, and expert maps. Each person selected was briefed, and the actual escape had to be done in broad daylight because everybody was locked in after the last roll call.

The escape of a young naval lieutenant, Dennis Kelleher, illustrates how the plan was carried out. The slight bend in the wall afforded concealment from the two sentries stationed at each end of the moat. A big, tall man stood close to the wall, and the chap due for escape was hoisted up on his shoulders. Then watching the movements of the sentry, he wormed his way up the incline, crossed the roadway, and disappeared. This was the trickiest part. To distract the sentry's attention, a fight was staged or an argument flared up, or even a dance was performed. We had a chap with the small piece of a Scottish bagpipe, I think called the chanter. Anyhow, he played a tune on this gadget, such as "The Campbells Are Coming," and by his tone gave the proper warning—the sentry is losing interest, the sentry is sleepy, the sentry is ready to resume patrol. These tunes conveyed the alert to those supervising the escape. The navy chap got away nicely, and the sentry was thrilled as he watched Scottish dancing. I met Dennis later and learned he had stowed away on a Swedish freighter and managed to get back to England.

The next part of the jigsaw was to replace those who had gone so that our roll call tallied. Inside the fort was a large galley, and a chute for potato peels led outside the wall to a trough. The drill was to get small chaps into the first group to be counted and, once they dispersed, one, two or three—whatever was needed—scampered to the galley, jumped into the chute, and rejoined a group that was short of men. This system worked fine, and eleven men got outside before one of the prison's senior officers blew the whistle. He used one of those super-long cigarette holders. One day, as he was watching the parade, he turned round to throw away his cigarette. He spotted one of our chaps emerge from the potato chute and rejoin a unit. Holy Moses! Blow the bugle! Everybody halt! Those inside came out and assembled in the moat. Then, a very serious head count revealed eleven men short. The young officer who had boasted, "Nobody escapes from here," looked as though he had wet his pants. He declared, "My military career is ruined." This upset all of us, as one can imagine.

We stayed in the moat while a thorough search was made and were then notified that we would move the next morning. One chap who felt particularly frustrated was an Australian fighter pilot, Jeff Chinchen, who was next in line to go. Well, the escape committee had another idea. The fort had small recesses along the main corridor that were probably used years ago to store rifles or ammunition. It was decided to hide Chinchen in one of these small recesses, which the Germans were bricking. The bricklayers were local men and by no means disposed to be friendly with the Germans. A proposition was made to use sloppy cement and enclose Chinchen before sealing up the recess. This was okay with the bricklayers. The pilot got inside; the last bricks were put into place; and, with little air, he stayed there until after the main column moved out. Here again, a head count showed one man short, and panic almost ensued. Dogs were brought in. One sniffed a long time outside Chinchen's hiding place, but the German just growled and thought the dog was crazy.

When the place quieted down, no more patrolling or dogs around, Chinchen pushed down the brickwork, walked right past the sentries, and headed for Switzerland. He made it to the Rhine River but had to go upstream for crossing, and the riverbank was closely watched. After picking off a small branch to conceal his nose, he swam across the river and landed in Basel, Switzerland. He was befriended by a Mr. Adam, who in turn had to be careful because his wife was pro-German. Chinchen rested up and finally returned to England to fight many more battles. He later became a member of Parliament for Queensland, Australia.

German sentries kept swarming over the building, but we were allowed to pick up the few items we owned. Then, forming a column with rows of four, we marched out of the camp. The fourth man in each row on alternate sides was a German, and none appeared too friendly. This forced march of about 10 miles ended at the Rhine River, where we awaited another train. The Gestapo took charge and immediately began searching our baggage. I lost a short piece of pipe, but everybody lost something regardless of its worth. As usual, nobody knew where we were going, but our reputation had evidently spread. We had as many military escorts as there were prisoners. They included a goodly mix of Gestapo, whose uniforms resembled those of the Italian carabinieri.

The train had typical cattle cars. A sentry was placed in each car, and a single telephone line enabled him to report every hour. The flatcar with sharpshooters was missing, but the weight of guards offset this shortage. We entrained, feeling very low, because the train was taking us over the Rhine and further north. For no good reason, I decided to get out of that damn train. We cut the wire over the small window. With the sentry half asleep, my friends lifted me up and passed me out the window while we were passing through a tunnel. I dropped to the tracks.

I was told afterward that the alarm went off and everybody with a rifle was shooting. I caught an explosive bullet in the elbow joint, and my tunic was full of holes. The tunnel sentry came running, eager to make a capture. My arm was bleeding badly, and somehow he flagged down an ancient motorcycle with a sidecar. I was placed in it and hustled off to a two-floor building. By this time, I was not keeping track very well. The next thing I knew, I was in a barrack room full of black French troops from Senegal. Quite nearby was a white-covered table with a priest mumbling something, which I learned later were the last rites. It was very kind of him but not necessary for this occasion. The black troops helped me sit up, and I was given a cold drink that helped to restore my sense of proportion.

A German officer came by and asked who I was, what rank, what army. He had escorted me over from the casualty station and complimented me on a quick recovery. It turned out that he had been a university student in England and his wife was English. He quickly arranged for me to be moved and placed in a private room. I was not in any mood to argue, but I requested some clothes. The best they had to offer was a skimpy nylon shirt and a pair of large clogs. My mind got all twisted trying to figure out the events of the past few hours. The English-speaking officer informed me that my right arm had been cut off without the aid of anesthetic. Of all places to make an escape, I had been right on the Siegfried Line, which was Germany's second line of defense. Two days later, I felt rested up. That evening, I was asked if I would like to be moved to a hospital for English prisoners not many miles away—that surely would be great.

Next morning, a big hulk of a soldier knocked and motioned for me to follow him. I still had on my short shirt and oversized clogs, but I followed this guy out into the cold, with the wind whistling around my butt, the clogs sliding every which way, no shave, or even a wash. Here I was, thinking about the immaculate dresser I used to be. Now I was the most bedraggled poor guy in Europe and, despite the agony and discomfort, I began to laugh at myself. The sentry stopped dead in his tracks and mumbled something, but he never offered a coat or anything to keep me warm. I was taken to a checkout point, given some papers, and loaded into an ambulance. The driver must have trained at Indianapolis. Fortunately I was on the floor, but the SOB did not do my temperature any good or my disposition.

The head doctor took charge. I was given a bath, and somebody shaved me. After a cup of hot chocolate, I was put to bed. I slept for about fourteen hours straight. The doctor kept close tabs on me but ignored my roommate, an American bomber pilot named Purefoy, who had been badly burned.

I finally said, "Doc, I'm okay, why not pay attention to this guy?"

Three days later, the doctor explained that the report brought with me listed me as being *non compos mentis*, or crazy. He wrote to the hospital and asked for specific symptoms. The reply was a classic: "The prisoner, while being escorted across the parade ground, began laughing in an uncontrolled manner, despite obvious pain and discomfort."

My new hospital was in a spot named Winesberg in Germany. Here again, I had another reunion with chaps who had been with me for months—from the toe of Italy to mid-Germany. It was marvelous seeing them again.

The Winesberg camp had a mixed bag—many South Africans, Americans, Australians, and English. It was well run, and the food supply was adequate. One nice feature about being in the hospital was special rations, especially body-building items. I needed these because my weight had dropped way down to 97 pounds from my usual 145. In fact, I was so weak I was scared to bend over. If I dropped anything, I'd wait for two chaps to stand by while I went down in a squat position to pick up the item, and then they helped to lift me back upright. The doctor washed and dressed my wound. Good medication and food, plus sunshine, greatly helped my recovery, and I resumed walking again with my old buddy Eddy Ward and his Ethiopian friend Senussi.

The war was definitely going our way, and the Germans were very friendly for a change. I was there about two months, having been discharged from the hospital and able to bend over with no fear of not getting back. The chaps had me lecturing about Malaysia and the fortress of Singapore. The Japanese had overrun all that area, and it looked like Australia was about to be captured. My knowledge was fairly good, having lived in the Orient for many years, and I was considered by these young troops as an authority. I felt embarrassed by the faith they placed in me, but the big thing was to keep them informed and as happy as one could expect.

Two to three months were about my limit in any one camp, with the exception of Sulmona. I had filled my time in Winesberg and, sure enough, I got orders to move, this time due north where all the naval types were being assembled. By now, packing and saying good-bye were routine. I had stored up quite a bit of supplies, including extra chocolate and, because I did not smoke, many cigarettes. My critical report card had been mislaid and, in essence, I was clean. A prominent bandage indicated that my arm was not there and not to bang into me. The two guards escorting me were equivalent to our marines, with anchors on their tunic collars but in the same German dun-green color scheme. We marched to the railroad and were assigned a special car.

The German trains were subject to much bombing. Each train ran what might be called a section, or 100 miles, when the crew were changed and the train returned to its starting point. Another train took its place for the next 100 miles. We had lengthy stops while these changes were handled. My guards were in a friendly mood, and my liberal offering of cigarettes and coffee was working just fine. The cars had a small map that showed the route being taken. During one layover, the idea occurred to me to switch over at Hanover and try reaching Holland. We were in Heidelberg when the two sentries eased up enough for me to talk to civilians—not much, but this can be significant in planning an escape.

When the train was ready, we climbed aboard and were off to the north. Next stop Kassel, which was rather large, and the central concourse was busy with hundreds of people shuffling about. I was amused at the various types of salutes I was getting—the straight arm, the bent arm, the open-hand Fascist, and the touch of the cap. We were standing near a steel telephone booth when the air raid alarm sounded, and the people quickly vanished. My two guards left me, and I knew damn well bombs would be falling soon. The telephone booth offered flimsy shelter. Nearby, I noticed people getting into an opening that turned out to be a baggage tunnel. It was not very deep and not much of a shelter, but bombs were exploding, the whole earth shaking, and for a while all hell was let loose. The tunnel had white tiles. Some popped out of place and hit people, who, for the most part, promptly fainted. When the all-clear sounded, we moved out and my two guards came back, greeting me like a long-lost friend. The telephone booth was twisted out of shape, the whole station was a mess, and much was still burning.

Two engineers were busy studying the damaged tracks. When they determined which one could be restored the quickest, a large number of Russian prisoners were brought in and they started tearing the damaged track apart. New rails were stored by the platform. As a strip of rail ties was cleared, about twenty men were lined up and their orders went somewhat like this: bend over, take hold, lift, move to the right (or move to the left), straighten up, lower, let go, straighten up. The prisoners were then moved over to another piece of track, while others drove spikes. With all this fantastic coordination, a train was ready to load within ten minutes of the all-clear signal. I found out that the Russians were housed in a train a mile or so from the station and they moved in while bombs were falling.

My guards and I were now buddy-buddy, and we settled into a new train, ready for the next 100 or so miles. According to the map, we then should be in Hanover. The countryside looked peaceful enough. We were in the middle of the German industrial belt, but there was little sign of bomb damage. I noticed a great deal of similarity in the people waiting to board our train—the majority were women, mighty tough-looking babes, nobody smiling, and face washing had gone out of style. Best of all, the incessant "Heil Hitler" had gone.

When we reached Hanover, a repetition of earlier stops followed. My guards were experts at getting the attention of women, while I just wandered about. The very thing I was wanting appeared, a train to The Hague in Holland. Whoopie! I went up on the platform, but the idea fell flat. Police were guarding the exit of every car, and they inspected papers for each passenger.

I returned to my guards, who now seemed to resent my butting in, so I went back for another look. Two girl porters were having much trouble getting the wheel of a small trolley out of a bomb hole. The train guard put down his lamp and helped the little darlings get going. I saw the open door of the baggage car, jumped in, and hid behind a stack of mail. The guard got on board, closed the big doors, pushed his cap back, and lit his pipe. Meanwhile, my heart was thumping away, making more noise than the wheels. The guard continued to shuffle papers, talk to himself, and look at labels on a few packages. This was a fast train and apparently had the right of way—Holland, here we come.

The routine of the guard at the occasional stops we made followed a set pattern. He tossed out a few parcels or a bag of mail, then walked toward the engine, but he got back before the train started moving. He placed his lamp just inside the door, took a seat near a small desk, and lit his pipe.

Dawn was starting to break—high time for me to leave the train. I watched my fellow passenger do his routine. The next time he started walking toward the engine, I jumped off and walked the other way off the platform. The ground led slightly uphill from the railroad tracks. I spotted a small house with a light and headed straight for it. My knock brought a chap in his underwear and, with my few words of German, I indicated that I was a POW and in need of a friend while escaping. He hesitated a few moments, then gave me the welcome sign and guided me to the table, where he had been having breakfast. He gave me a bowl of thick soup or porridge. Whatever it was tasted good. I then asked permission to use the toilet—ya ya. I thought I had found a friend, but while I was in the john he had telephoned the police, and I was escorted to the local pokey.

The policeman seemed huge, but he spoke English with a Brooklyn accent. As a boy, he had worked in America at a shoe factory. His advice to me was priceless: "The only man we know around here who is Nazi is that man—next time you come here, don't stay with him."

Well, I gave him the assurance I would certainly avoid him and asked where I was. "This is Daventer, Holland, and when this war is over, I'm going back to Brooklyn."

The Gestapo were notified. For three days I was grilled and beaten up. One SOB was particularly mean, and I'd like to meet him some fine day. The big question was how did I get so far and escape all the safety precautions. Of course, I told them the truth and how I had traveled in the baggage car from Hanover without any assistance from anyone. Their point was to find out if anybody had assisted me, and Lord only knows the trouble they would have been in.

When the Gestapo realized there was no underground connection, they sentenced me to ten days' solitary confinement in a brand-new jail, built of concrete and steel and soundproof. Even the big steel doors were on beveled hinges that allowed the door to drop into a slot when closed. The small one-way window was about eye level, and the only opening was a narrow slit that was sheltered by an awning. The furniture was a thick board suspended by a chain at each end. One hour about noontime was to be used for toilet, eating, and, if there was any time left, exercise. I recall marching around in a tight circle of men, with a sentry stationed in the center who watched over us like a watchdog. We were forbidden to talk. From what I could see, the ten or twelve chaps out exercising were either American or British.

The Gestapo grilled me a few times but ultimately gave up. My two ex-guards were sent to the Russian front, and the train guard was fined heavily for allowing me to be on board without his knowledge. I was returned to Germany and again headed north toward Bremen. Damn funny, years before, just after World War I, I was a crew member of a freighter that brought about 10,000 tons of Australian wheat to Bremen as a gift from the Australian government to the German people. Here I was back again, but there were not many thanks.

We changed trains to a local track and headed inland to Westertimke. Camp Marlag 0 had been described as a wonderful spot designed and used by naval cadets. Not so; it was a lousy cinder patch full of naval types and the most desolate country existing. I was placed in the schreibstube for search. While I waited, a chap signaled me in Morse code. I could tell by the sound of his taps on a pipe that he was nearby, and so I asked him to identify by voice. Yes, he was next door; his name, Guy Morgan; and he was doing solitary on bread and water for trying to escape. He was a war correspondent captured in Czechoslovakia and had been shot in his right arm. I asked what sort of camp this was and received the depressing news that it was lousy— formerly a swamp that had been filled with cinders. I asked what the country surrounding was like. Bloody awful, but he'd never been outside the gates.

The only people allowed out were doctors and the clergy. I asked how well off they were for doctors.

"Hell, we are loaded with specialists, damn good surgeons, dentists, eye specialists, internal medicine, and God only knows what, but we have no ministers."

I told him, "You have one now."

It was 0400 when I had entered the camp. The Gestapo came in to search me about 0500 and told me to go into the main officers' camp and report. Morgan had told me that the senior officer was a Commander Lambert. I was duly passed through several gates and into the officer compound. Morgan was right—it was a miserable dump.

When I knocked at Lambert's small room, he growled, "Who is it?" He had just awakened and suggested we meet in the galley for a cup of coffee. This lantern-jawed officer, who had been captured while on a raid to a French port, was rather formidable. I told him about hearing Morse code from Morgan, and he said Morgan was doing time for plain stupidity—"Serves him right."

I was pleased to meet the head chef, John Wells, who explained how they were able to serve one substantial meal a day by sorting out the food parcels and getting supplements from the black market. The camp was well organized and contained about three hundred officers, mostly British, but we had representatives from many lands, including Iceland. The big handicap was being restricted within the high barbed-wire fence that was surrounded by a 10-foot ditch, plus guard towers, dogs, and a mean SOB of a commandant who was a dyed-in-the-wool Nazi.

I admitted to Lambert that I had told Morgan and the questioning officer that I was a pastor. He was pleased and said I could take the service on Sunday morning, but now I had better see the doctor and get that wound okayed. The doctor was in another camp with the enlisted men. Because of a lenient commandant, it was fixed up rather nicely. The commandant was a German naval commander who had been staff captain on board the crack transatlantic liner *Bremen*. He spoke fluent English, had numerous friends in the United States and the United Kingdom, and seemed damn sorry to be at war with us.

The problem with my arm had developed because of lack of use. I had kept the stump close to my body for both warmth and protection, and the joint had calcified. The job was to break up the calcium deposit and get the regular fluids back to oil the joint. This was damn painful. About the only way I can describe it is like a cook stirring a heavy soup. The sound was like breaking eggshells, and I could only stand the treatment for an hour, by which time my body was soaking wet with sweat.

They kept me in the hospital for a week, where I had a complete physical by an eminent surgeon, Dr. Harvey. Then, I returned to my original camp to take up the duties of pastor and enjoy the special accommodation for men of the cloth. Church services were held in the mess hall, and the music was played on an accordion obtained through the black market. We had hymn books and several Bibles supplied by the Swiss Red Cross. Services began at 1000, usually with a few hymns, then I would read from the scriptures and say a prayer, then another hymn, after which the service was open for debate. It's a shame nobody kept notes on the subjects. The hottest was comparing our various religions—the Germans professed their beliefs, and we fought them, although we had the same or somewhat similar beliefs—a crazy world.

I told Lambert about being in Winesberg and how one room held twelve ministers, covering all faiths. He approached the commandant and requested a transfer for one of them, to which the crusty old bugger agreed. Three weeks later, a pastor arrived but he was not from Winesberg. Of all things, he was a Dutch Reform Boer who could hardly speak English. I was happy to hand over the dignified office and move out of the single room. I helped him with the first two services, and he then wanted to visit another camp to give Easter service. This chap left by train around 1000 hours, and we never saw him again. We think he was killed by a bomb that hit the train.

The group we had in this naval camp varied in rank, age, and origin. Everyone had fascinating stories to relate. Two young lieutenants had been awarded the Victoria Cross for attacking the super-dreadnought *Tirpitz* in one-man subs.

Some had been in the camp three or four years, ever since we attacked the Germans in Norway. Many survivors came from torpedoed ships, crashed aircraft, and bombed submarines.

I met two Roman Catholic priests who had been captured off the South African coast when their ship, the Egyptian SS *Zam Zam,* was sunk in those waters. I had resumed my clerical role and was entitled to go outside for walks with the two priests, plus another character from the Salvation Army.

One of the priests had been a street urchin who hunted with the mob. He had been in the pokey a few times for stealing but let out on parole. One day, as he was being chased by the law, he jumped a high fence surrounding a monastery. The priest at whose feet he landed offered to shield him and, later in the chapel, lectured him about altering his ways. He evidently had been duly impressed.

In his French Canadian accent, he said, "You know, Palmer, that man changed my life. I began to study and after three years of intense study was ordained."

I asked what he was doing on an Egyptian ship off South Africa. He said that he was now a missionary and had been going to relieve somebody in Africa. He was a dedicated missionary, but I could readily see how his earlier life had been by just watching him when he played softball. He would run straight into the chap on base, knock him over or deflect the ball, and then, with a mischievous grin, apologize to the injured player. When he had difficulty in getting hot water for shaving, he requested suppositories made of wax; by lighting one of them, he could readily get boiling water.

I asked him, "When you get released, will you go back to Quebec?"

"Oh, no, Palmer, I must continue to the mission where that chap is still waiting." This remark convinced me that he was genuine. He taught me how to preach and gave a few hints on delivering a sermon. I wished him well— he was a great person.

We had a sailor who worked as a janitor in the camp office, and he was a valuable asset to our escape committee. He copied signatures from blotters, timetables, troop movements, and the Nazi swastika to perfection, all helpful for forging passports. Well, the commandant had married a rather attractive woman and brought her into his office to work. The first morning, she said good morning to the sailor but got no reply. Next morning, the sailor again ignored her greeting.

The third morning, she stood right before him and said, "I always thought you Englishmen were trained to be polite—why do you ignore me?"

He said, "Ma'am, when I was captured, they read the conditions we were to live by. One of them was about our relationship with German women. We were not to talk with any and if caught, the punishment was one year in prison. We were not to have intercourse with any and if caught, five years in prison, and if she became pregnant, we would be shot."

Then the sailor added, "When I look at you, it is not worth the risk."

The woman was furious and called the guards. Off went the sailor to the pokey, and we lost our source of supply!

Lambert ran a tight ship, but we always had people trying to escape. When the roll call revealed one man short, Lambert could put on a priceless act. Of course, he knew damn well who had escaped, but he would recount the numbers, check the lists again, and finally inform the officer conducting the count that he was quite right—someone had gone, but he had no idea how that could happen.

The method used to escape was unique and later publicized. Everybody took a hot bath once a week. The bathhouse was a brick building just outside the fence. The drill was to get a group of thirty lined up, complete with towels, soap, and clean underwear. They would be counted going through the front gate, then counted again at the second gate, and finally, before they went out the main gate, a third count was made. We learned that each guard was held responsible for his count and handed each other a receipt. The group marched to the brick bathhouse. Each man undressed and took up his position under a shower head—first came cold, then medium, then hot, and back again to cold. Everybody helped dry each other and then got dressed. The person chosen to escape hid up in the ceiling, and a dummy was quickly rigged up. The dummy had to be good to fool those three guards. It consisted of a wire coat hanger, over which a greatcoat was hung, and a papier-mâché head, complete with hair from the barber shop, eyes made from Ping-Pong balls, and painted eyelashes, topped by a naval cap worn at a jaunty angle. The dummy was placed in the center column, and two men slipped their arms into the sleeves of the greatcoat to hold the coat hanger. When everybody was out of the bathhouse, the gang marched to the main gate where they were counted, then into the *vorlager* for a second count, then the main compound for a final count. This method worked OK; when night fell, the chap in the rafters climbed down and vanished. At the next roll call, Lambert put on his act, examined the papers, and apologized.

The plan blew up when a small sentry, who had been a waiter, thought there was a new man in the lineup and approached him for verification. He was greatly surprised to discover that the new man had a paper face and no feet. His training immediately came into action: blow the whistle, put on the steel helmet, and start hollering. The other guards came running, and all hell broke loose. The dummy was examined by the Gestapo. Everybody was mustered outside on the parade ground. Three truckloads of police, covered with canvas screens, came into the grounds and fanned out to search every hut. We had seven huts, plus a kitchen and mess hall. They found three cleverly concealed radios, and we lost contact with the BBC for a while until a discard unit was repaired.

There was no idleness in the camp. We were engaged in all manner of activities. Boat building was popular—one chap even made a small motor with melted lead from the foil of cigarette packages. It worked fine. Our other activities included knitting, shoe repair, wood carving, painting, sketching, and much studying about every subject, but mostly Board of Trade navigation and seamanship. We had an arts and crafts exhibition in August, and the theatrical group put on good shows about twice a month. We got German news via a loudspeaker set up in the compound. It was fun to listen to the Germans and then listen to the BBC. They both claimed advances, but place names belied their positions. Our war correspondents analyzed the assorted claims—both sides were lying.

The frequent rumors about being repatriated started up again. We had several visits from the Swiss Red Cross. One visit was laughable. Two chaps quickly dressed up in the civilian clothing that we had long before traded from the Italian Embassy staff. While the Swiss chaps were inside interviewing, our two chaps, one carrying a briefcase, walked up to the gates, saluted, and walked right out. When the Swiss tried to get out the gate, they were promptly arrested and put in the pokey until their true identities were established. I never did hear about what happened to the two phony diplomats, but Europe had already been invaded and hopefully they got away.

Guy Morgan was back in the hospital. He had sustained a broken arm earlier in the war and had broken it again. To compound this injury, he then fell out of bed and broke a tooth. It seemed that misfortune hovered over him like a halo over a saint. He was busy writing a book, and we became good friends. The rumors of repatriation had become incessant. I was on the list for interviews by the Red Cross (I had been on the list before but my bellicose branding had ruined my chances), and the doctors also placed Morgan on the list. To emphasize his arm trouble, they had inserted several sticks in the plaster cast that, when X-rayed, looked like the arrangement for a campfire. He and I both passed, and we began the long wait for final papers.

Since the bombing raids to Hamburg and Bremen had been stepped up, any train movement appeared to be well-nigh impossible. One daylight raid that passed right over our camp presented a sight rarely seen, or maybe never seen again. Eight hundred American B-17 Flying Fortresses came in with fighter escort. The bombers flew in formations of fifty. Staggered in altitude, they made counting easy. The first flight heading for Hamburg was on the eastern horizon, and the last flight of fifty came in from the west. Of course, bombing continued day and night. The ground shivered and our wooden huts rattled, but we were able to adjust and even to sleep through the night raids.

The great day of departure arrived—9 September 1944. The gates of Naval Camp Marlag 0 near Westertimke, Germany, were opened for Guy Morgan, Skip Palmer, and six men from an adjoining camp, as we began the long journey back to our homelands.

As a fitting memorial to this period of my life, I include here a map of my journeys and some of the pages from my *Wartime Log for British Prisoners.* This log is a sturdy 5- by 8-inch album-type book, distributed by the Red Cross—a gift from The War Prisoners Aid of the YMCA in Geneva, Switzerland. It contains entries of many kinds from my friends at Marlag 0. This treasured book is still in my possession.

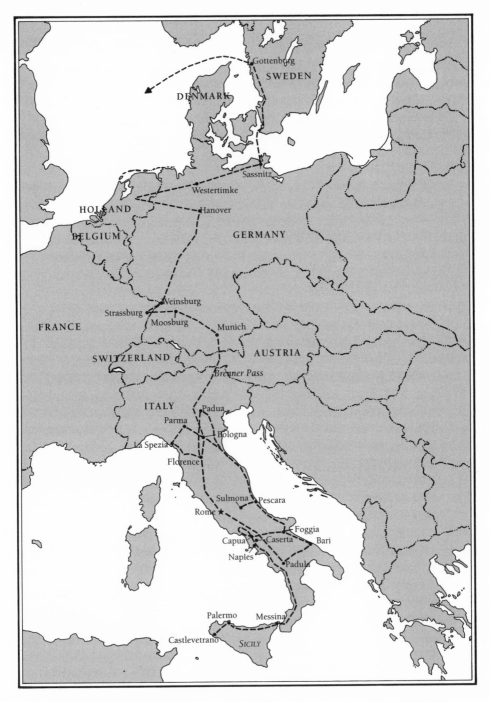

Palmer's journeys as a prisoner of war in Italy (prigioniere de guerra), 1941–43, and in Germany (Kriegsgefangener), 1943–44. Based on a map drawn by POW John M. Montgomery, 30 August 1944.

I also smuggled out a 15- by 24-inch oil painting of the sailing ship *Burrowa* (pictured in Chapter 1). It was created by John Crossdaile solely from descriptions of the ship by myself and others. Because only the last letter received by a prisoner could be taken out at the time of repatriation, I wrapped the painting around the stump of my arm, put on my coat, and carried the painting to freedom. It is now framed and hanging in my den.

Let them in, Peter, they are very tired;

Give them the couches where the angels sleep.

Let them wake whole again to new dawns fired

With sun, not war. And may their peace be
deep.

Remember where the broken bodies lie . . . . .

And give them things they like. Let them make noise.

God knows how young they were to have to die!

Give swing bands, not gold harps, to those our boys.

Let them love, Peter—they have had no time—

Girls sweet as meadow wind, with flowering hair . . .

They should have trees and bird song, hills to climb—

The taste of summer in a ripened pear.

Tell them how they are missed. Say not to fear;

It's going to be all right with us down here.

Anonymous poem. (*Wartime Log*, p. 27)

55

Retrospect.

Of all the lands I've ever Known!—
Coral beaches white as bone,
All the hot lands, & the cold,
Nights of stars and moons like gold,
Tropic Smells, and blood red wine,
Whispering palms and singing pine,
All the islands of the Sea;————
I'll leave you to guess where
            I'd rather be.

Milag Nord. Germany. 1944.

J. F. Power ("Chippy")
86803.
Shipwright Diver
ex R.N.R. 1934

"Retrospect" by J. F. ("Chippy") Power, Milag Nord (hospital), 1944. (*Wartime Log*, p. 55)

" Time they say, must the best of us capture
and travel and battle and gems and gold.

no more can kindle the ancient rapture.

For even the youngest of hearts grows old

But in you I think, the boy is not over,

So take this medley of ways and wars

as the gift of a friend and a fellow traveller

of the fairest countries under the stars."

Sincerely & fraternally yours
Jamie.

"Time" by Jamie (last name unknown). (*Wartime Log*, p. 61)

In This Book... Cap
YOU may have

Schooners and

Auxiliaries

and

Sweepers,   Liners

and

Junks.

But when you reach
the Outside World
I guess the type of
craft you'll prefer
will be
a

Clipper !

(and don't tell me you won't!)   S. J. Hugill
                                  Milag Nord
                                  Germany
                                  1944

Sketch by S. J. Hugill, Milag Nord (hospital), 1944. (*Wartime Log*, unnumbered page.)

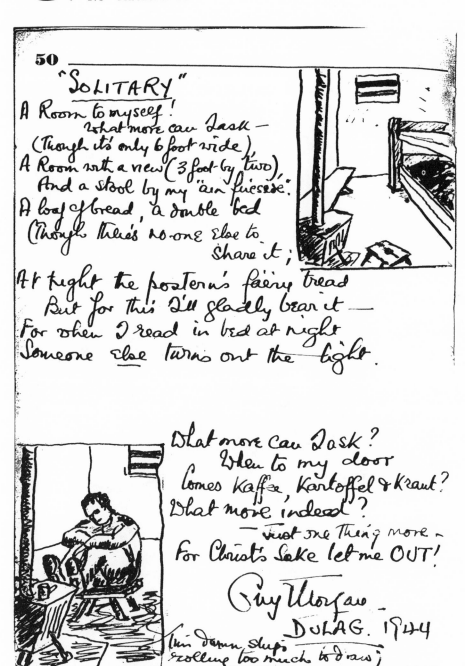

50

"SOLITARY"

A Room to myself!
        What more can I ask —
(Though it's only 6 foot wide),
A Room with a view (3 foot by two),
And a stool by my "ain fireside".
A loaf of bread, a double bed
(Though there's no-one else to
                Share it;
At night the postern's fairy tread
    But for this I'll gladly bear it —
For when I read in bed at night
Someone else turns out the light.

What more can I ask?
    When to my door
Comes Kaffee, Kartoffel & Kraut?
What more indeed?
        — Just one thing more —
For Christ's Sake let me OUT!

Guy Morgan.
        DULAG. 1944

(This damn ship's
rolling too much to draw;)

"Solitary" by Guy Morgan, a newspaper reporter from London, 1944. (*Wartime Log*, p. 50.)

The Snuffle-hound, whose fearful aspect is a warning to all erring and belated Kriegies!

John Worsley
Marlag 'O' 44

A German guard and his watchdog. Sketched in 1944 by John Worsley, who later opened an art studio in London. (*Wartime Log*, p. 17.)

Hong Kong junk. Watercolor by John L. Crossdaile, 1944. (*Wartime Log*, p. 52.)

Antung trader junk. Watercolor by John L. Crossdaile, 1944. (*Wartime Log*, p. 53.)

10

THE LONG ROAD HOME

After almost three years in twelve Italian and German POW camps and two jails and threats of execution, I was ready for the 2-mile hike to the train that would carry me to freedom. Guy Morgan and I took one last look at the many good friends we were leaving and at the lousy cinder patch that was Marlag 0, with its rusty barbed wire and beat-up frame huts. Hitler was declaring another war on all prisoners—shoot them all—and I understand the bastard would have done just that had not one of his generals ignored the order.

Morgan and I, along with the six enlisted men, reached the train. It contained several hundred prisoners—some blind, some amputees, a few crazy—but whatever, the big joy permeating the train was freedom.

I had been nominated senior officer and, as such, occupied a special car with the senior German officer. Although he spoke English, we had little in common. He knew the war was lost and that he would soon face the consequences, whereas I was heading out to celebrate victory. He had a wad of Reich marks and proceeded to issue a 20-mark note to everyone on the train. I had the temerity to ask whether the money was any good. This question shocked him badly: "Why, of course, best currency in existence."

The train crawled along. We reached Hamburg and could clearly see the devastation—whole blocks of buildings were nothing but rubble. We could see people having supper in one house that had only three walls standing.

When the train moved out, everybody heaved a sigh of relief. To our astonishment, it went only a few miles before reversing and backing up into the dilapidated station again. We didn't know why, and our blood pressure mounted. The train finally got going, and we clipped along past Lübeck and Rostock, mostly dairy country. Gangs of Russian prisoners, building roads and repairing fences, were closely watched by the ever-present armed guards and their dogs.

At last, we pulled into Sassnitz for transfer to the Swedish Red Cross. We were lined up in alphabetical order and, as each name was called, we then approached a long table where Germans were seated. A clerk crossed our names off a ledger, and we were given cards stating that we were no longer under the protection of the German government—ho, ho! Next, we passed through a gate in a long fence and the same procedure followed, except this time the Swedish government took over the responsibility.

The Swedish Red Cross took marvelous care of us. Each prisoner was issued a small kit that contained shaving gear, toothbrush and cream, a mirror, new pajamas, two sets of underwear, two pairs of socks, a pair of slippers, hairbrush, and comb. As senior officer, I was escorted to a platform where Princess Silylla of Sweden greeted me and, of all things, gave me a bouquet of flowers. She then signaled two nurses standing nearby to escort me into a building, from which I could see a ship flying the Swedish flag.

The new nurses, known as *lotta,* looked just like angels to me—scrubbed clean faces, blond hair, full bosoms, and the slightest whiff of perfume. It was very disconcerting. "Long time, no she," said Morgan, who had adopted the position of being my adjutant. He hovered close by and remarked, "Keep it down, Skip!" It was a damn hard job keeping anything in mind except *one* thing.

I had previously said to Morgan, "I'll buy you a drink once we get on board and I have wiped the dust of this country off my feet." We boarded the ship and went aft to watch for the last line to be dropped off the pier, then headed for the bar. I asked the tender what he recommended—"Aquavit."

"OK, fix two please." I then handed him my 20-mark note. He was not surprised, but shook his head and opened a drawer that was full of similar bills. They were not worth a damn, and he declared the drinks were on the ship. Funny, those drinks were small and went down easily but, when we started to walk, things got out of hand. The corridors seemed miles long.

Another angel appeared and asked if she could help. She took us in tow up to the boat deck and seated us in comfortable chairs. A steward appeared with a tray of cookies and hot chocolate. Our immediate contact with life as we knew it and had been denied for so long had startling effects. We found we couldn't drink and our appetites were limited!

The trip across the Skattegat was perfect, the ship was all one could desire, and the Swedish princess took care of us like a clucky hen. We reached Malmo on the Swedish mainland and entrained to Gothenburg (Göteborg) the main seaport of Sweden. We found the Swedish train superb, clean as a pin and well run. We thought how fortunate Sweden had been in keeping her neutrality and not getting cluttered up with wreckage and ruined highways. Awaiting our arrival in Gothenburg were three large ships to carry us to England.

Our ship was the SS *Drottingholm* of Swedish registry. I left Morgan to find a cabin and look after our small baggage, while I helped with the troops. I think the real shock of war hit me when the blind prisoners were being led to the gangway, five men in a group. The leader had vision, but the four following him each had a hand on the chap in front and the leader called the shots, "Step down, step up, turn right, turn left, bend a little to avoid a lamp" or whatever. These poor guys were returning to a changed world, and I wondered whether they would know their loved ones.

Many interesting passengers were on board. I asked a Mrs. Cheney, who represented St. John's Ambulance, if she knew Peter Cheney, the novelist, and sure enough, he was her husband. I told her how much his detective stories were appreciated by the prisoners, and we arranged to meet later at the Overseas Club in London.

I mentioned to one lady who was from the Channel Islands that I had seen pictures of the Channel Islanders swearing allegiance to Germany with the Nazi salute. Her explanation was simplicity itself.

"We were ordered to appear in the town square where a platform had been erected," she said, "and the German in charge started reading out the requirements for what he called German security. We were required to bring in all animals, surrender all firearms, make payable to the Reich Bank any deposits we had, and they in turn would issue a receipt. Then the questions—'How many of you speak German? Indicate with your right arm extended.' Well, hardly anyone raised their arms. 'How many of you speak French?' Here he got quite a show of hands. 'How many speak English?' Everybody showed their hands, and on the platform were photographers and movie men taking pictures. When the print was released, it had the caption, 'Channel Islanders swear allegiance to Hitler.'"

We talked awhile about life on the islands and how she had been treated while in Germany—all able-bodied men and women were taken prisoner and put to work.

"I left my family in charge of Grandma. Would you like to see their picture?"

"Why, of course."

It was a trip because I hardly got inside the cabin door when she bolted me in and proceeded to take off my clothing. Of course, I never fought very hard—it was rather a pleasant experience. I never did see her family pictures, and we spent much time in the bunk for the five days of the voyage.

When we arrived at Liverpool, the pier was gaily decorated, a brass band was playing, and quite a number of relatives were awaiting our arrival. Their feelings toward POWs were kind and understanding. Morgan and I were given keys to the city by the Lord Mayor's office. We were both broke, so after four days we decided to head for London and try to get new uniforms, identification papers, and, most of all, money. The navy issued us transportation vouchers and, on reaching London, Morgan reported to his newspaper office while I headed to the Overseas Club. I had trouble adjusting to the traffic and street crossings, and the gasoline fumes gave me headaches.

I next attempted to get clothing, shoes, and other necessities, but this rather simple requirement was fraught with problems. Everything needed coupons, something I didn't have or know much about. I was sent to a huge building, Queen Anne Mansions, that had been taken over by the navy. This fifteen-floor building had been hit by a bomb, which had taken a slice about 50 feet wide right out of it. Power lines had been strung between the two sections, but there was no pedestrian way across the gap. I experienced no trouble entering the building, and the index in the lobby showed where various items were issued. Having lived for a long time in a state of semistarvation, I chose a room that issued food stamps. The ladies in two different rooms were very polite, but they had no coupons.

I had no more success in other rooms for clothing stamps, but this time I had to return to the lobby and walk to the other section of the building for the elevator there. Tired of this runaround and as a last resort, I thought I'd try shoes. Back to the lobby—shoes in the other building. The lady there was ready to pass me off, and here the fuse burst. My tirade brought out a young lieutenant from another room. After persistent questioning about my service details, he finally asked who my admiral had been. At this, I was suddenly interested and asked where Admiral Cunningham was now.

"He is the First Sea Lord at Admiralty House."

"Oh, that's fine—please get him on the phone," I requested.

He looked astounded. "Why, you can't speak to the First Sea Lord."

"Well, maybe not, but I'll try."

He was reluctant but finally made connection, not with Cunningham but with his secretary, whom I also knew.

"Palmer, we knew you were in London, but nobody knew where; the First Sea Lord wants to see you, where are you now?"

"Sir, I'm in Queen Anne Mansions trying to get a few coupons."

"Palmer, who is with you?"

I asked the lieutenant his name and informally introduced them. After much yes, sir; yes, sir; oh, no, sir; yes, sir, this guy asked me to follow him to the lobby. In a few minutes, a Daimler driven by a marine and his sidekick, another marine in dress uniform, drew up. I was given the red carpet treatment, safely stowed in the rear seat, and driven down the Mall in real style. I thought to myself—if the chaps could only see me now.

The admiral had me ushered into his office and asked a few questions. "I'm surprised you knew me," I said.

"Palmer, I never forget those who serve me well and you served me exceptionally well." He then called in his secretary and had him record my promotion to commander. I thanked him profusely and bowed out. A great sailor and gentleman.

The secretary called in a young sub-lieutenant and gave him a note, plus whispered instructions. We boarded the same Daimler car and returned to Queen Anne Mansions—but what a difference. I doubt whether the King could possibly have been treated better. I was given credit for my years in prison, plus six months' allowance for being wounded, and I think another plus for the runaround these civil servants had given me. My pockets bulged. Instead of a few stamps to get some meat, I had enough to get a whole cow.

I was asked to give a few lectures for the Red Cross, private groups, and several air force camps. I recall talking to a large gathering of American airmen, chiefly bomber crews. One chap asked me to point out the camp I left in Germany. A large blowup of an aerial photo showed our comparatively small camp, which was about halfway between Bremen and Hamburg. When I indicated the exact location, one chap said, "Hell, I've looked at that many times and figured if I had any spare bombs on the return flight, I'd drop them on that mystery camp." I explained that four hundred naval types lived there; we had grown very accustomed to the bombers flying overhead and most of us slept like babies, never thinking anyone would harm us. I implored them to be more careful the next time they were in that area. The reason for the lecture was to alert them, in case they were shot down, to avoid civilian groups as much as possible—they were very dangerous.

My second headquarters in London was Australia House on the Strand. The Red Cross had established a nice reception room there under the guidance of Betty Larke, whom I had known slightly in Sydney. She made my London visit something special. People in England who could afford the luxury sent invitations for military personnel to come and stay at their homes, with priority to those from prison camps. Betty showed me several letters. The one that sounded like a winner came from the Burleys, who lived 15 miles outside of London in Denham Mount, a beautiful house set in 40 acres of farmland. The Burleys, Fred and Denny, came from Australia. The household had two daughters, one son, and the parents. The house had been built by Christopher Wren, the famous architect who designed St. Paul's Cathedral. The nearest neighbor was Sir Laurence Olivier (whom I met on two occasions), and Lord Vansittart lived down the road. I liked Van, who had been British Ambassador in Cairo, Tehran, Paris, and Stockholm. He was loaded with orders for chivalry and academic degrees. Having retired from public activities, he and his wife had decided to economize by shutting off heating units to all but three rooms of their palatial home.

I stayed at Denham Mount, a lovely home in a perfect setting, for weeks and the home life was wonderful. It did more to get me back on the track, as it were, than all the solutions that psychology had ever developed. Air raids were still prevalent, and I remember seeing what was called a "buzz bomb" glide past my window as it headed for London.

The Navy had been silent far too long and the thought of my being released kept cropping up. I had new shoes, new uniform, and was almost back to my spick-and-span days. The people making my artificial arm sent me a note to be in their office on 16 October 1944 to try out my arm. I was by no means happy about getting one, but it was a must. I was given instructions on how to wear the damn thing and how the assorted fixtures were attached. "This one is for typing," said the instructor, "this for brushing your teeth, this hook to help you climb, this to hold a pencil or pen," and so on. I was given the full treatment, an arm with hand, two gloves, five attachments, and a book of instructions.

Soon, the Admiralty gave me rather complicated details about making a survey of Gibraltar, Malta, and Alexandria and reporting on damage, necessary repairs, available skilled manpower, transport, and other essentials. The task was monumental, but the time given would not allow in-depth research. I told the chap my feelings, and he confided that it was just something to keep me out of mischief. My orders were to board the cruiser HMS *Swiftsure* in Plymouth, and the date gave me five days to prepare. Actually, this was not necessary—my whole travel kit could fit into a small bag.

Among my mail was an invitation to a cocktail party being given by Anthony Eden, the frustrated prime minister who was waiting for Churchill to step down. I had never met Eden and was happy to visit and have a few drinks with him. He and his wife were exceptional folk, the party well run, and the few hours spent were truly delightful. I would have liked visiting with Churchill, but he was about the busiest person in Europe at that time.

The *Swiftsure* was ready to sail when I reported on board. The ceremony awaiting my arrival seemed excessive. The ship was reputed to have great firepower, and her sister ship had battled the fancy German battleship *Bismarck* in the Atlantic. I was quite impressed. The original plan had called for me to stop in Gibraltar, but this ship steamed right on by, with her first stop in Malta. With the aid of the harbormaster, I inspected the dockyards, slipways, and cranes and checked the work force, machine shops, and other facilities. This island had truly suffered from Italian bombs. Hardly a wall was standing, but the island construction of solid rock gave the Maltese a built-in shelter and the casualties had been minor. I flew from Malta to Alexandria and asked the pilot to skim the coastline and let me see if anything remained of the faithful *Maria Giovanni*. Alas, nothing was visible, but Tobruk was shaping up and some salvage was going on in the harbor.

I considered Alexandria my second home, and the many friends still living there greeted me like a long-lost brother. The docks and facilities were in good shape. The pier where I had loaded the *Maria* was badly damaged and several sheds completely gone, but, all things considered, Alexandria had come through smelling like a rose. I received orders to return to London and arranged for a trip via Morocco, with stops in Algiers and Rabat.

My next big venture was to attend Buckingham Palace, where I was to receive the Distinguished Service Cross from His Majesty King George VI. The invitation from Admiralty Whitehall read: "You are expected to attend an Investiture at Buckingham Palace at 10:15 A.M., on Tuesday, 12th December 1944. Investiture, 11 A.M.—Service Dress." Recipients were allowed to take along friends, and I chose Janet Burley, one of the daughters at Denham Mount, and Betty Larke as my guests. When all preparations were ready, the other recipients and I entered the main hall, a huge, beautifully decorated room. A military band was playing, and the guests were seated in rows like in a theater.

The King was standing on a raised platform. We approached by an incline where an admiral called the names of the recipients. Someone had already affixed metal clasps to our tunics, which eliminated using pins. The medals were simply hung onto the metal clasps. This parade moved slowly, or so it seemed, but eventually I was standing in front of His Majesty.

He asked, "Where did you lose your arm, Palmer?" I told him it was shot off in Germany.

"Your career reads like a novel."

"Yes, sir, I have had quite an experience."

We shook hands, and he pinned the medal on my breast. I headed down the ramp, where another chap unhooked the medal, placed it in a neat box, and handed it to me with a certificate. I passed up an invitation to have afternoon tea with Princess Elizabeth and Princess Margaret in order to meet three friends from China, who were waiting in a nearby pub. It had been a great day.

The next day, I called the navy office to ask for my discharge. "Oh, no, Palmer," came the reply. "We need you, just relax and enjoy yourself, and congratulations on winning the DSC. So long."

My next assignment was to be in Washington, D.C., to which I had no objection. The war in Europe was winding down. Germany was still sending buzz bombs but retreating steadily. Hitler still rampaged and was making a spectacle of himself and the whole nation. Lord Haw Haw was as mad as ever, but things in and around London were slowly getting back to normal. My phony arm was not acting the way it was supposed to—the locking device gave me much trouble, even though the manufacturers had diligently explained to me how it worked. I was about to board a bus when it locked, and my arm was stiff and straight out at a 90-degree angle. I quit the idea of boarding the bus, turned around and returned to my room where I shed the damned thing, tucked my sleeve in my pocket, and headed out again on my trip.

In Southampton, I boarded the SS *France*. War brides, wounded and discharged veterans, and other passengers were being loaded. This ship never had escorts, or if she did it was just out of the English Channel to the open sea, where her speed and zig-zagging frustrated any U-boat.

On arrival in Washington, I reported to Captain Laird of the British Admiralty Delegation at its headquarters in the Arlington Hotel. The hotel had been taken over by the British and the rooms converted into offices, not the best arrangement but adequate for the duties. The accommodation Laird had found for me was no good at all—a flea-bitten dump in a hell of a neighborhood. I was lucky to spot an old Yangtze River gunboat friend, Fen Brode, who was on Admiral Edward King's staff. Fen had a sumptuous apartment on Connecticut Avenue that had been a ladies' dress shop and was far too large for Fen—would I care to join him? Would I! My assignment was to lecture to groups about conditions in prisoner of war camps. That took me to Philadelphia, Baltimore, New York, Charleston, and a few other places. There was no set time to go or come, my travel vouchers were always ready, and the pay-master always had money available. Any spare time was spent exploring this fabulous city.

One day while in the Mayflower Hotel, I saw a chap I thought I knew and went across the wide lobby to introduce myself. "I'm Alf Palmer from Shang-hai, China, and I think I know you."

My friend, who was a very big man, looked me over and politely said, "No, Alf, we have never met, but it is nice of you to come over. I'm Jim Far-ley, the Postmaster General." We shook hands and promised to renew our acquaintance in China.

In April 1945, I was given two days' notice to pack. I had to be in San Diego within ten days, where I would proceed to Australia. The Royal Air Force Transport operated out of San Diego, and I embarked on a four-engine transport with my bags, which had grown with the accumulation of items intended as gifts for my Australian friends. The plane was loaded with essen-tial spare parts, and the only other passengers were two Australian Army types. The pilot was a young Scotsman and his copilot a New Zealander. When gassed up, the plane was just about able to get off the ground. Our first stop was Honolulu, and then on to Canton Island; New Zealand; and Sydney, New South Wales.

The jump to Honolulu was easy, but to Canton Island we met the mother and father of all storms, plus vivid lightning. Our heavily loaded craft pitched and bucked like a wild bronco. The copilot had picked up a bug in Honolulu. He was in bad shape and had flaked out on the cabin floor. I had taken up with Scotty and sat in the copilot's chair. The situation was tense, and nobody was talking. Scotty asked if I had ever flown a plane. I acknowl-edged the fact that I had had several hours' flying time on an old four-bladed DeHavilland open cockpit single-engine many years ago. I don't know to this day whether he thought he had an ex-pilot alongside or not, but he pointed out a few buttons and particularly a red light that blinked occasionally.

He said, "I'm fighting sleep, and if I doze off you keep her on course, but watch that light and if it stops blinking, call me right away."

With these brief instructions, he was sound asleep, and I'm flying this crate over the Pacific in one hell of a raging storm. I kept her on course, the automatic pilot worked OK, and Scotty slept like a baby.

At Canton Island, the United States had a small base, plus a doctor who diagnosed the copilot as having ptomaine poisoning. A stomach pump cleaned him out, and some medicine, plus twenty-four hours' rest, made the chap as good as new. The full day's rest was welcomed by all of us and, of all things, the birds put on a rare show of how not to fly. These gooney birds never graduated from flying school. They would come in to land, but they spilled over on their beaks and floundered about as though they were drunk—very funny to watch. The birds seemed self-conscious but walked away to roost.

New Zealand was the copilot's home country—he had fully recovered and wanted to be discharged—but no way, he was told to stay where he was. He helped us reach Mascot Airport near Sydney without further incident. I was made honorary pilot.

We found that Germany had thrown in the towel (7 May 1945) during our flight across the Pacific, and now we were gearing up for Japan. I frequently thought about the Japanese people, whom I had gotten to know in a vague sense. The individual Japanese was about as polite a person as one could possibly meet, industrious, and curious as a monkey. Given some authority and a uniform, however, he became a changed individual, like a goldfish turned piranha.

At Sydney, I got orders to proceed to Brisbane, Queensland, and take over command of HMS *Furneaux,* which was a repair depot located in New Farm, officially known as the Royal Naval Fleet Repair Base. This was an oddball setup with a crotchety old character in charge, a retired naval captain, who had been called in during the war. I knew right away I was not going to like him, but fortunately his office was quite a distance from my base. I had an excellent master-at-arms who helped me lick the place into good shape. The work went ahead like clockwork, and the only group giving me trouble was the women's section—Wrens who looked after mail, stores, canteens, and bookkeeping. There were only thirty-five of these young women, always into mischief but lovable.

Brisbane was one of the large staging posts preparing for our war against Japan. Aside from my main base, with 2,000 feet of wharf space on the river, we also had a large ammunition dump and a rest and rehabilitation camp on the ocean front that had accommodations for five hundred, plus eleven tennis courts, canteens, and baseball diamonds. All of this required a lot of authority to keep law and order. I had neglected these outside areas until the main base was in order. Then, my first lieutenant and I decided to inspect them and get to know the people living around there.

The crotchety captain suggested that a formal visit be made to the mayor of each surrounding township. Most of these small places did not have a mayor, but Southport boasted one. A notice was mailed to him to announce our forthcoming visit. My lieutenant and I dressed in whites and, complete with gloves, sought out His Honor. The mayoral mansion was just an ordinary cottage, designed for tropical living, that was built up on piles for air circulation. This particular house was on a slope with only a few steps up to the front door. We rang the doorbell. A rather heavily built man wearing suspenders, an open-necked shirt, and absolutely no badge or insignia came to the door. I introduced myself and my lieutenant, handed him a fancy printed greeting form and asked whether he had received my note. Yes, he had, then over his shoulder he hollered, "Hi Mum, two blokes here from the Navy."

Mum, wearing an apron, duly arrived and, without any formality, invited us in to have a cup of tea. This helped to deflate our egos. The gloves came off, high-collar buttons were undone, and all formality was abandoned. His Honor was quite a person. He had seen service in New Guinea, Borneo, and some other place I forget and had been wounded, which he proceeded to prove by hoisting his pants. Mum made strong tea, baked some scones, served homemade jelly, and, when we departed, gave each of us a large jar of her quince jelly. We figured our mission to Southport was successful.

The armed forces in and around Brisbane were at least twice the population of the city and suburbs. We had a complete infantry corps of the U.S. Army camped in Ascot Racecourse, much smaller detachments of the Australian Army, Dutch units, the British Army, and the local garrison. On the naval side, there were two U.S. cruisers, two Dutch gunboats, a British aircraft carrier, three Australian destroyers, and a French gunboat.

Following Japan's surrender on 15 August 1945, dismantling of our repair base began. Shipment of machinery and transfer of personnel elsewhere became a headache. When the job was near completion, I hired the Brisbane City Hall, which was quite large and truly a jewel, and sent out invitations for a farewell dance on Wednesday, 3 October 1945. The arrangements were made by the men of the Royal Naval Repair Base to return hospitality enjoyed during our few months in Brisbane. A ship's bell hanging in the vestibule was sounded every half hour and fourteen hundred guests attended the ball. The mayor posed with me on the stage, congratulations were made, and the final curtain was lowered on our establishment in Queensland.

I received orders to report to Headquarters Sydney. I knew the time had come for me to leave this land that I loved. Looking out the train window and seeing the farms roll by, I was convinced that great potential was in store for my country.

My orders were to prepare to go north to Borneo, on an assignment to survey naval facilities in the Far East, in association with General Bres of the U.S. Corps of Engineers. After getting my travel vouchers, I boarded a plane in Mascot for the long jaunt to Borneo, via Cloncurry and Darwin. Scheduled arrival time at Cloncurry was 0700. The moment we were airborne, I pushed some mailbags into a corner, put on a heavy coat, and curled up for a sleep.

We had only six passengers, and I'm sure they figured I was crazy. But, for a twelve-hour flight, there is nothing better than some shut-eye. My fellow passengers got the right idea over the mountains, when they damn near froze. As dawn started to break, I awoke and took an interest in the land below. I had never seen inland Australia and thought it to be a vast desert. Not so. The ground we were flying over was lush, with numerous large trees, tall grass, and small creeks.

Time to land, and we were lost. The sergeant pilot had no idea where we were! The estimated arrival time of 0700 had long passed; in fact, it was almost 0900 when the copilot came into the cabin and ordered us to prepare for a crash landing. This was an experience I had not had but, as they say, an old dog for a hard road. I gathered up mail bags, jammed them up near a bulkhead, loosened my buttons, buckled up the seat belt, and awaited the inevitable. The sergeant pilot was very skillful and brought that heavily laden plane down as gently as possible with wheels up, but when he hit the ground the noise was simply awful. One minute we were gliding, and the next all hell broke loose.

The port engine had broken away and we missed trees by fractions, but after about a mile of sliding the plane stopped dead. The copilot came back and opened the door—there was Australia right level with the sill. No need for steps, just walk out. We could see our track way back where the weight of the plane had plowed a deep furrow, with one engine looking lost near some trees. This was where I pulled rank and ordered one chap north, one chap west, and so on. That left myself and a young lieutenant who had banged up his nose and was bleeding profusely. The pilot and his sidekick were destroying codebooks and getting their ship in order for abandonment. The agreed signal for anyone locating a road or other human was to fire a Verey pistol, and I would reply in kind for them to get bearings. The heat was oppressive but, in the shade of the wing, it was bearable.

I guess an hour had gone by without any signal or sign of life when two aborigines came into view. They were scantily dressed, skinny as rails, and quite tall. I had never met these natives of Australia and recalled my mother warning me about black people living in the bush country. Well, here was the real thing, and I wondered whether they were friendly. These two came right up to the plane and in unison said, "Good day." That eased the tension. They stood with one foot resting on a thigh just above the kneecap. This accentuated their height, and they stood on one leg for quite a while. I asked where they came from.

"Oh, we work at a station nearby." I might add their idea of nearby was 10 miles away. "We knew you were going to crash and we ran over."

"Where are we now?" I asked.

"Oh, Mount Isa is just over there." Again, just over there was 37 miles off.

I fired some Verey lights to bring in the other four chaps. One of them had met two odd characters tending their traps. They had an old Model T Ford but would not deviate to help us. Instead, they promised to telephone the nearest police post, which they did, and an army truck came out to help. We had crashed about 0930, and the two aborigines had arrived about noon. The army truck came just before dark and drove us to Mount Isa. It had been quite a day.

The truck left before dawn the next day, with the copilot as guide, to pick up the mailbags and our baggage from the wrecked plane. I booked departure for the following morning on a narrow-gauge railroad to Cloncurry, another new experience. A rather small train, three carriages plus a baggage car, small coal-burning engine, and unique types operating the system, but it worked and off everybody went. We made a short stop at a priceless way station known as Princess. Whoever gave it that name had a keen sense of humor. This place of about twenty houses and a general store-bar-grocery-hardware was beyond description.

While the engine was being filled up with water, we went into the bar. There was no ice, but the beer was wet and appreciated. On the shelf, we had noticed bottles of liquor—Johnnie Walker, Haig & Haig, Canadian Club, and Plymouth gin, among others—and asked the owner whether they were genuine and for sale. Yes, true to label and priced right. Well, this was equivalent to striking gold. I bought three bottles of scotch and two of gin, but the others had the same idea and, after a few more sales, the owner clamped down. I guess he realized what value he had. Those who were in the Pacific knew only too well the cost and scarcity of these items. A friend of mine had traded three bottles of scotch for a brand-new Chevrolet and had the audacity to complain about getting only a half tank of gas with it.

The train eventually steamed into Cloncurry. Although a huge city in comparison to Mount Isa and Princess, it had no appeal for me. I had visions of Hong Kong and a sumptuous dinner a friend had bet me while I was in Sydney. Admittedly, I was running late, but it eventually paid off. We went on to Darwin, a soggy mess, and landed there for fuel. This was the monsoon season. North Australia does not suffer greatly from this phenomenon, but it can get pretty well shaken up. I had never been to this northern city before. I remembered, as a school student, drawing in Darwin on the maps, a sizable town with a background of wealth, chiefly in cattle, to sustain it. Ships came into the port at high tide, secured to the jetty, and found themselves sitting on the bottom at low tide because of the fantastic rise and fall.

Borneo was right smack in the monsoon belt, and landing there was a hit-or-miss proposition. We landed at the airport in Brunei (then the capital of the state of Brunei), with jungle all around and rain to beat the band. There were buildings and things to see, but the dispatch rider came aboard and delivered his messages. I was satisfied to leave the place strictly alone. My orders were to proceed to Saigon. When the rain permitted, we took off again, despite the turbulence.

Saigon had not changed a great deal from my visit there on the HMS *Cockchafer* at the beginning of the war, but lawlessness now prevailed. Some of the buildings had been shelled. Electricity was limited, there were no elevators, and amenities were few and far between. The curfew started at sundown, and the streets were patrolled. The precautions against theft were staggering. Trucks were parked beside the road with all wheels removed. Store windows were covered, with shutters, locks, and chains on everything. Lying in bed, one could hear rifle shots frequently. There was no law worth mentioning. We were warned never to go out alone, but preferably in groups of three or more, to keep out of dark alleys and doorways, and never to accept invitations to strange houses.

The unfortunate aspect was that the two French factions—the Vichy French, who had capitulated to and worked for the Japanese since 1940, and the de Gaulle Loyalists, who had come in 1944—despised each other. Humiliating gestures were commonplace. Women accused of collaborating with the Japanese were paraded naked with their hair shaved and ridiculed by the natives and the French. The Vichy and de Gaulle factions were required to work in harmony on the accounting for stores, oil, transports, foodstuffs, and other matters, but come lunchtime the de Gaullists went into the club and the Vichy-types ate at a greasy spoon or had a sandwich in the basement.

The many conflicting forces in Indochina had resulted in a disaster waiting to happen. The Vichy government in France, when it surrendered to Germany early in the war, had agreed to the Japanese occupation of Indochina (which later would be divided into three countries—Laos, Cambodia, and Vietnam). After Gen. Charles de Gaulle, leader of the French Resistance, liberated Paris in 1944, he sent out key men to Saigon to set up a new government for Indochina. They came by fast corvette, while the bulk of the staff, plus troops, followed in two cruisers. The Vichy administrators stayed on, and French Legionnaires, who had remained neutral throughout their country's crisis, now flew in by plane. Added to this confusion were the French soldiers, who hated the French marines. The lack of training and discipline of the French troops, or their "just don't give a damn" attitude, was the basic cause for the unrest and costly wars in Southeast Asia.

The only stabilizing force was the British Army, which had fought in Burma and landed in Indochina soon after Japan's surrender. The British troops kept what little law existed. It was busy disarming the Japanese Army stationed in that area, estimated at half a million. The Japanese guns were stacked in a warehouse, and every ship still able to float carried these men back to Japan, many of them standing up all the way.

Native guerrilla groups had been trained by U.S. Office of Strategic Services (OSS) people to harass Japanese patrols. They became experts and accounted for the deaths of thousands of Japanese sentries who had been left to guard isolated points inland—railroad bridges, water and power plants, and highways. When the Japanese withdrew, the guerrillas still had their weapons and killing skills but nowhere to go, so they harassed the French for want of something to do.

I sent a young lieutenant as an observer on a French cruiser that was to steam up the local river as a show of force. He reported back that, after going about 50 miles or so, somebody in a small village took a rifle shot at the cruiser. The cruiser dropped anchor, swung around her main armament of 12-inch guns, and fired smack into the village, not once but several times. The straw huts flew skyward, the natives vanished, and the whole area was a shambles, where minutes before had stood a peaceful village. One crackpot who owned a rifle had disputed the intrusion of this big cruiser. Of course, when the real enemy was knocking at their door, the French lay low and pleaded neutral. The show of force, the flying of the tricolor flag, the haphazard manner of the French troops, the enmity among the various factions within the French government, and no real stability had turned these peaceful natives into a hostile mob. From such incidents grew a devastating war that involved many countries and resulted in the slaughter of millions.

I witnessed the formal changeover of the country from the British to the French. It took place before a large cathedral that fronted on a wide boulevard and across from a park area. Two flagpoles had been erected before two wicker chairs, one for the new de Gaulle governor and the other for the commanding officer of the British army. Bleachers had been set up for officers; as the senior naval officer present, I had a front-row seat. The line of march brought the British forces past the reviewing stand, thence right to the docks where three transports waited to receive them.

The air was festive. Thousands of natives in their best gaudy attire were watching the parade from the park. The British Army was led by a brass band, with instruments polished. The leader wore a leopard skin apron and white gauntlets and beat time with a fancy staff. The troops were first-class soldiers. They had been fighting for years and were in excellent condition.

Their uniforms were clean, shoes shined, everyone in step, and rifles angled in unison. The natives cheered and threw flowers. When the British Gurkha troops came along, they broke into the ranks and kissed the warriors from Nepal, India. They felt something of kinship with those brown people. The British general took the salute, the Union Jack was lowered, and a formal document was handed to the French governor.

After a brief spell, the French troops arrived and, frankly, I was ashamed of being a white man. I could not believe that such a motley bunch was worthy of being called an army. The band played off key, the instruments were green from neglect and the players out of step, and no effort had been made to keep their uniforms clean. These were the remnants of a defeated people. They had beards, long, short, trimmed; moustaches, sideburns; headgear that suited the character, on the back of the head or sideways; some without headgear; and some of the men were smoking. They had no pride, no spirit, and apparently their officers had little control over them. I wondered how they ever got this mob assembled into a line of march. The French governor took the salute, the tricolor of France was unfurled, and then all hell broke loose. The natives stoned them, took their rifles, and spat on them. Vive la France! They were an army of bums.

Events of the recent past were the cause of their discontent. The Indochinese people had lived under French rule for many years and had been promised protection from all enemies. When World War II started, the Japanese had walked right in. In fact, the French gave them a welcome. Under French rule, the local people had been required to work ten hours a day, but, when the Japanese took over, they worked twelve-hour days for very little pay. The Allies had promised them self-determination; now they saw themselves being sold down the river. The British had put on a fancy show and driven the Japanese out of their country, but then betrayed them by handing the country back to the French, whom the natives hated. When the stabilizing influence of the British departed, the whole country was in turmoil. Nobody knew who was getting screwed, or why, or how, and nobody was paying attention.

My chief concern was to leave this vale of tears and get to Hong Kong, chop chop. About a dozen of us religiously went to the airport each morning. On the blackboard for sailing time, someone had written MAG DROP. I never knew what that meant, other than not going. After six or seven days, the MAG forgot to DROP, and we were actually ready to go. The natives in revolt had placed a price on the heads of anybody with white skin. An officer was worth $10,000, a noncom $5,000, and the going rate for a soldier about $1,000. It was hardly worthwhile living.

We finally reached Hong Kong. What a change from Saigon—law and order, but crowded; bulging at the seams would be appropriate. A British naval force had arrived on 30 August to reoccupy the colony. The Japanese had wrecked much of the city and erected a huge monument atop Signal Hill, a monstrous edifice without beauty of design. My ship, HMS *Tamar*, which had taken me from Hong Kong to Singapore in 1939, had been sunk and much of the dockyard smashed. The population explosion was very much in evidence, plus the stiff upper lip tradition, which had been fully restored. Government House was much improved from what it had been, and the governor's mansion was completely refurbished. The naval base looked the same. I took an inventory of some old anchor chains, anchors, steel plates, and bric-a-brac of bygone days that were still carried on the books. Although the Japanese had swiped much of this junk, quite a lot remained.

The Hong Kong Hotel, known as the Grips, was in full swing. The old restaurants were jammed with patrons at all hours. Aberdeen fishing village had a new floating restaurant, the brightly lighted sampan of the Sing Song girls slowly wended its way through the rows of anchored junks. My friend kept his promise—we had a sumptuous dinner and relived past events.

My next assignment was Shanghai, and it seemed the navy was running out of things for me to do. The naval base, such as it was called, was inside the British consular compound. We had an impressive array of brass for an insignificant establishment—a captain, two commanders, and several types who spent their days translating Russian newspapers into English. The chaos that existed in Shanghai was probably similar to situations that occurred in Europe after World War II.

It was not until 8 August 1945 that the USSR had decided to declare war on Japan, just one week before Japan surrendered. The Red Army then invaded Manchuria and, two weeks later, Stalin announced victory there. Many thousands of Russians—businessmen, guards, police, bus drivers— were now living in Shanghai. I got to know many of them and thought them really nice people. The newspapers maligned them on every occasion but, to me, these stories seemed biased, obviously trying to drum up trouble. Right after World War II was over, many people around the world—British and American—wanted to continue the war against Communist Russia because of its aggressive policies. Capt. R. Kruzen of the USS *Birmingham* had made detailed plans for this event, but too many others ruled against it because they were war-weary. I wondered, why all the bitterness? The small group at the navy base was quite alert, intelligent, and possibly included the best-informed chaps on Russian Far East politics. I plied them with numerous questions, but it was obvious I must learn the hard way.

The Russian Consulate was just across Soochow Creek from the British compound. Our consul received an invitation to attend a celebration. I was chosen to join him as an aide. The morning of the special day saw thousands of Chinese parading along the Bund with posters, banners, flags, and small handbills denouncing the Russians, the Imperialists, and foreigners in general. I apprised the consul of the display, but he decided to attend the party anyway. A British marine eased our car out the main gates, and we steadily traveled over the bridge toward the Russian Consulate. There was no display or hostility shown. A few people banged their hands against the door panels of the car, but the traffic opened and allowed us to pass.

The Russian Consulate building, like many of Shanghai's older buildings, was slowly sinking. To enter, one went down a few steps to a semibasement. There were two moon-faced guards at the bottom of the steps. Across the room, two more guards with expressionless faces stood at the foot of the stairway leading up. These two characters, with their hands in their pockets, showed no recognition or sign of respect but allowed us to proceed to the main floor. What a transformation: large tables loaded with food, hovering waiters who smiled and poured drinks, everything spotless, and much formality. In the bay windows, however, photographers were taking pictures of the mob waving banners out in the street. Three or four days later, the newspapers had pictures of the demonstrators blazoned across the top of the front page. The scary caption quoted a Russian spokesman: "If the Chinese cannot protect our representatives, we will send in troops." This was the last thing desired by anyone except the Russians.

I found out later that the Chinese demonstrators were hired by the Russians for the occasion; each received $1 after the ceremony. The Russian consul must have known about the phony demonstration, but he carried on as though nothing was amiss and toasted everlasting friendship. These people were experts in deception and practiced it across the board—taxi drivers, guards, waiters, whatever.

We knew the Russians had inside information about the Japanese trying to negotiate a separate peace, but they kept it to themselves. At the last minute, they had decided to join the Allies in the war against Japan, and one week later Japan had surrendered to the Allies. The terms of the peace treaty called for a three-way partition—American, British, and Russian. This three-way division was never designed to operate the way that the Russians interpreted it. They were practical and picked the best of everything—railroad engines, streetcars, tugboats, barges. Anything worthy of inspection was whittled down and the best shipped off to Russia.

I was dispatched to Mukden, the capital of Manchuria, with the intention of curbing this sacking. The British Consulate in Shanghai gave me a valid passport but, when I arrived at the Mukden airport, the Russian officials refused to acknowledge its validity. After I had spent four days in a cold corner of a hangar while I waited for my credentials to be examined, the local general decided to interview me. A big gruff chap, he was so covered with medals I wondered how he ever got into his coat. He informed me, through an interpreter, that he knew why I was there and I was at liberty to make notes, take pictures, and so forth. He was very annoyed to learn that I had been confined in a cold hangar and ordered space to be made available in the best hotel in town. He added I was the first person to come before him with an obvious disability and asked where I had lost my arm. He had been on the Eastern front fighting the Germans and loathed them. He issued me a passport that was magical in its effect.

My room in the Yamata Hotel was pure luxury, complete with servant. The first morning revealed who was in charge: a Russian sergeant. He came in, announced who he was, then started to examine the room. When he learned that my shoes had not been polished, the Manchurian servant was called in and reprimanded with much agitation.

The general gave orders that I was not to be molested. Although I never saw or noticed anyone following me, I'm sure that I had a shadow somewhere. I saw a big, bewhiskered Russian riding a velocipede. He was the funniest sight: this huge man astride a small bicycle; fully clothed in Russian uniform, greatcoat, rifle, bandolier; and a full beard and fur cap. The bicycle was not traveling fast, but the wind parted his whiskers. He looked ridiculous, and I could not control my laughter. The Russian realized I was laughing at him. He slowed down and, before the bike stopped, jumped off and let the thing fall over with the miniature motor sputtering. The rider approached me with arms akimbo. Before I had an opportunity to get out my passport, this giant of a man burst out laughing, slapped me on the back, recovered his bike, and rode off.

I imagined I was all alone, but there suddenly appeared three secret police armed with the latest automatic rifles. One of them spoke English and plied me with questions. "What did I say?" "What did he say?" "What are you doing out here?" When I produced my passport, they all saluted and vanished from sight, but I knew I was being carefully watched.

Each day found me looking over old papers and studying the Russians. Orders came for me to investigate shipments being sent into Mongolia. Nobody knew just where—"You find out, Palmer." Maps were nonexistent, and the obvious place to aim for was Ulan Bator, the capital, and also a rail center.

Ulan Bator, which means "Red Hero," is thousands of miles away from anywhere, and at least a thousand miles north of Mukden. I had noticed many trains loaded with machinery but had no idea where they were going. My passport smoothed the necessary regulations; eventually, I was fitted out with tickets and bits of paper that would enable me to travel into Mongolia, a country I had never visited.

I was quite surprised at the size and modern appearance of this city buried in Central Asia and yet quite historical, dating back to Genghis Khan. It was a communist satellite in name only. The Russians had never been able to get these people to toe the line; they are independent, and Mongolia is first on everything. My hotel was ultra modern, built by Chinese, nicely furnished, carpeted, and with a superb view. The main square had a statue of Sukhe Bator seated on a prancing horse. This was a good indicator of the life style of the inhabitants. Livestock exceeded humans twenty-five to one, with sheep, horses, and camels topping the list. The large government buildings, rows of apartments, and department stores looked odd against the tents surrounding the city. The tents were made of felt fitted over a wood frame and most of the population lived in this type of dwelling, known as *gers*.

Mongols love their horses. Small fry jump on a pony for a gallop to the local store, school, or a visit with friends. Fermented mares' milk is intoxicating, and it appeared to be the favorite beverage. Aside from horseback riding, wrestling is the favorite pastime. Everybody knows the best grips, and kids practice them. I learned that the people lean toward Russia politically but pay no respect to the dictates of Moscow. They are very proud and independent, but being wedged between Russia and China gives them few choices.

My chief mission was to snoop around and find out where all the loot from Northern China and Manchuria was going. Of all people, a young Mongol chap in the hotel provided a wealth of information. The railroad was single track, and, during my trip, the train was frequently sidetracked to allow another train to pass. In and around Ulan Bator, however, there seemed to be a surplus of tracks, and much of the equipment on these sidings was being checked, inventoried, and made ready for final shipment into Russia. Items included cranes, locomotives, boilers, earth-moving equipment, trucks, streetcars, and assorted hardware. With the help of the young man, I made a listing of what I saw. After eight days in this vast, remote country, I was ready to head south and submit my report to the captain.

Shanghai was still in turmoil but, having lived in that city for many years, it held an appeal for me. I now had time to reexamine it, and it was in a sorry way. The Bund, the world-famous thoroughfare that skirted the Whangpoo

River and the large commercial houses, followed a gentle curve. Prior to the war, there were lovely lawns, gardens, and shrubs, plus two four-lane roads, sidewalks, rickshas, tracks, and piers. The Bund was now a mess, with hundreds of bamboo shanties and thousands of residents fighting for space.

Under Japanese occupation, the Chinese had been unable to buy anything. When the war was over, the U.S. Pacific Fleet arrived in port with thousands of sailors loaded with money, and the Army and Air Force came in from the back country. The Chinese quickly unearthed their hidden treasures of silks, carved chests, embroidery, jade, ivory, exotic gowns, beautiful crockery, and other unusual items. There was much speculation as to the value of the Chinese national currency. It fluctuated every hour on the hour, and prices for basic items were ridiculous—silk stockings reached over U.S. $100 a pair, and a pen and pencil set cost $125. But the people were always animated and appeared happy, with no knowledge of what was in store.

I was overdue for discharge and ordered to Hong Kong. The base commander, Capt. Clive Gwinnes, did the necessary duties. In 1948, I became Mr. Palmer, and my association with the ships at sea had come to a close.

On the mountain behind the city, Clive had a beautiful house that overlooked the fabulous harbor. As I sat on the porch of Katoomba above Hong Kong and reviewed my service career, I recalled arriving here from Shanghai in 1939. By various stages, I had gone completely around the world. I had been promoted, belittled, a prisoner, a minister, a casualty, decorated, and honored. Many people had shaped my life, and I had a strong desire to reach out and greet them. Life was full and exciting, but it was now time to hang up my sword, relegate the medals to a box, order some civilian clothes, and look to the future.

Everything in this story is true and factual, but shipwrecks, attempted prison breaks, and frequent moves made keeping a diary impossible. Consequently, much of it is from memory. As I wrote, one item revealed another. So the story unfolded, with assistance from friends and research. Hopefully, the reader has enjoyed my saga of the Seven Seas and the many countries in between, as I enjoyed living it.

Alfred B. Palmer

EPILOGUE

Alfred B. Palmer died 4 July 1993, at the age of ninety-four, too soon to see his book in print, but knowing that it would be published. He had retired to Clearwater, Florida, in 1965 and, in keeping with his earlier life, had spent much time traveling around the world—to Australia, China, Egypt, and Europe—visiting old friends and making new ones. Two months before his death, he had flown to London for a fifty-year reunion of POWs who had been confined in Camp Marlag, Germany. He was an active member of the Circumnavigators Club, the Cape Horners Club, and the Rats of Tobruk Association, along with civic and fraternal organizations. As his secretary, I soon recognized his indomitable spirit, ready wit, courage, and leadership ability that made him such an outstanding individual.

Over the years, he had received many commendations. One of his favorites was a letter received in 1943, after his repatriation to England. He had been asked to talk to various groups of service people about his experiences, and this particular letter was from the Staff Officer to the Lady Superintendent-in-Chief of the St. John Ambulance Brigade Overseas. She wrote: "Just to thank you and also to congratulate you on your splendid talk. Your natural humor and philosophy ring so true in spite of (or is it because of?)

the inferno you have sailed through. Wishing you all happy seas and trips from now on."

Early in the North African campaign of World War II, his unusual qualities were being recognized. Gen. Sir Archibald Wavell, General Officer Commanding, Western Desert, sent this signal to Commander-in-Chief, Mediterranean, on 16 December 1940:

> I should like to commend especially Lieutenant A. B. Palmer, RNVR, and the ship's company of X39 for their untiring efforts during operations at Sidi Barrani and Sollum. Lieutenant Palmer handled his ship with marked skill and has displayed outstanding seamanlike ability under adverse circumstances. This officer, engine room personnel and ship's company of X39 are worthy of the highest praise.

Of course, the announcement of his Distinguished Service Cross (DSC) award brought immediate congratulatory messages. One of the first was from Capt. Sam Raw, Commander of the HMS *Medway*, who wrote on 19 August 1941:

> Justice at last. Very many and most hearty congratulations on your more than well-deserved DSC for X39. Now it's the *Maria's* turn to add another one for your later exploits. We were all delighted to see your name in the list and are looking forward to seeing you on board to celebrate the great event very shortly.

Maj. John Devine of the 9th Australian Infantry Division, who was stationed in Tobruk the entire time that Lieutenant Palmer was delivering supplies there, saw his performance first-hand. In his book, *The Rats of Tobruk*, he notes:

> The most famous carrier of supplies to Tobruk was an Australian naval officer serving with the Royal Navy. . . . It was a sight to see this skipper bringing his ship safe into the harbour of Tobruk. . . . No one more deserved the DSC he received than did this captain.

One of Alfred Palmer's most treasured articles appeared in the newspaper *Tobruk Truth*, dated 4 September 1941:

> Here's a toast to "Pirate" Palmer. A Dinkum Aussie who is helping to win the war. BBC announced this week that Lieutenant Palmer has been awarded the

D.S.C. Everybody in Tobruk will join in congratulating Lieutenant Palmer, and if we had any beer we'd drink his health! Bluff hearty, thickset, Alf Palmer, of the booming voice, is known to hundreds in Tobruk merely as "Pirate" Palmer. He is an Aussie, one who has seen practically every part of the world.

Lieutenant Palmer, who is now an Australian Naval man, has been ferrying supplies into Tobruk on the captured Italian schooner *Maria Giovanni*, originally built for the wine trade between Italy and Libya. Practically every time the *Maria* comes to Tobruk she is subjected to merciless bombing attacks, and Lieutenant Palmer carries anything from prisoners to explosives—as he says, "everything that nobody else would think of carrying." He has Italian guns and ammunition, and has more than held his own with enemy bombers. No matter how badly the *Maria* has been damaged, Alf Palmer has always had her patched up quickly and ready for sea. . . . Again, Alf Palmer, congratulations!

Later, an important naval award, ordered by His Majesty King Edward VI, appointed Lt. Comdr. A. B. Palmer a Member of the British Empire (MBE) for "outstanding courage and devotion to duty."

Don Edy, one of the group of POWs transferred from Fort Bismark to the Winesburg Camp soon after the surrender of Italy, wrote about this trip:

Skip Palmer had tried to escape from a small window in his car as the train was rolling through a tunnel. His right arm was nearly torn off when he jumped for a side of the tracks and it had to be amputated near the shoulder. Skip says that a burst of machine gun fire did it but the Germans say he must have hit a jutting post in the tunnel. The whole camp was thrown into gloom over the news.

Skip soon arrived in the camp from the hospital and I went to visit him with some hesitation, not knowing how he would react to such a calamity. I need not have worried. Skipper greeted me with a wave of his stump, cussed the Germans and the Third Reich roundly, and then launched into a long and humorous account of his adventure. Skipper 'Alfie' Palmer was a grand man and a real person to know. Very few people went through the POW life as cheerfully, and as bravely as he did.

An item appearing in a Mediterranean Fleet Log described Alfred Palmer's requirements for his crew; amazingly, it describes his own approach to life as well:

Lt. A. B. Palmer required of his ship's company three things—that they should work willingly while work was necessary, shoot straight, and fight as long as they were conscious. He had only one punishment, dismissal from the ship. His infrequent dispatches, masterpieces of laconic recording of essentials, invariably concluded the same way: No complaints, no requestmen, no defaulters.

So I add my own tribute to Commander Alfred Brian Palmer, for his sharing with us the highlights of his remarkable career at sea, on land, in war, and in peace, and for being the very special person that he was.

Mary Curtis
Clearwater, Florida

INDEX

ABOUT THE AUTHORS

ALFRED B. PALMER grew up on a horse farm one hundred miles inland from Sydney. His fascination with the sea began when his father, a native of Kentucky, took him to Sydney harbor to meet friends arriving from the United States. As he watched the huge ocean liner ease into its berth, he determined that he would become a ship's captain.

After retiring from the Royal Navy at the end of World War II he became marine superintendent and director of the Chinese Relief Agency, an offshoot of United Nations Relief. He later became an engineer with RCA and Ford Motor Company, moving to the United States and becoming an American citizen. He retired to Clearwater, Florida, and died in July 1993 at the age of 94.

MARY E. CURTIS was born in northern Indiana and graduated from Nash Junior College in Cleveland. She spent twenty-seven years as an executive secretary at the headquarters of Westinghouse in Pittsburgh. Now residing in Clearwater, Florida, she pursues her interest in genealogy and is an active member of the Daughters of the American Revolution.

THE NAVAL INSTITUTE PRESS

THE PIRATE OF TOBRUK
A Sailor's Life on the Seven Seas, 1916–1948

Designed by Karen L. White

Set in ITC Berkeley Oldstyle
by BG Composition
Baltimore, Maryland

Printed on 60-lb. Glatfelter Sebago eggshell cream
and bound in Holliston Roxite B
by the Maple-Vail Book Manufacturing Group
York, Pennsylvania